Genesis Regained

Toronto Studies in Religion

Donald Wiebe
General Editor

Vol. 25

PETER LANG
New York • Washington, D.C./Baltimore • Boston • Bern
Frankfurt am Main • Berlin • Brussels • Vienna • Canterbury

David H. Turner

Genesis Regained

Aboriginal Forms of Renunciation in Judeo-Christian Scriptures and Other Major Traditions

PETER LANG
New York • Washington, D.C./Baltimore • Boston • Bern
Frankfurt am Main • Berlin • Brussels • Vienna • Canterbury

Library of Congress Cataloging-in-Publication Data

Turner, David H.
Genesis regained: Aboriginal forms of renunciation
in Judeo-Christian scriptures and other major traditions / David H. Turner.
p. cm. — (Toronto studies in religion; vol. 25)
Includes bibliographical references and index.
1. Australian aborigines—Religion. 2. Australian aborigines—Social life
and customs. 3. Self-denial—Comparative studies. 4. Charity—
Comparative studies. I. Title. II. Series.
BL2610.T85   200'.89'9915—dc21   98-44187
ISBN 0-8204-4404-9
ISSN 8756-7385

Die Deutsche Bibliothek-CIP-Einheitsaufnahme

Turner, David H.:
Genesis regained: Aboriginal forms of renunciation in Judeo-Christian
Scriptures and other major traditions / David H. Turner.
–New York; Washington, D.C./Baltimore; Boston; Bern;
Frankfurt am Main; Berlin; Vienna; Paris: Lang.
(Toronto studies in religion; Vol. 25)
ISBN 0-8204-4404-9

Book cover and CD cover design by Lisa Dillon

The paper in this book meets the guidelines for permanence and durability
of the Committee on Production Guidelines for Book Longevity
of the Council of Library Resources.

© 1999 Peter Lang Publishing, Inc., New York

Printed in the United States of America

for Graeme and Michelle

The most impressive thing about man, perhaps the one thing that excuses him of all his idiocy and brutality, is the fact that he has invented the concept of that which does not exist.

(Glenn Gould, in *The Glenn Gould Reader*, pp. 3–4)

Editor's Preface

In this work David Turner takes the research findings and theoretical insights of his work among the Aborigines of Groote Eylandt and Bickerton Island in northern Australia and applies them to other traditions. Though highly speculative in nature, this work raises the possibility of unexplored correspondences between aspects of four of the world's so-called "major" religious traditions. Utilising the Aboriginal concept of Renunciation, which in Turner's terms means "the giving up of everything of something to someone who has nothing of it," he reads Hebrew and Christian Scriptures, the Upanishads, the Qur'an and dialogues with the Abbot of a Zen Buddhist temple in Japan to locate what he regards as a "sub-theme" in these traditions. He then reads the terms of Canadian confederation in the same light before turning to a more "recreational" tradition—the game of Sunday morning hockey in his hometown of Perth, Ontario.

Perhaps Renunciation is really there, perhaps not, but one cannot fail to be intrigued by the possibility that the cosmology of the world's oldest continuing religious tradition might illuminate our understanding of texts and traditions we have come to take for granted.

This book sets forth a proposal which merits serious consideration. The work is a fitting conclusion to Turner's work on the Aborigines and a welcome addition to this series.

Donald Wiebe,
Trinity College,
University of Toronto,
September, 1998

Table of Contents

Illustrations

Cover: Hand stencil and x-ray painting of Macassan prau, Renunciative symbols in Aboriginal rock art, Groote Eylandt (see pages 34, 55, 57–58)

frontispiece: The cross as intersecting straight lines—an archetypal Aboriginal symbolic form represented in Christian iconography, St. Mary Magdalene's Church, Toronto

Acknowledgements

The summary account of Australian Aboriginal culture presented here has been compiled from material contained in my *Afterlife Before Genesis*, New York: Peter Lang, 1997. The section of Part V, entitled "Renunciation in the Indian Tradition," is a revised version of "BrahmanForm: the Vedic-Hindu Tradition in Aboriginal Perspective," published in *Man in India* (special issue in commemoration of the 70th anniversary of the journal, vol. 71, no. 1: 47–65, 1991). The section "Renunciation in Gujar Society" is a revised version of my article, "We Will Always Be Gujar: the Politics of Nomadism in Himachal Pradesh" published in a special issue of *India International Centre Quarterly* (Geeti Sen ed., August, 1992 and reprinted in *Indigenous Vision*, Geeti Sen ed., London: Sage, 1992). The section "Renunciation in Sunday Morning Hockey" is a revised version of "The (S)Pacific Effects of Sunday Morning Hockey: a Participant's Observation," published in *Culture* (vol. 12, no. 1, pp. 77–85, 1993).

All Scriptural quotations are reprinted from *The New King James Version, Holy Bible*. According to the Preface to this version, "The New King James Version follows the historic precedent of the authorised [1611] version in maintaining a literal approach to translation, except where the idiom of the original language occasionally cannot be translated directly into our tongue" (pp. v-vi). This satisfies my purpose here. In any event, it is beyond my competence to debate the details of text-translation with biblical scholars. If it eventually turns out that *The New King James Version* is not the version that best expresses what the authors of the texts therein originally meant (let alone what Jesus, assuming that he existed, originally meant), it is the version that best expresses what a great many of the readers of the Bible, including many Aboriginal people subsequent to contact, think they meant.

I owe a great debt of thanks to Don Wiebe, the editor of this series, for allowing me the latitude to express ideas in this volume which sometimes crossed the border of what he considered the proper academic study of religion. I have found Don to be someone who does not have to agree with you in order for him to support your work. What he requires most of all is logical coherence and a statement of premises from which the reader can proceed to draw his or her own conclusions. This volume also owes much to Heidi Burns of Peter Lang Publishing in Baltimore who not only encouraged me to proceed with it as an idea but who also copy edited the final version.

I would like to thank Christopher Trott for reading the manuscript in pre-published form and for offering many useful suggestions as to how the "argument" could be strengthened. I benefited from his training in both anthropology and theology. I also appreciate the comments of Canon Howard Buchner of Trinity College who confirmed me in the idea that the concept of "God" is more a problem than a solution to inter-religious dialogue and understanding. I would also like to acknowledge the support of two Catholic friends, Fr. Richard Whalan of Holy Name Parish near Kingston Ontario and Dan Bajorek of Toronto, on whom I "tried out" many of the ideas and experiences mentioned in this book over the years. In this connection my gratitude to Cynthia, Dave, Ece, Jeff, Jesse and Magdalena, students in my "Aboriginal Religion in Comparative Perspective" course at the University of Toronto in 1997-98 with whom I worked through the final draft of this work.

I would especially like to thank Nancy Lalara and Grant Burgoyne for their hospitality and friendship at Angurugu, Groote Eylandt, in July-August of 1997 where I completed the first draft of this manuscript. Perhaps this volume will provide a counterbalance to the pronouncements of the C.M.S. missionaries there who, for so many years, have been trying to undermine Aboriginal religion and culture.

Completion of this journey would not have been possible without its beginnings in 1969 with Ruth Charles who worked with me and supported me in that first year on Groote Eylandt and in subsequent follow-up research. This book is dedicated to our son Graeme and daughter Michelle who, each in their own way, represent the best of what the Aboriginal tradition is all about.

Prologue

For almost 30 years now I have been working to understand the way of life of the Aborigines of Groote Eylandt and Bickerton Island in northern Australia. The extent of this understanding has been expressed most recently in three volumes in this series published by Peter Lang and edited by Donald Wiebe. The first volume, *Life Before Genesis*, explored a theoretical insight into the nature of Australian Aboriginal society and applied that insight to a reading of the *Book of Genesis* in the Bible. In 1986 I took that insight back to the Aborigines of Groote Eylandt and Bickerton Island to discover that they had a concept of it and elaborated it in ways I had missed in my previous researches there. This was the subject of my second volume *Return to Eden*. The third volume, *After Life Before Genesis*, explored this insight in the context of Aboriginal music and "spirituality" and was to have been the last in the series. I had originally planned another volume pointing out the implications of my findings for other traditions, particularly religious traditions, but abandoned the notion as too ambitious and open to criticism, given the wealth of material written on these traditions. However, once I began thinking of the project as the formulation of a hypothesis rather than as a conclusion, I decided to proceed. The result is a four-volume series rather than a series of three.

The present volume takes the understanding of Aboriginal society and culture reached in the pervious three volumes including a theoretical insight into the nature of the human condition—and draws the implications for understanding other, primarily religious, traditions, in particular the Judeo-Christian. My thesis is that what I have termed the "lifeway" of Renunciation finds its most comprehensive expression amongst the Australian Aborigines but appears as a kind of "sub-text" in the texts and teachings of the so-called "major" religious traditions (not to mention in some episodes of "secular" history and contemporary events). However, the lifeway in question generally has been poorly articulated in xxii

these traditions largely because of the existence of other
lifeways and world views which interfere with its expression as
an idea and its manifestation as a practice.

If the lifeway of Renunciation is pluralistic and accom-
modates many in peaceful co-existence, its nemesis, the
lifeway of accumulation (though it may be better referred to as
a "deathway" considering the implications of its practice), is
monistic and incorporates many into one. The lifeway of
accumulation is inherently competitive and aggressive and
constitutes the mainstream within which Renunciation both
emerges and is destroyed. By setting the terms by which
reality is defined and recorded (as the "winners" in history
always do), the lifeway of accumulation masks our ability to
perceive accurately the alternative lifeway in question.

I want to be clear that what follows is not so much an
Aboriginal reading of the "revelations" of other traditions and
certain events in history as a *theoretical* reading which
includes an Aboriginal expression of the terms of that theory.

The theoretical perspective in question runs: *anti-thesis* —>
thesis —> *plurality*. In the Anindilyaugwa language of the
Aborigines of Groote Eylandt and Bickerton Island area of
northern Australia this would be an accurate translation of the
term *gemalyangerranema* which literally refers to the process
of taking something from nothing and twisting it in (with the
mind) to something already existing to make a new creation.
Another way of formulating the process is, "Nothingness —>
being —> relationship." "Nothingness" or "anti-thesis," the key
term in the theory, is synonymous with "contentless Form" at
one level, with "spiritual Presence" at another and is to be
understood in the Aboriginal sense as the "cosmic
substance(s)" that still exists after the "matter" of something
has been "removed."

**I write Form, Presence, Nothingness and Renunciation
with a capital in order to imply what the Aborigines recognise a**

dimension to existence that is something more than tangible matter as such. Hence the distinction in Aboriginal cosmology between the land as a material resource and habitat and the Land as bounded into a shape or Form; this quality can be perceived separately from tangible matter itself. For this reason I also capitalise words such as Land and Species when it is this "quality" that is being referred to and not the material aspect of the thing itself. The quality in question is critical to understanding Renunciation in the Aboriginal sense. Unfortunately the English language does not provide us with the linguistic tools necessary to discriminate such distinctions, nor to adequately express many of the concepts to be introduced here. As a result, I sometimes have to create new words (such as landForm, speciesForm, someNothing) to communicate what I mean. Quotation marks around a word in English will indicate that the word is only an approximation to what I mean.

The alternative theoretical perspective I originally brought to bear on Aboriginal society and culture and which eventually broke down under the weight of my experience in their society and culture was that which underlies the lifeway of accumulation, namely *thesis —> anti-thesis —> synthesis*. This is the process of acting in the world and thinking about the world in terms of mutually exclusive, conflicting—indeed warring—needs, interests, and categories. Its complements are ideas and practices of autonomy, self/group-determination, and movement to and from oneness or unity through incorporation, hierarchy, hegemony.

In this book I will first recount my understanding of Australian Aboriginal culture and society and show the lifeway of Renunciation full-blown as a living practice. Then I will read Judeo-Christian Scriptures for hermeneutical evidence of Renunciation in the Aboriginal sense, taking the text at face value as given to me by the biblical scholars responsible for the translation. The reading complete, I will briefly examine teachings of certain other religious traditions (Hinduism through the Upanishads, Zen Buddhism through dialogue with an Abbot, Islam through the lifeway of the Gujar of north India), before turning to two "secular" episodes of history (Canadian Confederation and Sunday Morning Hockey) to show how certain "forces" at work in history can "throw up" elementary forms of the Renunciative way of life.

I also want to be clear that my reading of Hebrew-Christian Scriptures in particular does not preclude the existence of other scenarios in the texts other than those I have defined as "Renunciative." The reading will, however, beg the question of whether Renunciation, where I claim to find it, is "really there" as a peripheral, if not central, message of the Hebrew/ Christian (and other) religious traditions or whether I am simply reading something in through coloured glasses. The same question might even be raised in my account of Renunciation in Gujar society, in the terms of Canadian Confederation, and in the way we play ice hockey in my hometown of Perth, Ontario. All I can say by way of anticipating such criticisms is that my reading does seem to make sense of certain materials in the texts and societies under investigation, resolves apparent contradictions in certain materials, and, if not always explicit, is at least implicit in them.

Mine or any other reading of Christian Scriptures in particular is complicated by questions as to the ontological status of the texts in question. Is the Bible a recording of things observed and experienced; is it a story made up to illustrate a point; or is it both? Was there really a Jesus; did he do and say the things Christian Scriptures say he did and said? Or was the whole Christian thing concocted by someone like Paul based on his own "religious experience" on the road to Damascus (Wilson 1996: 42)? It is now established that Paul's writings (if they really are his writings) were composed before the four canonical Gospels of **Matthew**, **Mark**, **Luke** and **John**. And as Mack (1995: 46) argues, even if Jesus did exist, his chroniclers seem to have recreated him and what he represented in the image that seemed appropriate to the founder of the various schools they "had become or wanted to become."

John's Gospel, the most different in style and content from the others, is generally accepted as being composed later, but a fragment of **John** has been dated to between 100 and 125 A.D. or earlier than the dates accepted for the three Synoptic Gospels (Wilson 1996: 21). We cannot even be sure that the authors of these texts were people named Matthew, Mark, Luke, and John. And unless we accept the authority of these texts, we cannot even be sure that Jesus existed, as there is no independent reference to him outside these texts in the period of his supposed lifetime. The Roman historian Tacitus as well as Pliny the Younger refer to Jesus only in the context of citing those of his followers who had been executed in their time, and a comment by Josephus (b. 37 or 38 A.D.) about Jesus appears to have been edited into the text much later by a follower (Wilson 1996: 42–43).

In consequence I will treat the texts in question as a vehicle for disseminating ideas and experiences documented for one tradition that can be compared to ideas and experiences documented for another tradition, namely the Australian Aboriginal.

In the final analysis I justify my reading as an act of respectful engagement with the texts and traditions in question. As McDonnell observes in his "Interpreting the New Testament in the Light of Jewish-Christian Dialogue Today,"

> There is no reading without interpretation; the reader creates meaning through engagement with the text; and reading is essential to the discovery of new truth . . . . The text remains the focus, in all its linguistic, structural and rhetorical concern . . . . But weight is now also placed on the self-awareness of the readers, on the possibility of transformation through their transaction with the text . . . . *the reader is part*

of a chain of interpretation spanning the ages. (pp. 26–27)

*   *   *   *

Throughout this book the line between the academic study of religion and "theology" (really "cosmology") is blurred. This is the inevitable result of having been taken in to the Renunciative way of life by the Aborigines to experience its more esoteric aspects first-hand. I have seen and heard the "Forms," "Presences," "Nothingnesses" in question, or at least have been led by their methodologies of accessing the non-discursive to experience what they say they experience through the means of these methodologies. I do not apologise for this. Indeed, I believe it enriches the work rather than diminishes it. You, the reader, though, need not believe what I have come to believe, namely that the basis of Renunciation lies in another dimension of life that is inaccessible to most people in our own contemporary, so-called "Western," societies. Renunciation is understandable as a practice without having personally realised its presumed basis. The consequences of its practice are still the same whether you have experienced or believe in this basis or not. This brings me to a related point.

I cannot avoid evaluating the consequences of Renunciation as a way of life in human terms, that is, in terms of how it would affect our current life on this planet. I am convinced that life according to the terms of Renunciation is better for us than life according to the alternatives. By "better" I mean, leads to a more peaceful and less confrontational world than the one we have experienced in the 20th century. Sure, there wouldn't be as many and as great a variety of baubles, bangles, and beads; but then virtually no one would care and virtually no one would be competing to produce them. Again, I do not apologise for taking a stand in favour of certain kinds of practices. Like Mack (1995: 310), I say "And why *not* learn to evaluate [religions and] cultures in the light of the social issues and global horizons that challenge our times? Why can't we learn to talk about religion and culture in public as we look for ways to imagine and create the sane societies we desperately need in our multi-national world?"

But you do not have to share my passion in order to understand the terms of "Renunciation" or how it comes into being and passes away in the world.

David Turner,
Trinity College,
March, 1998

ILLUSTRATIONS

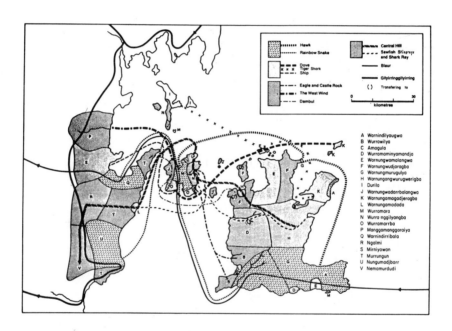

1. Songstreams of the Western Gulf, northern Australia

2. Dancing Curlew, 1969

3. Yidaki or didjereedoos and bark painting from north-east
Arnhem Land

4. Hindu temple at the ancient site of Brahmaur, Himachal Pradesh

5. Sougen at Kokokuji Zen Temple

6. Sakhi praying at Ranikot, Himachal Pradesh

7. Lanark County, Townships and Towns

8. Sunday Morning Hockey Sweater

frontispiece: The cross as intersecting straight lines—an archetypal Aboriginal form

I

Introduction

Renunciation defines the way of life of the world's oldest continuing civilisation—perhaps the world's oldest civilisation—that of the Australian Aborigines. Judged by technology, that civilisation is in our past, utilising as it did only stone, bone, and wood tools throughout its history. Judged by the ability of its members to peacefully co-exist, however, that civilisation is in our future, achieving something we only aspire to. The fact that this was achieved without constant advancement in technology perhaps gives us a clue as to why they managed to accomplish what we only aspire to. There might be something inherently destructive about the process of technological change; there is something in the lifeway of Renunciation that inherently renders the process of continual technological change unnecessary. What exactly, then, is Renunciation?

Let me begin by saying that I do not mean by this term exactly what you are accustomed to this word meaning. But the term comes closer than any other I can find in the English language to communicate the essence of the lifeway in question. Perhaps this in itself demonstrates my point that the lifeway in question is something only dimly imagined and imperfectly realised in our tradition.

The Oxford English dictionary defines renunciation as: "self-denial," "giving up of things." This is to see the giving up of things as the positive effect of negative denial. It is as if we give up reluctantly as a noble gesture; renunciation here is a form of sacrifice. We also use "renunciation" to refer to an ascetic lifestyle marked by self-denial and a rejection of worldly things. I am not using "renunciation" in either of these senses. But it is the only word we have that means a *total* giving up of something, a total giving up of *everything*.

In our conventional usage, renunciation or "giving up" could be seen as a form of sharing or reciprocity at one end of a continuum with hoarding and selfishness (accumulation) at the other. This would be to "give without the expectation of return." However, in my usage there is no expectation of return, certainly not from the one to whom you have "given up" everything of something. It simply comes from anyone who has everything of it when you have nothing of it whether you expect it or not. My usage reflects a situation where the bounds of selfishness and hoarding—of material attachment—have been transcended to the degree that *other*—particularly "empty" or "spiritually pure" other, as we'll see—is first rather than second in anyone's consideration.

Our conventional usage of the term "renunciation" reflects a way of life struggling—and only occasionally at that—to move beyond the bounds of selfishness and hoarding without even a clear or complete idea of what "being beyond" entails. We occasionally realise sharing (a 50/50 split) and reciprocity (I give to you if you give to me) but we contain these relations within the bounds of family, friends or work mates for reasons of predictability and security or we calculate comparative value in order to ensure we get full value for what we give in any market transaction.

Renunciation in my usage is entirely open-ended, applying to anyone anywhere, stranger or friend, who has nothing of something that you can provide. Nor does Renunciation equate with philanthropy or charity. Here, those who have everything (of something) may give to those who have nothing (of it), but the giver is not now left with nothing (of something) as they would be in a truly Renunciative relation. In other words, he or she remains in a situation of advantage despite the giving.

Reciprocity, exchange, whether direct (me to you, you to me) or indirect (me to you to someone else and back to me), codes according to this formula *thesis —> anti-thesis —> plurality* mentioned in the Prologue. Here, something that someone has (*thesis*) is given to someone else to incur a debt (*anti-thesis*) and move something of equal value back to the original person, thereby "resolving" the relationship (if of greater value the debt is on the original partner and the cycle continues until equalised).

Renunciation in the Aboriginal sense, by contrast, codes according to the formula *anti-thesis —> thesis —> plurality*. Here, the initiating force is the *absence* of something on the part of someone (*anti-thesis*) which is then provided by someone else who has it (*thesis*), to establish a part-of-one-in-the-other *relationship* between them.

In a Renunciative order, when you procure something you do not debate within yourself whether to consume it or horde it for yourself if there is someone around who has it not and needs it. You simply give it up. Let me illustrate with two examples involving my old Aboriginal friend Gula Lalara.

Gula, now in his mid-70s, lives on an outstation on Bickerton Island adjacent to Groote Eylandt off the coast of Arnhem Land in northern Australia. When I visited him in July of 1995 I flew into Bickerton on a small bush plane, disembarked and walked to the settlement. I saw Gula at a distance and he just sat there as I approached. When I reached him the very first thing he said to me was, "David, I have no money for food." Without even thinking I reached into my pocket, pulled out my wallet and handed him $20 of the $40 that was in there. Then we marched to the shop. I hadn't seen him in two years, my closest friend, and this was the extent of the "greeting"? To an observer this is a crafty Aborigine taking advantage of an anthropologist come for information. Not so. The fishing was bad and the barge that services the small shop on the island had not yet arrived. He had no food and no money to buy any.

But as we entered the store I broke out in a cold sweat as I realised I had committed a ghastly *faux pas*. I had *shared* my money with him; I hadn't given him all of it as I should have done. I quickly fumbled for my wallet again and fished out the remaining $20 and handed it to him. His face broke out in a wide smile of acknowledgement and he proceeded to buy what he needed out of the meagre supplies available. But this wasn't the end of it. As we were walking back to his place he asked if I had brought any food with me from Groote Eylandt for myself and Nancy, his daughter, who had accompanied me. I said, "No," and a look of panic swept over his face. This meant I had nothing (and therefore was entitled to everything). He fumbled about in his pocket for the little change he had left from his purchases and handed it to me. "Buy something for you and Nancy," he said, knowing full well what was left would purchase about a chocolate bar and a soft drink. Back I went and off he went. About half an hour later when I was back at the place where Nancy and I were staying, here comes Gula with something wrapped up under his arm. It was a big chunk of highly prized dugong meat he or someone had stored away. It was for us.

In 1992 I took Philippe Rouja, a former student of mine, with me to Groote Eylandt during one of my field trips. He made some good friends amongst the Aborigines while we were there and paid a visit with me to Bickerton to visit Gula now in his 70s and the most knowledgeable man in the region. Philippe was suitably impressed. Two years later Philippe was in Darwin on the way to carrying out his own research among the Bardi of Western Australia as a PhD student at Durham University in England. He had called an Aboriginal friend on Groote Eylandt trying to locate Gula to find that he was somewhere in Darwin at the time, so he set about finding him. Where else but down on the beach by the sailing club? And there he was. Philippe recognised him from behind by his coiffured mass of white hair as he sat there playing cards. Philippe approached, not saying anything, and Gula didn't turn around. When he reached him, Gula, without looking behind him but obviously addressing the remark to Philippe, said, "I need $20 to play cards with." Without even thinking Philippe reached into his pocket, pulled out a $20 bill, and gave it to him. Gula played until he lost it and finally turned around to face Philippe. Philippe said, "Do you know who I am?" And Gula answered, "Of course, you're Philippe, David's friend." Philippe took him to a nearby store and bought him $60 worth of groceries and left. Again, to an outside observer it looks like an Aborigine taking advantage of a do-gooder liberal white man. But that was not what was going on. Gula knew Philippe knew the Law and Philippe did. There was no expectation of return on Philippe's part or of obligation to reciprocate on Gula's. Quite likely Philippe would never see Gula again. It didn't matter. This is how you behave as an Aboriginal wherever you are with whomever you meet. There is no sense in which you are giving now to get a return in the future. It is simply what you do. If, in reply to Gula's request Philippe had said that he had been robbed and had no money for food and shelter, Gula would have found some and provided for him.

Renunciation in the sense I have defined it above and as expressed in these examples is termed *gemalyanggerranema* in the Anindilyaugwa language. The term literally means "create" in the sense of something new emerging out of Nothing (*nar' a:bina*—"not anything") and getting "twisting it in," or becoming part of, something already existent. Another word for *gemalyanggerranema* is *lyelingma*, which could be translated as "love" and carries the connotation, "expiration" or giving up one's "breath," though our concept of love does not contain the same instruction: "give everything of something you have to those who have it not."

Gemalyanggerranema, as I said in the Prologue, can be translated as *anti-thesis* —> *thesis* —> *plurality* or Nothingness —> being —> relationship where part of one becomes part of another. The logic that moves the two above examples involving Gula, then, is "You have nothing (of something), everything I have (of something) is yours," and "I have nothing (of something), everything you have (of something) is mine." In the Aboriginal usage what moves matter between people in this manner is spirit. You, then, are an active Nothing—enFormed spiritual Presence—that expels the matter you have to others who have it not.

Spirit is what remains when all matter of yours or any other thing's existence has been removed or eliminated. This I call the "someNothing" of your existence whose Form and essence derive from your own particular existence's existence but transcend it. (A parallel concept is that of "vital force" in the field of homeopathic medicine. Samuel Hahnemann, the founder of the field, concluded that a "spiritual vital force" remained after substances had been "so potentized they contained no detectable trace of the original substance" [Vithoulkas 1987, p. 28]. That something powerful still remained, was evidenced by the healing power of the presumably "empty" dilutions of these substances.)

To Aborigines, when you are born you incarnate out of Nothing from the "other side" while carrying something of it with you when you do (your "inner spirit," *amugwa*). When you die you (your inner spirit) transcend back into this Nothing, though leaving something of your spiritual Presence behind in the process—as you leave something of it with others and the places and things you encounter during your lifetime.

Renunciation, then, is not at one end of a continuum with selfishness and hoarding at the other end and reciprocity, sharing, and charity in between. It is rather outside—really over and above—a continuum composed of these four forms insofar as it requires the grasping of a transcendent dimension to reality, an idea or experience of Nothing behind or beyond material reality. It requires grasping that someNothing is left after every-thing has been given up or removed.

In this book I will use capital R "Renunciation" to refer to Renunciation in its Aboriginal sense as discussed above, and small-r "renunciation" to refer to tendencies toward this form in other traditions. The remarkable thing to me is that the Aboriginal people I am about to introduce you to actually live by this principle—it is not merely a lofty ideal to which they aspire. They see in the world around them evidence of Renunciation which they take as a sign of cosmological intent—a model of how we are to relate to one another and to nature.

Origins of the Aboriginal Way of Life?

We now know that the Aborigines have been on their island continent for at least 100,000 years and, if recent archaeological finds in the Kimberley region of Western Australia are correct, perhaps upwards of 200,000 years (*Sydney Morning Herald*, September 21, 24, 28, 1996; December 23, 1997; *Antiquity*, vol. 71, no. 271, 1997). If we assume that the Aborigines evolved from pre-human primates (as we assume we did), this means that they were in Australia as *homo erectus* and became fully human or *homo sapiens sapiens* in isolation from other developments elsewhere in the world.

Aborigines say they were always in Australia and didn't come from anywhere else. As fully human beings they certainly didn't. But did they come as *homo erectus*? Well, if they came to Australia upwards of 200,000 years ago they would have to have come as *homo erectus* and been technologically more advanced then than they were when first contacted by Europeans some two hundred years ago. When we found them they were in possession of the seaworthy dugout canoe but had learned this technology only a few hundred years earlier from Macassan visitors from Indonesia for whom they worked in search of trepang and pearl shell and with whom they often travelled (Macknight 1972). Before this they relied on unseaworthy rafts and bark canoes (with ranges of 5-8k and 30k, respectively). But then they had no need of large vessels in which to make long sea voyages. The Aborigines were content to fish off-shore in their bark craft and hop up and down the coast visiting their neighbours for ceremony, trade, and intermarriage. No invaders caused them to flee over long distances, nor did they invade far away lands. In fact there was no word for "enemy" in their languages, just as there was no word for "warfare."

It is possible that once having crossed the some 90 kilometres of open seas that separated Australia from

Indonesia some 200,000 years ago (the two major lowerings of the seas that may have occasioned travel by foot having occurred 140,000 and 18,000 years ago) in seaworthy watercraft, the Aborigines may have had no further need of these craft and let the technology lapse. We have evidence of technological "regression" in the Aboriginal archaeological record over the past 25,000 years (Pretty 1976 on the Roonka Flat site; Flood 1995 on the Kangaroo Island sites). It seems that their way of life needed technology but not progressive *changes* in technology. As we'll see, the arresting of technological change in favour of promoting peace and order is intrinsic to the *anti-thesis* —> *thesis* —> *plurality* (as distinct from the *thesis* —> *anti-thesis* —> *synthesis* process).

There is no doubt that the Australian Aboriginal way of life (and its variations) is very different from other ways of life recorded for hunter-gatherers. There is no doubt that it is very different from our own (differences in technology not-withstanding). But how significant is their degree of difference? There is no significance as far as their ability to procreate with us is concerned. That is, they are not a different species. But there is significant difference in their way of Life compared to almost any other in the world. Indeed, the difference is the way Aborigines handle "difference." Difference is used by Aborigines to relate positively to others. It is what is renounced to others. That is, you must first *have* a difference before you can give it up to someone else. In their way of life, then, differences are created, established, continued—even highlighted.

There is a remarkable example of this, unique in world prehistory as we know it to date. This was the coexistence in Australia for some 20,000 years of Aborigines we consider "modern" (fully *homo sapiens sapiens*) with a more robust type in many ways resembling Java man or *homo erectus*. During this period, the more modern type neither interbred nor assimilated nor exterminated the more archaic type (see Thorne 1977).

Despite living side-by-side for thousands of years, the Anindilyaugwa language of the people with whom I work has remained separate and distinct in its vocabulary from the Nunggubuyu language on the adjacent mainland. The two peoples solved the "problem" of communication by bilingualism—my language for you, yours for me.

Physical anthropologists and archaeologists debate the facts of technological regression and the co-existence of archaic and modern man, but their debates are fuelled by an assumption deep in our own way of thinking, namely that the evolution of species and of technology are inevitably progressive, moved as they are presumed to be by the law of natural selection. What is rarely if ever considered is that sub-species and even species might choose to co-exist indefinitely without competition for survival in "defiance" of the "law" of natural selection. Without competition, in the case of humans at least, technological change may be unnecessary to our mutual survival, each of us having abandoned the quest for self-sufficiency and autonomy and hence the need to progress technologically in order to extract more from available resources in time of crisis in order to maintain that autonomy.

If the Aborigines were different on their island continent in relation to people elsewhere, so too were the flora and fauna on which they depended for food. This is the continent of the marsupial and the eucalyptus. Marsupial animals split from mammals, our supposed pre-human ancestors, some 125 to 100 million years ago. Those in Australia became isolated and evolved giant species or Megafauna like the rhinoceros-sized marsupial Diprotodron and the three metre kangaroo. Some of these giants co-existed with Aborigines until about 20,000 years ago. The Megafauna posed no threat to humans. For the most part they were vegetarians. Only the marsupial lion (the size of a leopard), a giant lizard and the Tasmanian tiger (the size of a large dog) were carnivores. And the Aborigines, while carnivores, existed on a mainly plant diet (80% in inland areas).

Some Academic Issues

My account of Australian Aboriginal culture and of the lifeway of Renunciation I have abstracted from it must be qualified as derived mainly from a study of the people of Groote Eylandt and Bickerton Island in Arnhem Land. Does my account apply generally to Aboriginal peoples across Australia or is it particular to this one region? Is it contradicted by other accounts?

A great deal has been written about the Australian Aborigines and almost all of it is filtered through our own assumptions and has been distorted accordingly, even by anthropologists who have worked for years with these people. The old accounts made them out to be virtually sub-human (see early settlers' views in the collection *Seeing the First Australians* edited by Donaldson and Donaldson). The newest popular accounts attempt to assimilate them to Revised Standard New Age "universal aboriginality." An example is Lynn Andrews' *Crystal Woman*. But the worst is probably Marlo Morgan's *Mutant Message Down Under* as the author purports to be a spokeswoman for a lost tribe of Aborigines who are ready to reveal their secrets to the world—through her of course. And what is the secret message heretofore hidden from us? That we are all part of the great Oneness of Being and must get in touch with our inner selves (the child, the goddess, or whatever), within. All this supposedly emanating from didjereedoo playing Desert Aborigines who never used the hollow log musical instrument, with crocodile "Dreamings" even though they are 500 kilometres inland from the sea, and with telepathic powers resembling those of Whoopi Goldberg in *Ghost*.

Marlo Morgan made a lot of money and acquired quite a reputation as a "guru" on the public lecture circuit with this book, until it came to the attention of the Central Land Council in Alice Springs who represent most of the Western Desert Aborigines. They looked into it and found the Aborigines in the area she claimed to have visited had never heard of her, let alone designated her as their spokeswoman. The Land Council has lawyers, the lawyers recommended taking legal action, the Aborigines offered to debate her on American T.V. talk shows. She declined. She now prefaces her book with a statement that it had really been intended as a work of fiction all along, though that's not how it is written and not how people read it. Despite all this, the publisher still prints the book, and she still makes a lot of money.

A different kind of account, however, is Bruce Chatwin's *The Songlines*. First, he did his homework and visited the late T. G. H. Strehlow's archives in Adelaide to get his information on Aboriginal culture. Strehlow was born and raised among the Aranda and spent most of his working life with them. Then Chatwin simply went to Alice Springs for a few weeks, hung out in the bars and on the fringes of Aboriginal communities, and wrote up an anecdotal book about it—an exceptionally well-written book and accurate as far as it goes (except for one paragraph about me which would take a book to explain). But it cannot go beyond the limitations of its sources because the source is not Chatwin or the Aborigines, but Strehlow. Strehlow, too, had his problems translating Aboriginal realities into English and most of his works are all but written in Aranda (see his *Songs of Central Australia*). Neither Strehlow nor I can write as well as Chatwin, but this is largely due (I hope) to the fact that Aboriginal reality does not code in English categories or logic. Theirs is a world predicated on an underlying "two," if you will (actually "two or more"). There is no concept of "oneness" or "unity." If Aborigines don't compete, neither do they co-operate. If they don't horde, neither do they share. If they don't have private property, neither do they have communal property. If they "give," they don't "reciprocate." If they are tenacious about boundaries they are indifferent to what is contained within them and allow (controlled) movement within and without. If mothers are mothers, they are not the mothers of their own children (as the fathers are not the fathers).

Our language is predicated on a way of life in which

concepts such as competition/co-operation, hoarding/ sharing, private/ communal, are based on realities that have emerged in our history to define competing interests and aspirations of which traditional Aboriginal society has no experience. Our notions of "motherhood" and "fatherhood" are rooted in a materialist conception of relationships in which biology is seen as defining the essential nature of the person.

What, then, is the basis of my own claim to write with authority on the Aboriginal way(s) of life? Well, I have been there, I have lived among them on and off for some 30 years, I have been initiated into their society and what I have written about them to date has been read by some of those who can read English (for instance, Nancy Lalara) and given their seal of approval. For the benefit of the "scientific community" I have statistically validated my account of their so-called "kinship and marriage system" (in fact a system based on "spiritual" rather than genealogical connections); I have exhaustively mapped an intact eco-zone (Bickerton Island) to locate Land/People boundaries and resource distributions in relation to sites of spiritual significance; and I have based my conclusions on their music on an analysis of over 600 songs recorded during mortuary ceremonies in 1969.

But I emphasise that I write about their way of life not as a spokesman for the Aborigines, but rather from my own point of view as an affiliate of their society, in particular the society of the people of Groote Eylandt and Bickerton Island of the Northern Territory (though being an affiliate there makes me an affiliate pretty much anywhere else in Aboriginal Australia). I was not born and raised among them.

I was, in fact, born in Macclesfield, Cheshire, in England and came to Canada with my parents as a child after World War II where I was raised in Perth in the Ottawa Valley of Ontario. I went to Carleton University in Ottawa and from there went to Australia where I arrived in 1968 to do my PhD at the University of Western Australia and was promptly sent to Groote Eylandt by my supervisor Ronald Berndt to "get it right." The previous two anthropologists who had been there (Fred Rose and Peter Worsley) were Marxists who, Prof. Berndt thought, had probably got it wrong. In fact, their work went a long way to help me get it right. Despite returning to Canada in 1974 I have been travelling back and forth to Australia since 1983 as my need to know continues and the Aborigines' need for political help arises. The last stage in my understanding was reached in 1992–95 when I was transcribing songs with the help of my old friend Gula Lalara, the last remaining songman on my tapes. It was then that Gula told me that their music was the *first* thing I should have looked at when I arrived in 1969 and not the last some 25 years later. To them, music in the sense of Formed sound, locates the origins and is the foundation of their way of life. Music, unlike anything else on "this side" of existence, is "non-existent" yet Formed as Melody and songLine. It is as close as one can get to the "other side" of existence without actually being there. The term *gemalyanggerranema*, ultimate Creation, in fact applies first and foremost to the process of musical creation.

I don't claim to be an expert on all Aboriginal societies everywhere in Australia. I've surveyed many others in the Northern Territory as part of a project I did for the Government on local government (1986), but nowhere else than on Groote Eylandt and Bickerton Island have I developed such an intimate relationship with the people. Even in anthropological accounts of Aborigines in Australia (with the exception of the recent field researches of Deborah Bird Rose and Philippe Rouja and the analyses of Tony Swain), you will not find direct confirmation of the essence of what I am going to relate to you here, though you will find aspects in the writings of Maddock and Morphy, Stanner and Strehlow, the Berndts.

It's not so much that other ethnographic accounts got the wrong answers as that the right questions weren't always asked and indigenous experience was lacking. Most enquiries have been predicated on academic or other interests, whether these have been to fit the Aboriginal way of life into models of hunter-gatherer societies established elsewhere such as in North America or southern Africa (Lee and De Vore's *Man the Hunter*); into the Left's idea of "primitive communism" (Frederick Rose's *Australien und seine Ureinwohner*) or the Rights of "competitive individualism" (Geoffrey Blainey's *The Triumph of the Nomads*); into Lévi-Strauss's structuralism (my own early work); into neo-Marxism (see Tim Ingold's review of Testart in *Current Anthropology*, vol. 29, no. 1, p. 15); or into the requirements of the Land Rights Act, 1976, in order to legitimate Aboriginal right to territories which had been appropriated from them by Europeans.

We have also missed much of what Aboriginal societies are about because of our failure to take their own perspectives on their own ways of life seriously.

Yet we do have hints of evidence of Renunciation in the literature even if the examples are not elaborated and the basis for the practice remains unrealised. Strehlow observes:

> A local group might even have had to seek refuge for many months in the territorial area of a different local group hundred of miles away. Fortunately . . . many of the ranges in the poorest "desert" areas have always contained some permanent waters. Hence even in the worst droughts the survival of the Western Desert folk was assumed, as long as their social organisation possessed sufficient flexibility to enable any stricken local group to find temporary asylum within the food area of one of the more fortunate groups. (1965: 124)

Later (p. 144) Strehlow points out that "A man did not kill or eat his own totemic animal . . . . And since the various members of his own family might well belong to totems different from his own, he felt kindly disposed toward their totem animal as well." Strehlow does not tell us whether these latter were "therefore available to oneself as those prohibited to oneself would be available to others" as he does not tell us whether the food area to which those stricken by drought found refuge in the first example was likewise prohibited to its owners.

In a like vein, Donald Thomson in his book on the ceremonial exchange cycle in Arnhem Land (1949: 49–50) notes two of the six "chief ways in which possessions change hands" to be *yanna gurrupa:n*, "the for nothing gift" with no immediate, obligation to reciprocate and *ka:na:n-gurrupa:na*, "a free gift, pure and simple, without any reciprocal obligation." But he does not elaborate and goes on to discuss other forms in which reciprocity is expected, though he does detail the regional specialisation that exists in the production of objects for ceremonial exchange.

A passing example of renunciation from a non-academic source comes from Bill Harney in his *Life Among the Aborigines*, interestingly from Groote Eylandt. Bill Harney travelled the Territory in the 1930s and 1940s as a government appointed "Protector of Aborigines":

> An interesting custom regarding canoes when we were there was that a man who wanted a canoe would bring to us a chip from one of the paper-bark, Leichhardt, or milk-wood trees growing in that area. We would take the chip and in return supply him with some tomahawks, an adze and a little food, and he would go out and cut the canoe. After he and his kin had cut, trimmed and burnt it over a fire—a custom said to stretch and preserve it against the teredo worm—he would deliver it to us. We in our turn would brand and hand it back to him. By this custom we owned the trade that canoe caught, and he owned the canoe as long as he did not deceive us. (p. 111)

Harney thought that the custom originated with the Macassan visitors from Indonesia, but to me it is an expression of Aboriginal Renunciative logic—canoeForm expelling material, trade, contents. But this point cannot be grasped without an understanding of the Aboriginal perception of the Form or "Nothingness" of something and its relation to "content"; this Harney seems to miss. He notes collecting some of the Aborigines' sacred boards, saying that the Aborigines could grasp the image of, say, a turtle, and draw it on a board, but that they "were lost when it came to the abstract art. They had never reached that stage when the painted designs could recall in their minds the original story." The designs, in fact, are not intended to recall a story but rather to trigger a perception of Form.

The factor of "experience" is crucial to an understanding of the Aboriginal lifeway of Renunciation. The perception of Form or Nothingness that underlies Renunciation is taught through experience in ceremony and musical performance rather than described through concepts. It is how I came to understand it myself. Lack the experience and you lack fundamental understanding of Renunciation and how it differs from, say, hoarding or sharing. I put it that the phenomenon has been missed largely because the experience was not in the investigator's "methodological" repertoire. As Andrew McMillan, a writer, put it: "people bouncing from settlement to settlement, tribe to tribe, seeking a truth when their senses aren't attuned, and they cannot therefore, gain an appreciation of the bottom line. And without a sensual appreciation—stop, listen, taste, smell, learn—there's no telling what sort of impression they'll come up with" (1992: 132).

A final example comes neither from ethnography or observation but from Aboriginal lore. This is the story of the Dreamtime Djanggawul sisters and it is usually cited by "critical anthropologists" as an example of how, "in the beginning," men appropriated women's sacred "business" and maintained them thereafter in a position of ritual and social subordination. This excerpt comes from R.M. and C.H. Berndt's *The World of the First Australians*:

The two Djanggawul sisters came to Marabai where they built a shelter and hung inside it their sacred dilly bags (or long baskets full of emblems). They went out to collect mangrove shells. While they were away their Brother and his companions, men whom the Sisters had made, sneaked up and stole their baskets. The Sisters heard the whistle of the *djunmal* mangrove bird, warning that something was wrong. They hurried back to their shelter to find their belongings gone, and saw on the ground the tracks of the men who had stolen them. They followed these, but had not gone far when the Brother began to beat his singing sticks rhythmically. As soon as they heard the beat of the sticks and the sound of the men singing they stopped, fell to the ground, and began to crawl. They were too frightened to go near that place, fearful not of the men but of the power of the sacred songs. The men had taken from them not only these songs, and the emblems, but also the power to perform sacred ritual, a power which had formerly belonged only to the Sisters. Before that, men had nothing. The elder sister said: . . . 'Men can do it now, they can look after it . . . We know everything. We have really lost nothing, because we remember it all, and we can let them have their small part. Aren't we sacred, even if we have lost the baskets?' (pp. 215–216)

The key phrase in the tale from a Renunciative/Aboriginal point of view is not that the men took the baskets and their contents from the women but that "Before that, men had nothing" (in the way of sacred emblems and songs). Having nothing of them the men were, in fact, entitled to them. This left the women with nothing of them in a material sense but with something less tangible of them in the form of remembrances. Indeed the process of "losing" them actually sets up a relation of interdependence between men and women, each with their own "part" to play thereafter. The Women are indeed still sacred (as enFormed Presences) after this event, not "even if" but *because* they have lost their baskets. The critic might reply, "But the men did not give the women anything back in turn." The Renunciative answer is that they aren't supposed to. The Women, in the final analysis, do not complain about have nothing of the "something" in question, and even if they did, something else would not be expected to come back from these Brothers.

*　　*　　*　　*

If there is little precedent in anthropological pre-history for the understanding to be presented here with respect to the Aboriginal way of life, is there anything in the Western history of ideas that anticipates, or at least provides a familiar avenue into the subject? Don Wiebe suggested to me that I might find precedents in Plato's notion of "Forms." Indeed, proceeding as Platonic philosophy does from a "belief in a world of intelligible Forms or 'ideas' existing independently of the things we see and touch, and the belief in an immortal soul existing in separation from the body, both before and after death" (Cornford 1962: xxvii), would seem to be a point of articulation. However, there is much ambiguity in Plato and his interpreters about the status and character of Forms. Cornford, for one, states explicitly that Form does not mean shape but refers to essential properties that constitute what the thing is. The most important of these he says is "function" (p. 322). The Form of a bed, then, has to do with the fact that it is meant to be slept on. Plato often refers to Forms as "qualities" such as "temperance," "courage," "liberality," and their opposites. Then there is the vexing question of how Forms relate to Ideas. The ambiguities are summed up in this passage from *The Republic* :

> True; but when you are there I should not be very desirous to tell what I saw, however, plainly. You must use your own eyes.
> Well then, shall we proceed as usual and begin by assuming the existence of a single essential nature or

Form for every set of things which we call by the same
name? Do you understand?

I do.

Then let us take any set of things you choose. For
instance there are any number of beds or of tables, but
only two Forms, one of bed and one of Table.

Yes.

And we are in the habit of saying that the craftsman,
when he makes the beds or tables we use or whatever it
may be, has before his mind the Form of one or other of
these pieces of furniture. The Form itself is, of course,
not the work of any craftsman. How could it be?
(Cornford: 325)

The Aborigines perceive a kind of illuminated Presence
around a thing, defining it as what it is as distinct from
something else, though with an archetypal aspect that defines
it simultaneously as a certain *kind* of thing. I have translated
this as "Form," but "Presence" would do equally well; what it
really is, though, is the manifestation of an "intensity"—a kind
of "force-field" (or force-fields) which operates to shape things
in certain *kinds* of ways. I don't think this is what Plato is
saying, but there is no doubt that a reading of Plato would help
prepare one for the Aboriginal understanding. Could the same
be said, as Don Wiebe also thinks, of a reading of Mercia
Eliade's perspective on religion in general and Australian
Aboriginal religion in particular?

Eliade's approach to the study of religion is one with which I
am sympathetic. His aim, as he states in the Preface to
Shamanism (1974), is to approach religion as "religious
phenomena," to accept as "real" that "kernel [of human
experience] that remains refractory to explanation . . . . this
indefinable, irreducible element [that] perhaps reveals the real
situation of man in the cosmos . . . [and which] cannot be
exhausted by a psychological explanation" (p. xiv). In Eliade's
view, "From the most elementary hierophanies—the
manifestation of the sacred in some stone or tree, for

example—to the most complex (the 'vision' of a new 'divine form' by a prophet or the founder of a religion), everything is manifested in the historically concrete and everything is in some sense conditioned by history" (pp. xvi–vii).

In *Australian Religions* (p. xvii), he says, "Primitive man's . . . ethical, institutional, and artistic creations are dependent on, or inspired by religious experience and thought" (though I would drop the term primitive).

To Eliade the sacred in or about things is revealed by "mystical experience." He rejects a phenomenological approach to the sacred as it rejects comparison and is concerned solely with "approaching a religious phenomena (sic) and divining its *meaning*" (p. xvi, emphasis mine). In other words, meaning may be beside the point if apprehension of the experiential nature of the sacred as such is the issue. To pursue meaning would be to pursue an intellectual *interpretation* of the experience which would lead to reductionism.

Eliade's agenda here closely parallels that of the Aborigines' approach to things sacred. Indeed, Eliade's account of their view of creation in his *Australian Religions* is fairly close to the mark: "The act of 'creation' was not so much a cosmogony as it was a moulding and transformation of a pre-existent material; it was not a *creatio ex nihilo* but the shaping of an amorphous cosmic substance that had already existed before the appearance of the Supernatural Beings" (1973: 1).

However, the Forms of creation were already implicit within this "substance," and the substance in question had no singularity in and of itself. This is not an insignificant point and brings us to a major problem with Eliade's work when applied to the Australian material. This is his emphasis on "the sacred" in all things. Eliade's "hidden agenda" in *Australian Religions, Shamanism,* and in his other works (in particular Eliade 1960, 1979), is not merely to locate a common source for the "sacred" in all societies but also to locate that source as "the sacred" in and of itself—if not explicitly God, then some underlying unity or Oneness of cosmic-spiritual experience. In this respect so-called "archaic" peoples hold particular interest for Eliade. The more innocent and pristine the society, the closer he presumes its people to be to the "origins" of history and the more likely they are to be in touch with "the source" of creation.

Eliade looks for finds examples of High Beings and Gods in his Australian sources which is not surprising since they were reported by nineteenth-century ethnographers: "[The] Supreme God of the Kamilaroi, the Wiradjuri, and the Euahlayi dwells in the upper sky, seated on a throne; Bundjil, the Supreme God of the Kulin, remains above the clouds. Mythical heroes and medicine men ascend to these celestial beings by using, among other things, the rainbow" (1974: 134; see also 1973: 3–41).

Eliade also identifies Baiame as the "Supreme Sky God" of the Wiradjurri (pp. 135–39). But these "Gods" he dwells on to the exclusion of other aspects of Aboriginal spirituality and cosmology and ignores the fact that his sources are in the south-east part of Australia, the area with the longest and most intensive history of contact with Europeans. Here Christian missionaries had already been at work among fragmented groups of Aborigines for many generations. There is no record of "High Gods" in more recently contacted areas of Australia such as Arnhem Land and Central Australia.

In the same Preface (pp. xvi-vii) Eliade goes on to say that even in the "humblest hierophany," the Australians included, there is posited an "eternal new beginning," an "eternal return to an atemporal moment, a desire to abolish history, to blot out the past, to recreate the world" (p. xix). "For all history," he says (p. xix) "is in some measure a fall of the sacred, a limitation and diminution."

The Aborigines recognise no "Fall," no "resurrection" of culture or people into a better world, but rather posit *Amawurrena-alawuduwarra* to be "eternally uncreated spiritual Forms/Presences," there in the beginning, with us in the present, indifferent to humans' efforts at perceiving them and living in concert with them.

In the final analysis, then, Eliade's approach fails us.

*   *   *   *

What impedes the understanding, clouds the vision, scrambles the audition, when it comes to comprehending the essence of the Aboriginal way of life—even on the part of those attempting experience in indigenous terms—is another "way" whose outlines are materially-determined and to which neo-Marxist and other materialist paradigms can profitably be applied. This way, in the context of people living at hunter-gatherer levels of subsistence, I have termed "locality-incorporative." This way is predicated on one's situation in space rather than in abstract relation to space; on social relations of co-production and kinship, rather than abstract "spiritual" substance, defining individual and group identity; on autonomy and self-determination on an individual and group basis as driving forces in dealings with insiders and outsiders—indeed, as defining people as "insiders" versus "outsiders" as such. In this way, you are where you are and who you are with, and are dependent on the resource base where you are for survival.

I have documented this form of organisation with Paul Wertman (1977) in a study of the Cree of northern Canada, and these findings have been replicated by Guy Lanoue among the Sekani, Robert Adlam among the Tahltan, Barry Martin among the Iroquois and Chris Trott among the Inuit. However, a caveat must be introduced. These are "locality-incorporative" societies with "Australian" features, as if they are trying to transcend the limits of material determination to become something else. The Iroquois' "federative" aspect of their society and the Inuit's "namesake relations" are a case in point (see also my *Life Before Genesis*, Part I).

A consensus has developed among Australian Anthropologists (the aforementioned Rose and Rouja being notable exceptions) that Aboriginal society is a land-based society and their religion is a land-based religion. This view stems, I think, from choosing the land (read "environment") as the point of departure for investigations of Aboriginal society and culture as it has been so-chosen for the investigation of hunter-gatherers elsewhere. I rather see Aboriginal society and culture as "Renunciatively based."

One can, of course, examine Renunciation as it applies to land and resources, but one can also examine Renunciation as it applies to the Person and his or her possessions, to the Woman as it applies to her birthing of children, to man as it applies to his fathering, and so on. Proceeding from Renunciation one first considers the Form or Presence of the land, the person, the woman etc., rather than the matter contained within that Form or Presence. One then realises a cycle of "coming into being" out of one Form into another and back again. A person is born from the "other side" through the Form of the Land, into the Form of a Person and passes back through the Form of the Land to the "other side" on death. Why take the land as the point of reference for the whole way of life when it is but one aspect—merely a material aspect at that—of a much larger whole? It would be rather like judging polygamy and gerontocracy to be a case of old men controlling young women for sexual gratification simply because you observe old men with young wives. Had you examined the situation of old women you would find many of them with young men, because when an old man dies his young wives are passed on to his younger "brother" and so on and so on. Your judgement, then, depends on at what point in the cycle of re-marriages you enter the system.

Aboriginal society and culture, then is, as I will show, Renunciatively-based as distinct from selfishness and hoarding-based, reciprocity-based, sharing-based, or charity-based.

I was fortunate in having arrived on Groote Eylandt in 1969 in the early stages of prolonged contact when the Aborigines were questioning for the first time basic assumptions underlying their way of life. They made me party to their questioning by utilising me as a source of knowledge about European customs and institutions. They had moved in from their traditional lands into settlements in the 1940s, though missionaries had been at work among them before that. Manganese mining had begun on the island in the mid-1960s and the impact was just beginning to be felt. Only Bickerton Island adjacent to Groote Eylandt remained ecologically untouched and it was here—and on the people who had emigrated from here to Groote Eylandt —that I focused my research. Eventually, having learned the language and gained their confidence, I was able to talk to and learn from the *warniyarengga*, the "proper old wise people," born and raised in the bush and speaking no English.

The way of life of the Aboriginal people of the Groote Eylandt and Bickerton Island area is without the layered elaborations of the mainland peoples and may well represent Australian Aboriginal culture in its most ancient and original form (see Swain 1993). This way of life seems to have been modified historically in two directions. On the one hand are elaborations *over and above* the basic Land/People system we find on Groote Eylandt, Bickerton Island and the adjacent mainland. These are named moieties and semi-moieties which combine Land/Peoples into two and four "Companies," respectively. Then there are named "sections" that combine alternate generations of people in the same Land/People and Company of Land/Peoples into one category, producing a "father-son couple." These elaborations are found today in northern coastal areas.

On the other hand are the *subtractions* from the fundamental shape of the Land/People system of Groote Eylandt and Bickerton Island that mark other ways of life on the continent. These involve a weakening of the abstract, spiritual, aspect of the Land/People relation to allow for more pragmatic, co-residential, principles of land tenure. This characterises the way of life in the Western Desert. I will discuss the Land/People system of the Groote and Bickerton people in the next chapter (for a more detailed discussion of the elaborations and subtractions see my *Australian Aboriginal Social Organisation* and *Afterlife Before Genesis*).

In a way it really doesn't matter if what I am about to describe was once general throughout Aboriginal Australia. The fact that it existed even in one small corner of it seems to me extraordinary and the implications for understanding our own situation are still the same. Judged in terms of the peaceful co-existence of people(s), it would seem that something better than the European record *is* possible and existed somewhere for thousands of years and, in theory, can be emulated under different historical conditions. The Renunciative lifeway, I posit, is *not* tied to a particular mode of production like hunting and gathering or a particular stage of the technical means of production like stone and bone technology. It is a potential for getting along together; we are all perhaps capable of realising it if we but choose to do so.

Aboriginal Forms Of Renunciation

The "Dreamtime"

"In the beginning, now and forever more," is *Amawurrena-alawuduwarra*. *Amawurrena-alawuduwarra* can best be translated from the Aboriginal as "Creation-substance power" *Amawurrena* is the passive aspect, *alawuduwarra* the active. *Amawurrena-alawuduwarra* is the "substance" or "content" of the Nothingness of "anti-thesis" of original Creation. Implicit within it (although "it" isn't really an it) are differentiated, archetypal Forms which, in the beginning of Creation, remained silent and unincarnated. Then these Forms began to sound and become visible, moving in waves of varying shapes (melodies or songLines) which formed the spiritual substances through which they moved. Where these Forms periodically came to rest, the enFormed substances that they contained began to solidify into more precisely defined shapes (supra-natural Beings), incarnating as landForms, natural speciesForms, and human-Forms, each further differentiated in turn. Hence emerged the Lands as landForms—the landScape—out of which in turn emerged material entities on "this side" of existence: the land itself, natural species, and people. Though these material entities incarnate, pass away, and die to sometimes incarnate again on "this side," their source, *Amawurrena-alawuduwarra*, in its manifold Forms, continues to exist as an Eternal present not only on the "other side" but also as an enForming Presence on "this side" (called *awarrawalya* by the Aborigines).

In other words, the Eternal Formations *extend through* from the "other side" to "this side" to bridge the two dimensions of reality. From within the Formations on the "other side," individual bits of Creation-substance are "expelled" across to "this side" to animate or inForm the individual material incarnations (referred to as *amugwa*) that are constantly appearing as material entities through the reproductive process. Each person/species (and inanimate object during the initial phases of its incarnation), then, is enFormed by archetypal spirit and in-Formed by a personal spirit.

When the material body dies, your personal spirit returns to the "other side" along the archetypal en-Formation or "pathway" through which it entered the world, perhaps to reincarnate at a later date if you had not progressed through all the stages of initiation to become a fully initiated, "wise old," adult.

On the "other side" these enFormations are in constant motion while you, your inner spirit, remain in place. The enFormations now pass around you or through you, perhaps shaping and reshaping you in the image of whatever it is they represent, be it a humanForm, a speciesForm or a landForm. It is these archetypal Forms (really forces for Forming), that "expel" or Renounce, you, your inner spirit, over to "this side" to be born. This occurs when Form happens to coincide with the individual spiritual content appropriate to its shape. (It is interesting to note that if the archetypal spirit-Form of, say, an animal species were to succeed in reshaping the individual spirit-content of, say, a human being into its own image and propelling it over to "this side" you would have a form of reincarnation familiar to the Hindu tradition).

On "this side," by contrast, the enFormations assume a fixed position, "bounding" land, natural species, objects, and humans and it is the inFormed inner spirit that moves as the body within which it is contained moves. Though the archetypal enFormation is fixed in place, its Presence is nevertheless felt on you while you move and on death you should be in the presence of the enFormation that "channelled" you to "this side" so that you can be "channelled" back again along the same pathway or songLine.

Existence as a whole, then, is like a rubber band passing through a waterfall, the rubber band stretched to its limit and then rotated from one side of the waterfall through to the other. Each of us comes across to "this side" at birth, is Formally embodied, lives, dies, and then returns to a fixed position on the "other side." Both "sides," then, exist side-by-side in mirrored image.

(Judith Asher, a former student of mine, graphically demonstrated this during one of my graduate classes at the University of Toronto by clearing off the top of my table, placing one of my chairs there and then telling us to draw "not-the-chair" that is, "the space around the chair and its parts." Try it—you'll *see* what it means. The space around the chair is sort of the chair in mirror image: not-the-chair, but its shadow on the "other side.")

The process of incarnation of material reality from the "other side" to "this side" (of "not-the-chair" to "the chair"), then, can be expressed formally as *anti-thesis* (Nothingness) —> *thesis* (being) —> *plurality* (or part-of-one-in-the-other relationship through the Renunciation of (spiritual) "content" between Forms). The Aboriginal word for this process, as we've seen, is *gemalyanggerranema.*

*　　*　　*　　*

It is not really accurate to refer to the above account as "Aboriginal cosmology" as if it is an *idea* about something. Aborigines do not so much learn *about* it as learn to actually *see* and even *hear* the enFormations or archetypal spiritForms as they manifest themselves on "this side" as illuminated, outlined, Presences. And they see them all the time in everyday life. Some Aborigines describe it as a "smokiness" around a Person or thing, others as a "lightness."

In Songs about the Rainbow Serpent that I recorded among the Aborigines some 24 years ago the phrase *megamaing-gamandja,* "the waves are laughing, the waves are laughing," cropped up again and again. I had always wondered how waves could laugh and so in 1986 I asked Murabuda of the Wurramarrba about it. He couldn't really *tell* me in words, he said, but if I went down to the sea in the dry season when the east wind was blowing its strongest and the tide was coming in and I looked out over the open water I would see what they saw and understand how waves could laugh.

The appropriate circumstances materialised late one afternoon while I was on Bickerton Island. I borrowed a four-wheel drive and drove across to the south-east corner of the island, a place called A:nemurremadja that looks across to Groote Eylandt. I parked the vehicle and set off on foot over the dunes to the beach and looked out over the wide expanse of the Gulf of Carpentaria. The waves were laughing. I don't know how to explain it. But they were. And I just sat there on the beach chuckling away to myself—laughing with the waves. I felt a rush, a joy, as I entered into a state of identity, not so much with some *thing* outside myself, as with a *quality* of some thing outside myself.

What I actually saw was waveForm, its Abiding Presence, repeated over and over again countless times as a separate dimension—as an illumination—over and above the flow of the waves themselves. The experience really had five levels. First was the experience of water—matter—itself as it formed into waves (as it is always doing). The second was the impression of waves as such. The third was the perception of waves as a discernible form. The fourth stage was the perception of the Form of each wave as another plane of existence over and above the water itself. Add to this scene of waveForms the dynamic of "spitting" as the Aborigines call it—the wisp of whitecap on each wave suggestive of force and motion—and the overall impression is not so much of water—matter—passing through waveForms, as of waveForm(s) *expelling* matter—spitting it out—one to the other. (A fifth and final stage would be the Form of those Forms, a singleness of Form that defined each and every wave as a wave. *But this would be my conceptual imposition on the scene*—an intellectual projection beyond the scene, not something I actually saw. It occurs to me that monotheism, the idea of one God, and monism, the idea of an ultimate One in any form, may have had its origins in such a mis-projected perception of reality.)

In 1987 when I re-visited the place on Bickerton Island where the Aborigines said the man Nambirrirrma had come down from the sky to confirm the descent and marriage rules to the Aboriginal people in the pre-European period, I had an experience similar to that of "laughing waves." Nambirrirrma was described in the story about him as a stranger who spoke the Aboriginal language and knew the rules of relationship who descended one day from a cloud on the rain to two witnesses belonging to two of the Lands/Peoples of Bickerton. He reiterated the Law to them, they brought other people from the island over to meet him, arranged a wife for him, she bore a child and he died, then his son died. Both are buried at the place where he had originally appeared (see *Return to Eden*, chapter 5 and "The Incarnation of Nambirrirrma" in Swain and Rose, eds. 1988).

I had not been able to locate the site—merely a depression in the sand back from the beach filled with shells—and was walking along the beach feeling disappointed when I turned and looked out onto South Bay. Suddenly the Bay seemed to "horseshoe" in perfect symmetry and its outline—indeed the whole surface of the sea—seemed to rise above the scene as a separated, illuminated dimension. The water and shoreline were still visible; it was just that the scene now had this other dimension added to it—that and the impression of being able to fold one side of the scene down the middle over onto the other. I turned and walked directly inland a short distance and there was the site.

I have called my experience of "laughing waves," of the "horseshoeing bay," experiences of Form. They could equally be termed "of Presences," or "of Nothingnesses"—active Nothing-nesses—behind the discrete entities that we normally take to be material reality. To Aborigines, and now to me, such experiences are seen as evidence of another dimension to human life and nature that is without material content but which shapes that material content in various ways and forms. One may or may not wish to call this aspect of something "spirit"—the Aborigines do.

During a special remembrance ceremony called Amund-uwurrarria, held some five years or so after a person has died, images are carved, not of actual ancestors or ancestresses, but of the *archetypal* or *prototypical* spirit-Forms (whose representations I am forbidden to recount except to say that they are neither human nor natural in appearance). Each image represents an archetypal spirit-Form and a line of spiritual descent through all the generations of people in the Land who have gone before as well as those living in the present.

The purpose of life on "this side," according to the Aborigines, is not only to realise the nature of the "other side" while you are here, but also to bring life on "this side" into mirrored harmony with it. This is to reinforce, through practice of the Law, a mutually-Renunciative, Form-expelling-content, process. Here, Form or Presence, both outer and inner, "naturally" acts to "repel" or "renounce" material substances with which it is associated (much as the body eliminates the waste residue of life-sustaining food) whether these be resources bounded by the Land, a child born to Woman or the catch procured by the Hunter or Gatherer.

As these substances move between Lands and People they establish a part-of-one-in-the-other relationship between them and are the very foundation of the Aboriginal way of life.

Boundaries in this area seem to have been placed around resources such that no one Land contains sufficient resources of such a range that the People owning the Land can be self-sufficient within. Indeed, each of the Lands of Bickerton Island seems to contain an abundance of but one critical resource—yams in one case, year-round fresh water in another, wild apples in a third and a particularly abundant fishing ground in a fourth. Though the resource in question is found in abundance there, it is actually *prohibited* to those associated with the Land as having been spiritually identified with them in the Creation Period and given to them to sing. Thus you "own" the resources of "your own" land not for your own use and enjoyment as in our society, but for the benefit of someone else somewhere else. In this case, it is for those who themselves have "nothing" of the resource. They, in turn, sing and "possess" still other resources to which you are entitled because you neither "own" them, nor sing them.

When a woman bears a child, the moment it "materialises" out of the womb and is in her "possession," it is given up, again to someone who has "nothing," that is, her husband's Land/People's women and it is this Land/People from which it gains its spiritual identity. Likewise, when your husband's sister bears a child she too must give it up to someone who has "nothing," namely you (assuming she married a man in your Land/People on your generation).

When I go hunting and obtain a catch, the moment the catch is in my possession it is no longer my "own" but must be given up to someone who has "nothing," not my closest or even my more distant relatives, but those with least—the very old and very young whatever their Land/People identification.

It is a moral prescription in this society that you give the things in your possession to those with nothing of them in their possession. But in a more profound sense, a person's enForming Presence—the Nothinging side of one's nature —expels matter from one Person to the other; in the Aboriginal framework, Form *must* expel matter to maintain its spiritual purity.

Without an experience of Nothing-nature or Form/ Presence there cannot be a concept of Renunciation since no matter how much you give up, something still remains, namely the "matter" of the person giving.

Bridging the Two "Sides": Journey to the "Land of the Dead"

After someone dies, Aboriginal Songpersons accompany the spirit on a journey across to the "other side" of existence, that is, back to "this side" but in a different dimension. They begin their journey with the dead person's spirit at the place where the body has been buried (in the pre-European period it was placed on a platform) and sung to a special "Big Name" place (*alara*) on the coast in his or her Land. From here the Songpersons take the spirit out into the ocean where it transforms into a fish and from there to the island of Amburrgba, North-East Island, then just beyond and under the sea to Wuragwugwa, a kind of "gateway" to the "other side."

I used to think that Amburrgba was some kind of Land of the Dead where the spirits of the ancestors resided. But if this was so, how did the spirits of the dead ultimately end up back in their own respective countries? It took me many years to understand the Aboriginal perspective on Creation space and geographical space. To them they are entirely different things, the one following natural contours, the other following spiritual ones. Spiritual contours are lines while geographical contours meander following the natural landscape. But the *boundaries* on geographical space which demarcate the different Lands and People and differentiate them from one another are lines of Creation substance.

The Land of the Dead, then, is the "same" as the land of the living but in a different dimension and in mirrored image. If archetypal Form is the spiritual mediator which allows passage from one dimension to another, the physical mediator is the source of material life itself—water.

Across the water through which the dead person's spirit is taken is the juncture of three parallel roads. Here sits Nangberdangberda playing the didjereedoo, the Aborigines' hollow log musical instrument (a one-in-two instrument played by breathing in and out at the same time and sounding more than one pitch simultaneously). One of the roads is for the spirits of humans, another for those of dingoes or wild dogs and a third for those of other animal species. As the Songpersons carry the spirit through the water toward Nangberdangberda he looks down and sees something bright "swimming like a fish." He reaches for his hooked spear (Ma:nunggwa) but just as he is about to hurl it at the object it transforms into "the shape of a human." Nangberdangberda now uses his spear to lift the spirit out of the water where he lays it on the ground among a swarm of ants (Yua:ba) which bite and revive it. Nangberdangberda now shows the spirit the appropriate road to the "other side" but warns that it will soon encounter enemies who will want to fight it.

Walking down the road the spirit eventually comes upon two old women making damper or unleavened bread from burrawong seeds (Munenga). They ask it, "How are the people you have left behind?" And it replies, "I left them in good order." They give it food and water and warn it of the dangers that lie ahead. (I might explain at this point why I am using "it" in reference to the spirit. Strictly speaking human spirits are gender neutral. It is the human body that is sexed and a child has no gender until its body is ready to be born. When the names of babies about to be born are dreamed or intuited the *n* or *d* prefix indicating male and female respectively is omitted from the name until the child emerges from the womb. For example, *amagalya* would become Namagalya or Damagalya. Gender identity, though, seems to linger on for a time in residue form during the transition from "this side" to "the other" on a person's death.)

As it walks along, the spirit sees smoke rising in the distance and remembers the warnings of the old woman and Nangberdangberda. From the other direction a frilly lizard, Dugulawawa, sees him coming and, picking up his hooked spears, tells his brothers, "This is my enemy, I am going to fight him." Dugulawawa runs toward the spirit and spears it in the thigh, but Yuwadja:ra (a small lizard) and Derrangga (another small lizard), as well as Yaradja (goanna) and Yigarma (skink), pull the spear out and carry the spirit to their home where they keep it for two days until it recovers. They then tell it to leave because the frilly lizard wants to fight it again. Later, Yimarndagwaba, blue-tongued lizard, sees the spirit approaching and, picking up his fighting staff, runs toward it. But just before he is able to strike a blow against the spirit, Demernganiya:ndawiya, dragonflies, stop him and tie him to his fighting staff. The spirit now passes by unharmed and eventually comes upon a large billabong or pond where it refreshes itself by having a drink, a swim, and eating some lily roots.

Eventually the spirit encounters a man standing beside two trees, one tall and one short. The man tells it that it must climb one of the two trees if it is to continue its journey. If the spirit climbs the short tree it will return to the land of the living and just sort of hang around the world of the humans it has left. If it climbs the tall tree it will continue on its journey through to the "other side." (Here the Songmen relinquish control of the Song and the spirit is left to make a choice, an indication that consciousness and rational thought are still present.) Its choice is determined by the emotional state of the people it has left behind. If people, particularly the Songpersons, are sad and crying then the spirit will return to stay with them. But if they are not the spirit will continue on its journey.

(My old Aboriginal friend Gula made an interesting observation about grieving. In European society, he said, they try to reassure the dying that death is not all there is and that the dead person will be all right afterwards. In his society the dying person reassures the living that he or she will keep an eye on them after he or she has gone.)

At this point the Songpersons and spectators sit about for a few hours watching for signs among themselves as to what decision the spirit has made. People don't like spirits hanging about so they do their best to control their grief. Usually the spirit climbs the tall tree and continues on its journey. When they are sure it has climbed the tall tree the Songpersons pause for a few days then recall all of their ancestral spirits from the "other side," including that of the dead person, and sing them on a journey through their countries and from there to the ceremony ground to witness the next stage of the mortuary ceremonies, the burning of the possessions of the deceased.

After this journey is completed the Songpersons take the spirits on a longer journey along the various Creation tracks or songLines before holding another stage of the ceremony called Mamungba when a lock of the dead person's hair is sung into a dillybag and then physically transported to a special place in his, her, or a closely related, country. Then, some years later, comes the final stage of the ceremony, called Amunduwurrarria, in which all the ancestral spirits and the archetypal spiritForms are honoured and the deceased is finally released to the "other side"—in some cases to be reincarnated back to "this side." This is only if the person has not passed through all the requisite stages of the life cycle to become, as the anthropologist A. P. Elkin once put it, "an Aboriginal man (or woman) of high degree" (1977). What this means is to have to come to a full understanding of Creation and its implications, including a direct experience of the "Dreamtime" through what Elkin (in "Part 3") terms "mystical experience" (e.g., of my "laughing waves" through to the "other side"). This whole sequence of mortuary ceremonies can take up to five years before the person is finally laid to rest.

What are we to make of this journey to the "other side"? In the first place there is no clear evidence, to my mind, that it is an imaginative construct invented to reassure people that life continues beyond death. The tale does not code according to what I call "mystification-logic" which runs, *statement of opposition —> mediation of opposition —> weakening of opposition —> illusion of solution to opposition or problem.* This is to present a problem, pretend to solve it, then convince people the problem is solved by obfuscating its terms and glossing its severity. This logic proceeds by a process of analogical or metaphorical reasoning (see Lévi-Strauss 1967, 1968, Turner 1979).

The above journey to the "other side," by contrast, seems to unfold according to another logic: *mediation —> weakeners or constraints on violence removed —> opposition begins to emerge —> separation and withdrawal from the implications.* This is survival-logic, a logic whose action-implication is to separate and withdraw from possible trouble. This is the logic of thought in a society where human relations are *already* mediated and people accommodated in part-of-one-in-the-other, Renunciative, terms. Thought here proceeds analytically rather than analogically to imagine what would happen if the part-of-one-in-the-other mechanism were removed, and it concludes "chaos and confusion," and separates and withdraws from the implications. It is this logic that moves Aborigines to "separate and withdraw" from Europeans and the schisms they bring. And it is this logic that moves them to go off by themselves to the beach and contemplate the sea when trouble does start brewing around them.

Yandarranga, or Central Hill, originated in the "Dreamtime" on the mainland adjacent to Groote Eylandt and moved eastward toward the coast. On reaching the homeland of the Ngalmi people he sat down, but it was too dirty for his liking so he moved on to the land of another people on the coast. But he began to sink down in the mud and so moved out into the sea where he made the way across to Bickerton Island and the land of the Lalara people. From here he cut south across the island to the country of the Wurrenggilyangba where he "threw out his anchor" and stopped to dry himself off. However, he again began to sink into the mud and threw off some rocks—his "sons"—so that he could move on. At another place in this country he discarded some wild apples and met the Blind Woman, Diminba. As he was helping her dig some yams he began to sink down again and could barely get free. But he finally did and made his way out into the sea and across to Groote Eylandt. Angry at his departure, Diminba picked up her spears and began throwing them at him, but, being blind, she missed. Where the spears fell, new places were created. Grieving, she began to cut herself and her blood washed all the way over to Groote. When he reached Groote, Central Hill began to sink down and he again threw off some more sons. They told him to keep moving and he did—all the way on to Warnungangwurugwerigba country on the east side of the island. There he finally settled and made an inland salt water lake where he could catch lots of fish.

The go-between that is being removed here is Central Hill himself. That is, he is threatening to settle down in each of the countries he visits in turn. He seems to be confusing his own territory with territories he is merely visiting. With some prodding from his "sons" he is pushed on to his final destination—the land of the people who actually relate to Central Hill as their principal Creator Being. The "hell" that is about to break loose in the myth is a relationship formed on a co-production, rather than Creative Substance, basis. Central Hill and Diminba gather yams together. The attachment hints of "marriage." Marriage, though, is prohibited between people of the same or closely related Creative substance. In the story, Central Hill's and Diminba's relationship is anomalous in other respects: he is gathering, she becomes a hunter, whereas in reality man is primarily the hunter, woman primarily the gatherer. Central Hill finally seems to realise the problem: he separates and withdraws but Diminba literally can't see a problem at all. But then her blindness also excuses her mistake. In the end the real design for life is set back in place as Central Hill settles down in his own country.

The analytic, deductive, thought in evidence here is definitely rational thought. Here it is being applied to preventing problems from emerging rather than to their management after they emerge.

In the tale of the journey to the "other side," conflict is potential from the outset of the tale of the journey to the "other side" and the spirit is warned to anticipate it. Conflict is in part realised, but never fulfilled. Mediators always intervene to help the spirit separate and withdraw, or at least move on to join other spirits who have passed the same way before. Moreover, the violence potential in the tale is always on an individual-to-individual basis (except when Dragonflies collectively capture Blue-tongued Lizard, but this is to protect the spirit).

In the tale, then, we don't have opposition or illusions of solutions to problems; we don't really have mediation or separation and withdrawal in the sense that intervention is preordained, not negotiated, and the spirit doesn't so much withdraw as proceed somewhere else. Even the thought-logic of an accommodative society like that of the Aborigines which proceeds from "mediation" and ends in "separation/ withdrawal," then, seems to be absent. It is almost as if the tale is a stylised version of a very real afterlife journey through one's worst fears about the possibility of violence breaking out there what with real social constraints now left behind, a journey that ends in a Place or dimension where those fears— and perhaps consciousness itself—are finally laid to rest.

The "Other Side" Manifest as a Way of Life on "This Side"

Formal Organisation

There are some 20 separate Lands/Peoples in the Groote Eylandt, Bickerton Island and adjacent mainland area. SongLines establish their whereabouts and link them into four Companies (as the Aborigines call them in English), in turn linked into two separate sides or moieties which can be conveniently identified as Bara or West Wind on the one hand and Mamariga or East Wind on the other (Plate 1). One of the Lands/Peoples on the Bara side, Wurugwagwa Company, for example, is the Lalara whose proper name is Warnung-amadada (they-people-belonging-to Armadadi, a place on the mainland from which they originated before migrating to Bickerton Island in the pre-European past). This is the Land/People I was at first fictively affiliated with when I arrived on Groote Eylandt in 1969 and then was actually affiliated with (with certain qualifications) when I was initiated into the society in 1986. The Lalara sing a sector of the Central Hill (Yandarranga) songLine and of the songLines of Sawfish (Yugurrirrindangwa), Stingray (Yimaduwaiya) and Shark Ray (Yilyanga) which connect them to the Ngalmi of the adjacent mainland, the Wurrenggilyangba of Bickerton and the Wurramaminyamandja and the Warnungangwurugwerigba of Groote Eylandt. They all form one Company.

The boundaries of the Lands in question were laid down by Songs in the Creation Period to create/reflect Forms apparent to the people who subsequently appeared. When people did appear it was *through* the *Amawurrena-alawuduwarra* of these Forms that they inter-related rather than directly as individual-to-individual or as group-to-group. In other words, they related to each other as Persons rather than persons.

That is, their individual identities emanated from the Forms and spiritual substances—the Presences—in the Land (space) which enveloped each of them like a skin as they emerged into being through the process of birth (time). These Presences were constituted of the "stuff" of original Creation, were experienced as a reality in the present, and were the foundations of the model on which people based their lives.

Though you cannot marry someone on the same side or moiety as yourself, this is a consequence of applying the rule that you *do* marry someone in a Land/People your own has married two generations previously. In this region, then, it takes four Lands/Peoples to make a system, hence the four Companies. If you ask why the descent and marriage rules are the way they are, Aborigines may tell the story of that man Nambirrirrma who incarnated on Bickerton Island in the long, long ago, to reiterate to the Aborigines that this was, indeed, the way it should be (see *Return to Eden*, pp. 87–100). Or Aborigines may say that they marry the way they do "to keep the lines straight" (*mederrperra*). What they mean by this is *spiritual* lines.

The preference in marriage is for a man to marry a number of women in the Land/People the man's grandfather married two generations ago. These women should have the same spiritual identities and actual sisters will, of course, always meet this criterion. Not only will their primary spiritual identities be the same because they all have the same father, but also their secondary identities—the spiritual bits and pieces that "rub off" on them from their mothers (while they are in the womb), their father's mother's (which rubbed off on the father while he was in the womb) and their mother's mother's (which rubbed off while their mother was in the womb). When the husband dies his wife or wives are passed on to his eldest brother for the same reason—two brothers will, by definition, have the same spiritual identities and histories (through the mother, father's mother and mother's mother again); hence the new relationship will have the same spiritual continuity as the old one. Marriage in the present duplicates one in one's own Land/People two generations ago .

There is also a tendency here for a man to marry a woman some 25 years younger than himself. This may seem like older men exploiting younger women for sexual purposes until it is realised that the woman and her "sisters" pass on to the husband's younger brother when the husband dies. Eventually, through this process, older women come to be passed on to a younger man. In other words, the tables turn. How you judge the custom, then, depends on at what point in the *woman's* life you examine her situation. The Aboriginal perspective on gender "inequality" is that while men achieve spiritual understanding through a long process of learning, women are born with it—possessing the ability to create life within themselves. Given this perspective, an older man and a young woman are at equivalent stages of spiritual development.

Sexual relationships between men and women outside marriage are temporarily tolerated if the parties have the same spiritual histories as the persons to whom they are married, but not if they don't. A long-term relationship with a person whose spiritual identity is different from that of their marriage partner will fracture or scramble the continuity in which the married pair are primarily involved, not to mention "scramble" or disturb the person's spiritual relationship to their marriage partner as well as scramble his or her own spiritual integrity given its relationship to that of one's marriage partner. Infidelity in Aboriginal society is politically dangerous because it threatens marriage relationships arranged sometimes a generation in advance. These arrangements have important implications for access to resources and ceremonial participation (determining as they do the Lands you will frequent with your spouse and those you will perform *for* in ceremonies). Infidelity is spiritually dangerous because it threatens the integrity and continuity of the cosmological order as it flows across from the "other side" to "this" and across the human generations.

Hearing the "Other Side" on "This Side": Music

Musical Form

Music, like spirit, is simultaneously on both "sides." It is the original sound-shapes of Creation which manifest themselves in a variety of different ways on "this side" in performance. Like the original sound-shapes, musics are not fixed but fluid in Form as they are picked up from the "other side" by humans on "this side" and modified or re-Created as they are transmitted down through the generations while being enacted in performance.

The sound-shapes are embedded in rhythm ratios manifest in the articulated beats of the song-voice, the tapping sticks and the didjereedoo that identify the original sound-shapes of emerging Creation. A "Dreaming" on Stingray, for instance, emerges out of 4:2:1, on Curlew out of 4:1:1/4 and on Hibiscus out of 3:1:1. In performance these rhythms emerge as the sticks establish the initial beat (opening up a warp in space between the two sides), as the didjereedoo follows on (and the player summons up his inner spirit and projects it through the warp), and, finally, as the voice (of the person who operates the sticks), follows the sound of the didjereedoo with the song (and his or her own inner spirit). (The didjereedoo, by the way, is only played by men—just compensation for their innate spiritual inadequacy relative to women!)

Out of this rhythmic interplay of sticks, didjereedoo and voice emerges a dynamic, melodic, Form—really a force for Forming (third diagram below). This is constituted out of two separate melodic Forms or forces for Forming, the didjereedooLine and the songLine. The didjereedoo melodic line is this:

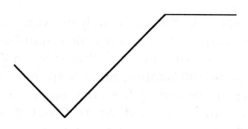

The songLine is this:

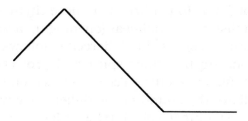

Together, they are this:

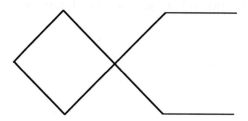

The didjereedooLine begins on a mid-point note, descends to a low note, then levels off to follow its own particular melodic course. The songLine begins on a mid-point note, ascends to a high note, then heads off to follow a particular melodic course of its own. The only rule in Song composition is that each Song must be different from every other. A Song must be *made different* from other Songs through the creative activity of the person to whom it has been passed from someone in the previous generation. This process is also referred to as *gemalyanggerranema.* This is to reproduce the process of original Creation in which something emerged from Nothing(s) and entered into a Renunciative relation with everything else. In the process of Song-making, one literally "dreams up" a few bars of a tune of one's own, takes something from one's father's or grandfather's tune, and "twists it in" to make a new creation or Song. The Song is then itself renounced, or performed, for those who have it not. Here are five examples: two on Midjiyanga (Ship), and three on Yandarranga (Central Hill).

46

Nungwa:nigba's Tune For Midjiyanga

Numera:nigba's Tune For Midjiyanga

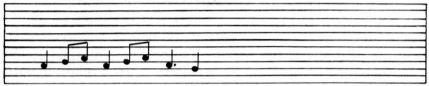

Gula Singing Sectors of Yandarranga: a. Ngalmi Sector

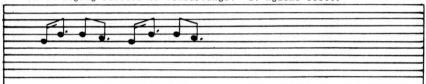

b. Warnungamadada Sector

c. Wurra:nggilyangba Sector

Musical Content

Secondary to the shape of a Song are its words. A Song is known by the shape of its *difference* not its meaning, though the meanings of Songs on different Dreamings are different. The words are selected to fit the Melodic contour of the Song as the Songperson follows the pathways of *Amawurrena alawud-uwarra* traced by the Creation Being in question as the song persons take the spirit of the dead person through his or her country. Words are selected which *sound right* on the melody in question. The words are a *vehicle* of the music.

This subordination of word to melody contrasts, for example, with mediaeval Gregorian chant and Plainsong where the melody is subject to the linguistic requirements of the Psalm text being sung, reflecting a theological commitment to the power of the meaningful word over the meaning-less note.

Let me illustrate the point by presenting Gula's Song on his Tune for Alumera, Silt-Churned-Up-by-Stingray:

48

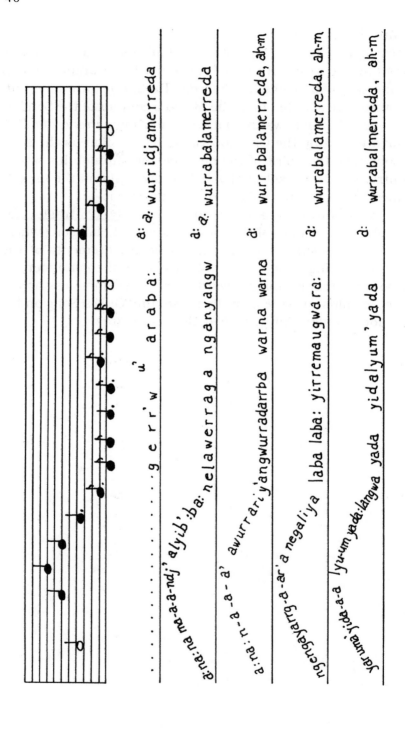

nenggaːaːaːa nigulʹyada agaːna yaga narberna yag   aː aː wurrabalmerreda, ah-m

agaːaːnaːaːa nemangadja arrerra merndagburridjawiyawiy   aːdː nawabaleleda

naːgeriyaːaːa da wadugwa laba baba: nerring balidja: aː wurrabalamerreda, ah-m

meragaraːaːa didja yada nageriyada laba baba: aː meragardidja yada

wurrubugwaːaːa yaa wambilyaː laba . . . .

50

..... *gerrawularraba*
you from the Lalara Land

wurridjiramerreda
the water is clear
and black

---

a:na:namadja   *a:lyibilyiba*
at this place   on one side

nelawerraganganyangwa
the sea is pulling my
(dust)

wurrabalamerreda
black dust

---

a:na:n' awurrariya
I (am singing) badly

wurradarrba warna warna
(I will make it) short this
one

wurrabalamerreda
black dusty sea

---

ngenengayarrga
I have been singing too long

negalyiya   *laba laba*
my brother   look   look
(the other songmen)

yirremaugwara
we are still following

wurrabalamerreda
black dusty water

---

yaruma   *yidalyuma yada*
big   river (Angurugu
                  on Groote)

langwa yada
belonging to

yidalyuma yada
river

wurrabalamerreda
black dusty water

---

nengga:nigwulyiya yada
you of the Wurugwagwa Lands/Peoples

aga:na   *yaga*
but   those
           ones

nara' bena	*yaga*	*wurrabamerreda*
the two (river and sawfish)	those ones	black dusty water

---

aga:na	*nemangadja*	*arrerra*
but	it (the wind) hits the sea	wind

merndagburridjawiya	*wiya*	*nawabalaleda*
right in the shallows		it is becoming shallow

---

nageriyada	*wadugwa*
he (sawfish) doesn't know what to do	stopping on top of the sea

laba laba	*nerringbalidja*	*wurrabalamerreda*
look	the sea separates the sawfish	dusty area

Meragardidja jada	*nageriyada*
jungle near Angurugu	he (sawfish) doesn't know what to do

laba laba	*Meragardidja yada*
look	jungle

---

wurrubugwaiya wambilya
take over the song (to brother songman)

The words of Aboriginal Songs recount the activities of supra-natural Beings active in the Creation Period. These are the Ships, Central Hills, Stingrays, and so forth that emerged out of original Creation but before they incarnated as material animals, plants, natural formations, and humans. In this phase of being they are capable of extraordinary feats such as breaking rocks, walking on water, swimming over land and so on. In their journeyings and activities, these Beings established the boundaries between the different Lands/Peoples in the area and, by acting on these Lands, left something of themselves there which eventually established the spiritual identities of the People who incarnated in the various places.

But the Songs rarely mention the name of the Creation Being whose activities are being recounted; as a listener you have to figure out the identity of the Creation Being in question from the context described and from the Melodic contour of the Song. But as I had learned from various Songpersons, every context is ambiguous with respect to the Creation Being it represents. In other words, there is what you think is being sung by listening to the Song, and there is what is *really* being sung in the mind of the Songperson. What separates the men from the boys, the women from the girls and the men from the women is knowing what Song is really being sung. The Songpersons test out initiates and each other on this issue during every performance. One mark of an outstanding singer is to be able to mask Songs belonging primarily to his or her Land from old men and women in other Lands and even from other men and women in his or her own.

For instance, when is the Creation Being Derarragugwa, Dove, and when is it Spider? The term applies to both real-world species. More properly, when is the Melodic line in question Dove and when is it Spider? The new name for Spider is Dagwarargwa which literally means thread and refers to the weave in a piece of cloth, Dumbala. Dumbala is also the Sail on Midjiyanga or Ship. Thread is Ma:ra, String, and String is what Dove pulled around on her journey in the Creation Period. But it wasn't really String; it was a piece of Wurrumilya:a or Burney Vine. Wurrumilya:a comes under Spider because vines are where you find them. Spider Webs are like the weave in a piece of cloth, are made of threads are like the piece of vine pulled by Dove which is what Ship was pulled with. Dove String broke just like Ship Rope broke. So now we have a third possibility as to what is really being sung.

To know what is really being sung, then, you have to know not only all there is to know about Doves and Spiders and Ships, their habits and distinguishing features, in the Creation Period but also all there is to know about real world doves and spiders and ships, their habits and distinguishing features. What is at issue, then, is your discriminating ability.

Didjereedoo playing carries the same kind of secrets. Only the didjereedoo player knows for certain what Melody he is playing. Only the most knowledgeable and skilled players can really tell from listening. Only the most discriminating ear can hear three distinct notes coming out of the open end (the high note and the low note being but a microtonal interval apart). One of the functions of a bucket resonator (traditionally a hollow dug in the ground) at the open end is to throw the sound back at the player so that he can accurately hear what he is producing and hence control what the audience is hearing.

When they sing and play the didjereedoo, knowledgeable Aborigines experience a soul journey to the "other side" in which they follow the stuff of original Creation laid down by the particular Creation Beings with which they are in continuity. They hear and see the "other side" while on "this side" sitting in performance, the "other side" being a mirrored image of "this side" but in another dimension. They are paradoxically in two places—the same Place—at once.

Seeing the "Other Side" on "This Side"

Dance

Dance incarnates the Creation Beings recounted in the Songs and represents them to the Songpersons and participants at the very moment when the Spirit of the just-departed and those from the distant past are brought together to bear witness to the ceremonial event in question. danceForm compounds time and space by mirroring an unfolding lineal sequence of movements into a timeless, spaceless, non-lineal whole. This occurs on two planes, the one establishing and then dissolving the context in which the dancing takes place, the other informing the movements of the dance itself.

Each Groote Eylandt and Bickerton Island dance unfolds in basically the same manner irrespective of Creation Being sung. The dancers, moved by the rhythm of the sticks/didjereedoo/Song and following on the sound, rise and emerge from the periphery and proceed to the dancing area just in front of the Songpersons. As they do, what appears a loose, unorganised grouping, loping lazily along with little or no purpose, slowly forms into a line and begins a series of steps which has the effect of raising the dust from the ground to, like water and smoke, create a mediating zone of material-less substance amidst the dancers and between them and the other participants in the ceremony. Within this space the dancers perform their movements under the direction of a *djunggwaiya:* or "boss" of the deceased's Land/People (usually a member of his or her mother's Land/People). One or two dancers on either end of the line now move around behind the group, cross, move to the front and dance along with the rest of the group then proceed back in the reverse direction in mirror image, crossing and dancing again. The Song ends, the dance ends, the performance ends; the dancers give a shout. The dancers then disperse as they step out of the dance space and casually amble back to their place with the Songpersons.

The dancers, then, do not return to place in the same manner as they entered the dancing area, on the sticks/didjereedoo/Song. Rather they help bring the Songpersons "back" from the "other side" with their shout on their last step. Entrance and exit, then, mirror each other.

Dance involves three basic steps. Other more elaborate

movements associated with a particular Creation Being may or may not be performed depending on the occasion. The basic steps are the lope, hop, and a shuffle performed by knocking the knees together while shifting both feet from side to side. Though the order of the steps and movements is associated with the activities of Creation Beings, the movements themselves do not imitate the actual actions of the animals or natural species associated with the Beings. They rather enact Forms—Forms continuous with those present in the Creation Period (in contrast to many of the dances of the adjacent mainland Aborigines which do imitate actual species' actions). This makes the dances highly abstract, so much so that it is very difficult for the uninitiated observer to know exactly what Being is actually being danced at any given time. The problem is compounded by the fact that the Being danced does not have to be the Being Sung at that moment. In other words, as is the case with the meaning of the Songs and the sound of the didjereedoo, only the dancers themselves know for certain what they are dancing.

As with the songLine and didjereedooLine in relation to the identity of particular Creation Beings, there is no archetypal danceForm to identify a particular Creation Being. What is critical is simply that one dance be different from another. Take three Lalara Land/People dances recorded on video for the Australian Institute of Aboriginal Studies by the musicologist Alice Moyle while I was conducting my first research on Groote Eylandt in 1969. These are Duwalya (Curlew), Yimaduwaiya (Stingray), and Mabunda (Hibiscus). Only the three basic steps are involved, as the dances were performed out of the context of mortuary ceremonies. But the *way* they are involved illustrates my point.

Duwalya: (Plate 2): the sticks sound with the dancers seated on the ground. The didjereedoo begins to play. The dancers stand up and lope out as the Song begins. The dancers now move into a line and two of them on either end of the line (the *djunggwaiya:* or bosses), move forward and begin directing the performance as they all lope-step in place. The boss on the left (looking at the line from the front) and the dancer on that end of the line move behind the line on the lope-step as a dancer from the other end of line moves behind while the line remains lope-stepping in place. They cross behind the line, the ones from the left passing outside the one from the right. As they change places, they move to the front of the line and shuffle-step there along with the line. Then the lone dancer, now on the left, picks up the dancer from that end of the line and lope-steps back the other way with him as the two now on the right do likewise. But this time the dancers coming from the right pass outside the ones coming from the left. Back in place, they all shuffle-step, first facing outward and then facing inward, then outward again (the boss, though, always faces out). They all stop on a shout as the Song/didjereedoo/sticks abruptly end.

Yimaduwaiya: The dancers sit as the sticks begin and the didjereedoo enters, then they lope out as the Song begins. They form their line and the two come forward as before. Now just the two bosses at either end proceed behind the line on the hop-step, cross, the one from the right behind the other, exchange places, and do the shuffle-step as the line continues the lope-step. The two then reverse direction and cross again behind the line, the boss from the right behind the boss from the left, and return to their original places and do the shuffle step. The line continues to lope-step in place for a few moments then also moves into the shuffle-step, all facing outward save for one who turns inward.

Mabunda: the sticks tap, the didjereedoo blows, the Song begins, the dancers remain seated and then rise and lope out as before. While loping in line the boss on the right comes forward and draws a short line in the sand, marking part of the boundary of the dance area. The two bosses now turn and lope-step behind the line and cross as before, performing the shuffle-step when they arrive at the other end while the rest of those in line lope-step in place. The two then return behind the line to their respective places on the lope-step while the rest of those in line lope-step in place. Then the two do the shuffle step and the line follows suit. They all face out, then in, then out, then in, then out, finally turning their backs as the dance, Song, didjereedoo, sticks, end.

One is tempted to look for some deep, textual, meaning in these subtle differences, but all they really represent is different ways of mirroring movement and transforming lineal time and three-dimensional space into a fifth-dimensional moment reflecting Reality as a whole.

Art

Aborigines see soundForm. The basic ground-plan of the music as diagrammed above, in fact, contains most of the sacred designs used to identify sacred objects in their secret ceremonies. Though I cannot recount the details of which design represents which Creation Beings I can say that these designs consist of parallel lines, herringbones, diamonds, cross-hatchings or X-shapes (and, if we can represent the points of transition in the ground-plan in question from one phase to another with dots), then dots. These designs occur in ancient Aboriginal cave paintings, on bark paintings and body paintings and on the didjereedoo (Plate 3). They occur either as background material or within animal, natural, and human shapes. Each design represents, in the abstract, the spiritual substance of a Creation Being as such. The designs are, however, transferable from the Creation Being of their origin to other Beings. This makes it very difficult for observers to know exactly which design represents which Creation Being in the same way as it is very difficult to know which Song Melody in fact represents which Being or which didjereedoo Melody a performer is actually playing or which Being is being depicted in a dance.

To execute a painting, as to perform a Song or play the didjereedoo or enact a dance, is to incarnate Creation:

First a sheet of bark is smoked, dried and sung to imbue it with spiritual significance. On this surface is then depicted Creation, Nothingness, or *Amawurrena-alawuduwarra* itself as a "blankness" in solid black or red (remembering that this is but a *slice* of Creation connected to the Land/Person executing the bark and not a Oneness behind Creation). Upon this surface are now depicted the shapes of Creation Beings which are first outlined or enFormed (illuminated) in white. Then these Forms and/or parts of the background are "filled in" with abstract designs associated with particular Creation Beings emblematic of sacredness as such. Some paintings incarnate "outward" from here to a more material reality to depict natural objects, fishing or hunting scenes, or ceremonial performances.

These paintings, like singing and didjereedoo playing, were not done for fun or for trade. The paintings were made for display to initiates in ceremonial contexts such as Amunduwurrarria or Remembrance after which they were destroyed or returned to the Nothingness(es) from which they had come.

In more formal, analytic, terms the incarnation of a bark painting, like the incarnation of material reality in general, can be expressed by the terms *anti-thesis* (Nothingness[es]) —> *thesis* (beings) —> *plurality* (part-of-one-in-the-other relationship through the Renunciation of content between Forms).

If we look back to pre-historic rock art (cover), the oldest record we have not only of art in Australia but also in the world, we find another expression of this the incarnational/ Renunciative process. This is the hand stencil whereby the artist holds his or her hand (or some other object) palm down against the cave wall, spews liquid paint over it with his mouth, and then removes his or her hand, leaving an outline-impression there. This is to "renounce" the matter from the Form he or she has left there. In the same vein, x-ray art in a sense dissolves the shell of outer-matter on an object while leaving the outlined Form of the object intact, to reveal the inner-matter within.

Interestingly, the incarnational process which informs not only all aspects of the Aboriginal way of life but also their account of original Creation also seems to inform the account of original Creation in Judeo-Christian Scriptures (if not the subsequent way of life that emerged out of it). Though in the Bible the earth is originally described as "without form, and void," matter seems to have emerged from, as in the Aboriginal account, from an active Nothingness referred to in *Genesis* as "the deep." Though here, in contrast to the Aboriginal account the "hand of God" orchestrates the proceedings.

Renunciation in Hebrew Scriptures?

Genesis

> 1:2 The earth was without form, and void; and darkness
> was on the face of the deep. And the Spirit of God was
> hovering over the face of the waters.

In the midst of the waters emerged a firmament and the
firmament divided the waters above from the waters below and
the dry land appeared. And the dry land God called Earth and
the waters he called Seas.

From Nothing, then, beings have incarnated and the beings
are now brought into relationship.

God divided the light from the darkness and called the light
Day and the darkness Night. And God made two great lights,
the greater light, the sun, to rule over the day and the lesser
light, the moon, to rule the night. And he also made the stars
and let them be for signs—signs for a type of relationship
which as yet remains incomplete. Part of the light has been
placed in the darkness but part of the darkness has not been
placed in the light—as it should be in a part-of-one-in-the-
other Renunciative relationship. A part of *one* of the two
differences only has been given up to the other who has it not.

The earth then brought forth grass, the herb yielding seed
and the fruit whose seed is within itself. Then issued forth
creatures of the sea and of the sky and the great whales.
Finally appeared man and woman to whom was given
dominion over fish, fowl and every living thing. But only the
herb bearing seed and seed bearing fruit were given them as
"meat" for food. In return they were instructed to replenish the
earth.

Here then, a part of nature goes to man and woman and a
part of man and women goes back to nature. But the

Renunciative "intent" is destined to fail, for man and woman in and of themselves by the end of *Genesis* turn out to represent Renunciation unrealised.

> 2:6–8 but a mist went up from the earth and watered the whole face of the ground. And the Lord God formed man of the dust of the ground, and breathed into his nostrils the breath of life; and man became a living being. The Lord God planted a garden eastward in Eden and there He put the man whom He had formed.

. . . . in his own image. Man, then, emerged as Formed matter from the waters of original creation and is alone in his garden.

In the garden grew every tree that is pleasant to the sight and good for food. But the fruit of two of the trees in the garden were forbidden as food. These were the tree of life and the tree of knowledge of good and evil which God had planted in the middle of the garden. Some of the garden's food, then, is to be renounced (to others elsewhere?). Eden, it seems, is not alone:

> 2:10–14 Now a river went out of Eden to water the garden, and from there it parted and became into four riverheads. The name of the first is Pishon; it is the one which encompasses the whole land of Havilah, where there is gold. And the gold of that land is good. Bdelium and the onyx stone are there. The name of the second river is Gihon; it is the one which encompasses the whole land of Cush. The name of the third river is Hiddekel; it is the one which goes toward the east of Assyria. The fourth river is the Euphrates.

Man, it seems, is alone in a garden that is not only not alone, but may be in some kind of Renunciative relation to other lands elsewhere. Eden has the water source, is the source of life and knowledge; Havilah has gold, bdelium, and onyx. The others? We do not know. But Renunciative potential *is* at the source of the creation of Adam and Eve:

> 2:18 And the Lord God said, "It is not good that man should be alone; I will make him a helper comparable to him.
> 2:21–22 And the Lord God caused a deep sleep to fall on Adam, and he slept; and He took one of his ribs, and closed up the flesh in its place. Then the rib which the Lord God had taken from man He made into a woman, and He brought her to the man.

A renunciative process has begun—a part of man becomes woman—but no part of woman has yet come to man. Their relationship could tend toward unity or part-of-one-in-the-other, Renunciative, interdependence. But the scales soon tip toward unity: "Therefore a man shall leave his father and mother and be joined to his wife, and they shall become one flesh" (2:24).

The move toward unity, or incorporation, rather than Renunciation is set when Eve eats of the fruit of the tree of knowledge and shares it with Adam. This is not only to consume food meant for others elsewhere: it is also to return, not something of herself to Adam, but rather to share something they both have in common. The "error" is compounded when they realise the sexual nature of their gender difference and consummate their relationship. In a Renunciative world, by contrast, two persons of the same substance, from within the same Garden, are to be made available as sexual partners and spouses to others in Gardens elsewhere. For their "sin" God expels Adam and Eve from the garden—before they are able to learn the secret of the tree of life.

> 3:22–23 Then the Lord God said, "Behold, the man has become like one of Us, to know good and evil." And now, lest he put out his hand, and take also of the tree of life, and eat, and live forever—therefore the Lord God sent

him out of the garden of Eden . . .

The secret of the tree of life is that the tree isn't there—or rather it is there to be made available to someone else.

The course Adam and Eve set themselves outside Eden is without Renunciative direction. We find two people originating in the same substance, procreating a tribe living in isolated self-sufficiency, toiling in pain, suffering in childbirth and dying a premature death.

The Renunciative alternative is implicit in creation itself and in God's judgements distinguishing sin from obedience thereafter. Renunciation seems to be what the Fall is *not*. To me the **Book of Genesis** reads like an instruction manual as to what will befall if you choose isolated self-sufficiency over Renunciation as an individual or a group.

Outside Eden, Eve conceives and their family embark on a course of territorial autonomy and group self-sufficiency in which the drive for technological progress to extract more from the limited resources available to support a growing population independently of one's neighbours becomes a major priority. Hence, *internal* to Hebrew society, the conflict between succession to authority and succession of technology. In Hebrew society, the eldest succeeds, but the youngest comes by the more advanced technology. Hence the conflict between Abel the husbandman and Cain the cultivator (Cain killing Abel in the interests of his mode of production), of Esau the hunter and Jacob the husbandman (Jacob appropriating Esau's succession).

Then the world thereafter descends into a seemingly anarchistic state (6) God, declaring even the imagination of man's heart now to be "evil from his youth" (8:21). Resigned to this reality, he now gives man every moving thing that liveth to be meat for him. In other words, God accepts man's nature as a predator on other forms of intelligent life. But at the same time, God provides yet another clue, albeit a vaguely defined one, as to the possibility of an alternative path: "But you shall not eat flesh with its life, that is, its blood" (9:4).

Here God qualifies the *kind* of flesh that man can consume, if not a *species* of flesh, which is what it would take to make it a Renunciative prohibition. It now seems that not only man's, but also *God's* imagination is by now limited. This is further illustrated by the nature of the "re-start." This is to put the righteous Noah in a self-sufficient ark carrying two of every sort and some of all food that is eaten together with himself, his wife, his sons and their wives (7, 8). The presence of the wives—from the evil world he is trying to escape—dooms the "new start" to defeat within the frame of reference of the text; but in our terms, the "new start" simply reproduces the problem that occasioned it in the first place, namely attempted self-sufficiency and autonomy.

The ark and its inhabitants make their escape as the deep of original creation opens up and the earth is flooded and its inhabitants are drowned. When the waters recede and Noah and the ark's occupants are safely on dry land Ham commits homosexual incest against his father (a sterile self-sufficiency), and he and his line are cursed. Instead of a brand new start, then, old habits simply return:

The whole earth was now of one language and one speech and the people gathered together in one place determined to emerge as one people with one name, thinking this to be God's purpose for them (11). Determined to be as they imagine God to be they raise a tower to reach him at Babel, but God sees the error of this way and intervenes to prevent it:

(11:7) "Come, let Us go down and there confuse their language, that they may not understand one another's speech."

(11:8) "So the Lord scattered them abroad from thence over the face of all the earth, and they ceased building the city."

Here God works *against* monism and, by separating and differentiating them, provides the Israelites with another possible future. A critical component of this possible future —of the lifeway of Renunciation—emerges with Abraham, born of Shem, son of Noah. This is the idea of a God-given jurisdiction over a Promised Land.

> 13:8–9 So Abram said to Lot. "Please let there be no strife between you and me, and between my herdsmen and your herdsmen; for we are brethren; Is not the whole land before you? Please separate from me. If you take the left, then I will go to the right; if you go to the right, then I will go to the left."

> 13:14–15 And the Lord said to Abram, after Lot had separated from him: "Lift your eyes now and look from the place where you are—northward, southward, eastward, and westward; for all the land which you see I give to you and your descendants forever."

This Land, like Aboriginal Land, is defined by the visual field which establishes its Form. It is something within which Abraham and his descendants can live forever with a kind of jurisdiction that does not require occupancy of the land for it to be owned. It is God-given to them irrespective of who else comes and goes within it. It is a Form for enclosing resources which, in Renunciative theory, is to be made available to someone else (though this is never explicitly stated).

The problem of subsequent Hebrew history is that one such Land alone is not enough. Nor is two or more if they are within the same "tribe." The problem is external relations to other "tribes" and of the presence of other "tribals" within one's own Land. The Land God has Promised is occupied by others outside the "tribe"—the Canaanites—who do not recognise the Hebrews and their God-given claim and who will resist forever the Hebrews' right to assert that claim if it means abandoning their own.

By the end of **Genesis** the Hebrews' prospects for realising the Promise seem dim indeed. They are surrounded by hostile tribes, are driven from Canaan by famine, and end up living in a land governed by others—the Egyptians—far away from the one Promised to them.

* * * *

You must agree that there appears to be more to the **Genesis** story than at first meets the eye when you read it with the Australian Aboriginal lifeway of Renunciation in mind. This reading of **Genesis** is consistent with a situation in which a federation of Promised Lands (a part-of-one-in-the-other without loss of integrity of either) saw one of their number separate and embark on a course of isolated self-sufficiency apart from the rest. Thereafter this past receded into history and was only dimly recollected by the writers of **Genesis** (whose perspective seems to be that of God in the story). This seems confirmed by the fact that it is the terms of the Fall that are explicit and well formulated here and not the terms of "Paradise" preceding the Fall. On the other hand, the bits and pieces of Renunciative logic we find here may represent the working out of an imagined future without prior historical basis. But if this were the case we would expect the terms of this future to become more and more clear as we proceed through the Hebrew Bible and this is not the case.

Exodus to Chronicles

Renunciation recedes both as an imaginative construct and as a practice, as we follow the Israelites back from exile to the Land they have been Promised. That is, examples are few and far between, and all that is not an example reflects a movement toward autonomy and self-sufficiency. This movement is directed by a seemingly monist God who supports the Israelites in the elimination of any who would thwart their aims—such as the Egyptians during the Israelites' escape from Egypt. But as in *Genesis*, this is a God who also gives clues as to an alternative path: "And the Angel of the Lord appeared to him in a flame of fire from the midst of a bush. So he looked, and behold, the bush burned with fire, but the bush was not consumed" (**Exodus** 3:2).

From the midst of the bush God called "Moses, Moses, Here I am." In Renunciative terms, this is spirit/Form (the material-less blazing Presence of the bush = *anti-thesis*) expelling matter (the bush = *thesis*). Insofar as God's word is also expelled to Moses a partial relationship of *plurality* or part-of-one-in-the otherness is established. However, in the final analysis, the relation between man and God is hierarchical not plural. God says to Moses, "I AM WHO I AM . . . . Thus you shall say to the children of Israel, I AM has sent me to you" (3:14). It is I AM who sends the 10 Commandments to Moses and demands obedience from his people. These commandments contain no Renunciative prescriptions at all—though there is nothing which would preclude Renunciation; but there are proscriptions against selfishness and acquisitiveness (20:13–17), both of which would have to be eliminated before Renunciation could emerge.

In the discussion that follows I will ignore the monist, incorporative, "Me-or-We-over-others" episodes in the text and dwell only on what could be interpreted as Renunciative examples.

In the tale of Moses and the Midian women (**Exodus** 2:15–22), Moses is in a foreign land and encounters a group of women trying to water their flock at a well. But shepherds have driven them away and Moses intervenes to restore them their place and provide them with water, he himself watering their flock. In other words, Moses treats these women from a different land, not as alien or enemy, but as friend. Then he provides them with what they have not—protection and water. What Moses has not is food, shelter, and a female companion, and these are provided by the women's father, Reul, who in turn treats Moses, not as an alien or enemy but as an honoured guest. Though renunciative in form, the episode is an isolated one which Moses eventually leaves to rejoin his own people.

God's pledge to restore the Promised Land to the Israelites is repeated in **Exodus** 6:7–8 where God provides yet another quasi-renunciative "sign" of his covenant. This is the taboo on eating leavened bread for seven days which to apply after the Israelites have been delivered from Egypt (13:6–9). This, though, is not the renunciation of a resource to be made available to someone else as leavened bread is to be replaced with unleavened bread which can still be eaten. Where a resource is renounced, as in the case of the sacrifice of all firstling animals, it does not go to those who have it not but to the Lord (13:1–21). When the Israelites have no food and water, they come not from others who have, but from the Lord (16:1–21, 17:1–7). In the Aboriginal lifeway, Renunciation is not via a third party in the spiritual realm but *by* one's own spirit *to* someone else whose own spirit moves his or her "matter" in turn.

Some isolated renunciative-by-implication examples appear in the aftermath of the 10 Commandments given by God to Moses for his people, For instance, you shall not wrong a stranger; if you lend money to the poor you shall not be a creditor or exact interest; if you take your neighbour's garment as a pledge you must restore it before the sun goes down as he has none (22:21–27); offer immediately from the fullness of your harvest and the outflow of your presses (but to God not to man) (22:29); do not eat flesh torn by beasts in the field but cast it to the dogs (who have none) (22:31); if you meet your enemy's ox you shall bring it back to him (he now having none).

Perhaps more indicative of renunciative awareness is the shining face Moses exhibits after being in the presence of God (34:29). In the Aboriginal lifeway of Renunciation this signifies an aesthetic and spiritual quality representing "other side" existence. Recall the fruit of the trees of the Garden of Eden which are "pleasing to the eye" and which may also be thought of as therefore exhibiting this quality.

Finally, in **Exodus** is a repeat of God's pledge to restore the

Promised Land to the Israelites (33:1–3), that is, the Land in its God-given Form.

In **Leviticus** (6) we learn more about the sacrifices that are to be made to God. Some are to be burned in their entirety. In the case of others a portion is to go back to those making the offering. Anything left over after this is to be burned (19:6) or given to the priests (a quasi-renunciative prescription). **Leviticus** 11 lists food prohibitions that apply to all Israelites. These include such edibles as "all that is in the water that does not have fins and scales" (e.g., shellfish), the ostrich, the stork, the heron, the hare, the lizard, reptiles, etc. Domesticated animals like swine are also prohibited. In not consuming these—at least the non-domesticated species—they are by default therefore available to others elsewhere, though this is not explicitly the intent.

More explicitly renunciative is the directive (25:35–39) to help "brethren" who are poor by giving them shelter and paying them for any services they provide.

In **Numbers** there is what could be a prelude to renunciation, but it occurs within the Israelite nation and not between it and outsiders. This is God's instruction (1:52–54, 2:2–3) to subdivide the nation by army or tribe as identified by the standard or emblem of one's father's house and to respect each other's jurisdiction (19:14). This at least allows for the possibility of renouncing from one "difference" to another within the Israelite nation, even if the concept of an army is repugnant to the lifeway of Renunciation.

If there is no hint of Renunciation in dealings with non-Israelites, nor is there a hint of Renunciation on the part of those neighbours toward the Israelites. When Moses asks permission to pass through the lands of Edom (20:14–21), guaranteeing them that the Israelites will not use their resources or stray from the road, he is bluntly refused. But rather than fight his way through, he detours around the land.

In **Deuteronomy** (2:4–9) we do find respect for the

jurisdiction of a non-Israelite people, but they are identified as descendants of Israel in the long ago past and as such are "brethren." God decrees they be left alone and that anything needed from them is to be paid for.

After the Israelites cross the Jordan and move toward Canaan they leave little but bloodshed and violence in their wake as they lay waste the inhabitants of the land to gain their preordained Promise (**Joshua** 21:43).

It is not until we pass through the books of **Ruth** and **Samuel 1** and **2** and arrive at **1** and **2 Kings** to encounter the wisdom of Solomon and the ascension of the prophet Elijah respectively, that we come across further examples of "almost Renunciation."

In **1Kings** Solomon establishes his own renunciative potential by making a peace treaty with Egypt (3:1). Later he sits in judgement of two women, each of whom has born a child (3:16–27). One woman's child, however, has died (now she has no child and in a Renunciative system would be entitled to one from someone else). But she steals the other woman's child and replaces it with her dead child (the other woman now has no child and is now herself entitled to another from someone else). In the absence of evidence as to the identity of the child, Solomon tells both women that the only solution is to cut the baby in two and each take half (dividing property in two and giving half to each of the disputants would be the actual solution to a dispute over boundaries in a Renunciative society). But the mother of the child would rather lose her son than see him killed and tells Solomon to give the child to the thief. The thief is indifferent to the fate of the child and if she cannot have it she would see it dead. Thus Solomon identifies the mother and gives her back her child. The mother, having nothing, is indeed, entitled to "everything." It is under Solomon that Judah and Israel are said to dwell safely together, "each man under his vine and fig tree" (4:25).

In **1Kings** we meet Elijah who encounters a widow who has no bread and only a little flour and oil to feed her family. Elijah causes flour and oil to appear in endless supply from an empty bin and jar, respectively. Elijah then receives the cake which he had not but of which he was in need.

But a more poignant instance of renunciative awareness comes on Elijah's ascension to heaven. Elijah tells his disciple Elisha to remain behind while he makes his journey, but Elisha refuses and comes with him (**2Kings** 2:1–3). Three more times Elijah asks him and three more times he refuses. They therefore proceed as "two." Elijah then divides the waters of the Jordan (in two) so that they both can cross. Elisha then asks that a double portion of Elijah's spirit be upon him when he ascends (in theory leaving Elijah with less than nothing) and Elijah agrees, if Elisha will actually witness his ascension. This he does. Elisha now has what Elijah has not, his earth-bound spirit and his mantle, neither of which Elijah now needs. Elisha then tears his clothes into two pieces (2:12) and takes Elijah's mantle and divides the waters of the Jordan (in two) with it (2:14). Elisha now repeats Elijah's earlier "miracle" of creating something from nothing (4:1–7) = *anti-thesis* —> *thesis*:

Elisha then encounters a widow who has no money to pay her debts and the creditor is coming. She has only one jar of oil which is not enough to repay what she owes. Elisha instructs her to find some empty vessels and fill them from hers (the empty jars have no oil and hers have some). Only when the woman had filled all the jars was hers empty (as should be the case in a Renunciative relation). Elisha tells her to sell the oil, pay her debts and live off what remains.

In 4:8–37 Elisha has no food and a woman feeds him. Then her son dies leaving her with no one. Elisha restores him to life by lying face to face, hands to hands with him—in other words, "mirroring" him—a representation of the relation of the "other side" to "this side" in Renunciative cosmology.

We make our way through the books of **Ezra**, **Nehemiah**, and **Esther** before coming to another quasi-renunciative example in **Job**. Job is "perfect in his generations" and has more in the way of material possessions than anyone in the East (1:6–21) and is in God's grace. But Satan challenges the Lord that Job would curse Him if he were to lose all he possessed. So God dispossesses him. Job responds: "Naked I came from my mother's womb, and naked shall I return there. The Lord gave, and the Lord has taken away; blessed be the name of the Lord" (1:21).

But Satan again challenges God: take away Job's health and he will renounce you. God does, but again, Job accepts his fate as God's will. Job, then, begins with everything and ends up with nothing, though what he gives up does not, as far as we know, go to those who have nothing. But Job is now in the position of having nothing which, in a Renunciative system, means he is now entitled to everything. And God is the person to give it to him: "Who has divided a channel for the overflowing water, or a path for the thunderbolt, to cause it to rain on a land where there is no one, a wilderness in which there is no man; to satisfy the desolate waste, and cause to spring forth the growth of tender grass?" (38:25–27).

If God can take away everything by full-emptying to render one "nothing," he can also give everything to the "nothing" he has created and thereby fulfil. God restores to Job twice as much as he had after Job prays for his friends despite the fact that they had interpreted his poverty as a sign of God's displeasure with him (42:10).

It is important to note that no principle is abstracted and no implications are drawn from these examples of renunciation. But they do stand in contrast to a mainstream that is anything but renunciative. The mainstream of Israelite life at this point is preoccupied with the accumulation of land and wealth. Gain in these areas is interpreted as a sign of God's grace just as losses are interpreted as a sign of his displeasure. But, as we've seen, there are hints of another purpose behind "God's will", and it must be admitted (tongue in cheek) that before one can renounce everything to those who have nothing, one must first accumulate everything from them so that it can, of course, be passed on or given back.

We move through **Psalms**, **Proverbs**, and **Ecclesiastes** with barely a trace of renunciative awareness to arrive at **Isaiah** where it again begins to emerge, only to be extinguished.

In 1:16–17, the Lord, through Isaiah, instructs his people to wash themselves clean, cease to do evil and learn to do good, reprove the oppressor, defend the fatherless and plead for the widow. In the last two cases this is to attend to those who have nothing. To reprove the oppressor is to wish to take from those who have everything. This will herald a peaceful time when the law and the word of the Lord will make peace among the nations: ". . . . they shall beat their swords into plowshares, and their spears into pruning hooks; nation shall not lift up sword against nation, neither shall they learn war any more" (2:4).

In 5:8 there is a condemnation of accumulation and in 5:11 of intoxication, that is, proscription against taking all instead of giving it up as well as one against allowing polluting intrusions into the body of such quantity that they do damage. And there is to be a sign of a new world to come: "Therefore the Lord Himself will give you a sign: Behold, the virgin shall conceive and bear a Son, and shall call his name Immanuel" (7:14). Christians take this to be a prophecy of Jesus' birth, but it could equally be a prophecy of an Aboriginal-like situation wherein the mother is not the mother of the child she bears. "Her" child is that of her brother's wife, a child with the same spiritual identity as herself. In this sense she is a "virgin" with respect to the child she actually bears. Moreover, that child is from a Creative spirit, not from a human progenitor.

What future does this son who is to come herald?: "For before the Child shall know to refuse the evil and choose the good, the land that you dread will be forsaken by both her kings" (7:16). That is, the Promised Land will be given up or renounced to the Israelites by its present inhabitants. This brings us to the "suffering servant" episode of **Isaiah** which Christians also take to be a foretelling of the coming of Jesus:

53:3 He is despised and rejected by men, a man of sorrow and acquainted with grief.

53:10 Yet it pleased the Lord to bruise Him; He has put Him to grief. When You make his soul an offering for sin, He shall see His seed. He shall prolong His days, and the pleasure of the Lord shall prosper in His hands.

Sacrifice, particularly sacrificing one's life, is not really an aspect of the lifeway of Renunciation. Here one renounces "content" from "Form," "matter" from living "spirit," which one cannot do if one's life is taken away. But what exactly is "God's pleasure" in this case?

53:12 Therefore I will divide Him a portion with the great, and He shall divide the spoil with the strong, because He poured out His soul unto death, and He was numbered with the transgressors, and He bore the sin of many, and made intercession for the transgressors.

This reads like awareness of the power of suffering to throw up a "saviour" with a difference, but it does not locate the difference in Renunciation. "Divide a portion" is not to give up the whole portion, nor is "divide the spoil"—particularly if it is to be with the strong. Better is **Isaiah** 49:9–10 in which the "suffering servant" will tell people whose "pastures are on all desolate heights" (i.e., those who have nothing), that they shall neither hunger nor thirst nor suffer from heat or sun.

In **Isaiah** 14:1–2 God's promise to restore the lands of Israel is reiterated. And in the future everyone and everything will get what they have not (29:17–24; 35:6–7):

Lebanon shall be turned into a fruitful field,
the deaf shall hear,
the blind shall see,
the humble also shall increase their joy,

the poor among men shall rejoice,

Then the lamb shall leap like a deer,
and the tongue of the dumb sing,
For waters shall burst forth in the wilderness, and
streams in the desert,
The parched ground shall become a pool, and the thirsty
land springs of water.
A later passage continues along the same lines:

55:1–2 "Everyone who thirsts, come to the waters; and
you who have no money, come buy and eat. Yes, come,
buy wine and milk without money and without price.
Why do you spend money for what is not bread, and
your wages for what does not satisfy? Listen diligently
to Me, and eat what is good."

But the passage ends, "and let your soul delight itself in
abundance," although it does not say if the delight in question
is that it is yours to consume or that it is yours to give to
someone else.

In **Isaiah** 58 we find an explicitly renunciative statement in
connection with fasting:

58:3 "Why have we fasted," they say . . .
58:6 "Is this not the fast that I have chosen: to loose the
  bonds of wickedness, to undo the heavy burdens, to let
the oppressed go free, and that you break every yoke?
58:7 Is it not to share your bread with the hungry [in
Renunciation, *all* the bread would go to those who had
no bread], and that you bring to your house the poor
who are cast out; when you see the naked, that you cover
him, and not hide yourself from your own flesh?
58:8 Then your light shall break forth like the morning,
your healing shall spring forth speedily, and your
righteousness shall go before you; the glory of the Lord

shall be your rear guard [perhaps a metaphor for the guard set at the entrance to Eden]

58:10 if you extend your soul to the hungry and satisfy the afflicted soul [in Renunciation your soul would extend food to the hungry], then your light shall dawn in the darkness, and your darkness shall be as the noonday" [that is, become what it is not]. The new world to come is to be under God's glory and achieve reconciliation between the Israelites and the Gentiles:

60:2 For behold, the darkness shall cover the earth, and deep darkness the people; but the Lord will arise over you, and His glory will be seen upon you
60:3 The Gentiles shall come to your light, and kings to the brightness of your rising.

But the Gentiles are to be *under* God and Israel: "For the nation and kingdom which will not serve you shall perish, and those nations shall be utterly ruined" (60:12). Is it to be a hierarchical or caste-like relation between "nations," or is it to be equality in interdependence?: "But you [Israel] shall be named the Priests of the Lord, men shall call you the Servants of our God. You shall eat the riches of the Gentiles, and in their glory you shall boast" (61:6). But, in a strange way, the situation is to be a mutually beneficial one:

61:7 Instead of your [Israel's] shame you shall have double honour, and instead of confusion they shall rejoice in their portion. Therefore in their land they shall possess double; everlasting joy shall be theirs.

65:17 "For behold, I create new heavens and a new earth; and the former shall not be remembered or come to mind."

But even if the relationship between the Israelites and the

Gentiles is not to be one in which the former dominates the latter, there is nevertheless a flaw in this new heaven and new earth: "They shall build houses and inhabit them; they shall plant vineyards and eat their fruit" (65:21). In other words, people are to be self-sufficient. The point is emphasised: "They shall not build and another inhabit; they shall not plant and another eat . . . and My elect shall long enjoy the work of their hands" (65:22).

*   *   *   *

From **Isaiah** we make our way through **Jeremiah** and **Lamentations** and the fall of Jerusalem and the Israelites' exile to Babylon (52) to reach **Ezekiel** before we find another example of renunciation.

In 1:4–28 a whirlwind appears from the north as a raging fire engulfing itself [into nothing]. Brightness is all around it and radiating out of its midst. Out of all this emerges [incarnates] the likeness [Presence, Form] of four living creatures. Each is like a man and each has four faces and four wings. Their legs are straight and their feet are like calves' feet. They sparkle and their wings touch one another [are separate but linked]. Each man-face has the face of a lion on the right side and the face of an ox on the left [predator-prey in peaceful co-existence] and also the face of an eagle [perhaps symbolic of the Heavenly realm]. Above their heads is a firmament like the colour of crystal and under the firmament their wings are spread.

This sounds very much like the Aboriginal view of Creation, a Creation which in the beginning is plural, having no "One" behind "them." In this passage from **Ezekiel,** Forms or Presences emerge first out of Nothing, then become apparent or materialise into definite shapes and features. Each of these appearances is itself multiple, even combining human and animal characteristics. And the appearances are separate yet interconnected, as in "wing touching wing" [not quite, but almost, a-part-of-one-in-the-other].

But this image in Ezekiel is finally overwhelmed or appropriated by a "Oneness": a voice emerges from above the firmament, then appears the likeness of a thing and the appearance of a man above it. His lower body is fire with brightness all around; his upper body is fire the colour of amber. This double-Presence, so to speak, is the glory of the Lord. It is like the appearance of a rainbow in a cloud on a rainy day. (In **Genesis** the rainbow was the sign of God's covenant with humankind.)

In 3:1–6 God feeds Ezekiel with a scroll and sends him to Israel to instruct them in his word. In other words, God gives Ezekiel what he has not and Ezekiel gives Israel what they have not.

In 40, a New City, a New Temple, is envisioned that will house the people. This City is internally divided into Districts by boundaries (47:13), four in all along its four sides, then subdivided by lots and assigned to the 12 tribes, with one lot reserved for God and his temple. But this inheritance is to be for the Israelites and the strangers who sojourn among them who bear children among them, that is, women brought in from Gentile society. This might at first glance seem progressive insofar as there is a place for foreigners or strangers in this new order. But it is not progressive from a Renunciative point of view insofar as these foreigners are to be incorporated into Israelite society or made one with them. In a Renunciative arrangement these people would rather retain their identities of origin and enjoy their principal rights elsewhere, but be treated as guests in the host's jurisdiction.

Leaving **Ezekiel** and proceeding through **Daniel, Hosea, Joel, Amos, Jonah, Micah, Nahum, Habakkuk, Zephaniah, Haggai, Zechariah**, and **Malachi**, we find only two brief renunciative examples, but they are instructive:

The first is Daniel in the lion's den (**Daniel** 6), the second Jonah and the whale (**Jonah** 1). In the lion's den the lion "renounces" Daniel as food as the whale that swallows Jonah "renounces" him. But in both cases it is with the help of God, in the first through his intermediary, the angels, and in the second God gives a direct order to the whale. But both cases carry the implication of a spiritual force behind a renunciative process.

*   *   *   *

If renunciation makes only sporadic appearances in Hebrew Scripture, we are at least informed that these scriptures are not the final word on the subject. In the final chapters the Lord proclaims through Malachi,

> 3:1 "Behold, I send my messenger, and he will prepare the way before Me. And the Lord whom you seek, will suddenly come to His temple, even the Messenger of the covenant, in whom you delight. Behold, He is coming," says the Lord of hosts.

The message of the Messenger to come may or may not be r/Renunciation. We'll see. But before we examine this possibility we must examine God, the Oneness that seems to keep heralding/interfering with, the possibility of Renunciation.

It is evident from Hebrew Scriptures that their God reaches humankind by revealing his intentions to particularly gifted, chosen, persons like Moses. Interestingly, there is some evidence that these revelations may have been channelled through music. First there is the general call to praise God through music in Psalm 150:

> Praise Him with the sound of the trumpet;
> Praise Him with the lute and harp!
> Praise Him with the timbrel and dance;
> Praise Him with stringed instruments and flutes!
> Praise Him with loud cymbals!
> Let everything that has breath praise the Lord.

But a connection is also made between prophecy and music: "Moreover David and the captains of the army separated for the service some of the sons of Asaph, of Heman, and of Jeduthun, who should prophesy with harps, stringed instruments, and cymbals" (**1Chronicles** 25:1).

In **1Chronicles** 6, David appoints certain men over the service of song in the house of the Lord, noting that they had performed this service previously. But is the music at issue polyphonic, involving the articulation of separate parts into a complex of counterpoint and inversion, as in the Australian case, or is it something else?

> **2Chronicles** 5:12–13 . . . and the Levites who were the singers, all those of Asaph and Heman and Jeduthun, with their sons and their brethren, stood at the east end of the altar, clothed in white linen, having cymbals, stringed instruments and harps, and with them one hundred and twenty priests sounding with trumpets— indeed it came to pass, when the trumpeters and singers were as one, to make one sound to be heard in praising and thanking the Lord.

This is the music of unity and oneness, of an incorporative, self-sufficient society.

Where does this idea of One—this God—come from? The words ascribed to God in Hebrew Scriptures reach us through human beings who themselves reach God through devotion, music, and some form of mystical experience. We have Elijah's initially plural vision, his experience of the transcendent as a numinous, "fifth dimension," outside himself and described very much in Aboriginal terms. But then God enters into it and "spoils" the vision. To me "God" as a "Oneness" behind the scene is an intellectual projection beyond the scene of, for instance, Elijah's actual vision. In experiencing the multiplicity of Forms or Presences in a non-material sense, the mystic projects beyond this scene to imagine a Form of Forms "explaining" the actual multiplicity of Forms he or she has experienced. But this all-encompassing Spirit-Form or Presence is an *imposition* on the field of one's vision (or audition), not actually a part of the vision itself. But once this projection is built into a tradition it becomes an expectation of those seeking visions of the transcendent. This, then, is how they interpret what they see (hear, feel).

Of course this begs the question whether people in a Renunciative society also have a predisposition to experience multiplicity. But while we can logically infer how One might be mis-projected from and over-and-above the Many, we cannot logically infer how the Many could be a mis-projection from and below the One.

IV

Renunciation in Christian Scriptures?

We really cannot proceed here as we did in the case of Hebrew Scriptures, that is, in chronological order. In the three Synoptic Gospels and John we essentially encounter four versions of the same story, each covering the same time frame but differing in some of the details. For example, it is **Mark** who puts the emphasis on the crucifixion and resurrection, **John** on the more spiritual aspects of the tradition. So as not to become embroiled in debates about which texts were borrowed from which, or which are earlier than which, or what has been added or deleted from the "originals," I will take a thematic approach, beginning with the Synoptic Gospels and **John** considered together and proceeding through **Acts of the Apostles** and the **Epistles** considered together and, finally, the **Book of Revelation**. The themes I have chosen such as SpiritForm, ChurchForm etc. derive from our discussion of the Aboriginal lifeway of Renunciation.

The Synoptic Gospels and John

1. SpiritForm

In the Beginning was the Word, and the Word was with God, and the Word was God. He was in the beginning with God; All things were made through Him, and without Him nothing was made. In him was life, and the life was the light of men . . . That was the true Light which gives light to every man who comes into the world. He was in the world, and the world was made through Him, and the world did not know Him . . . And the Word became flesh and dwelt among us . . . full of grace and truth. (**John** 1)

Here, as in Hebrew Scriptures, God is writ in the singular, as is "Logos," "the Word." Word is sound, indeed, a soundForm. Out of soundForm is to come the "true light"—flesh in the person of the man Jesus who is full of grace and truth and who will "light" every living person. This all has a certain renunciative ring to it, though the meaning-less Word, the Melody, has more significance in the Aboriginal lifeway than the meaning-full word.

When the prophet John encounters Jesus prior to his baptism he observes (1:32), "I saw the Spirit descending from heaven like a dove, and He remained upon him." The process of incarnation described here is reiterated by Jesus who says (3:5–6), "Most assuredly, I say to you, unless one is born of water and the Spirit, he cannot enter the Kingdom of God. That which is born of flesh is flesh, and that which is born of the Spirit is spirit."

In Renunciative cosmology you are both yourself in material form on "this side" and yourself in spiritual Form on "the other." This is hinted at in the portrayal of Jesus as the "son" of God: God "renounces" or "slices off" a part of Himself from the "other side" to "this side" to be "twisted in" to a human being born through the virgin Mary. Mary, as in Aboriginal cosmology, is more a receptacle within which Jesus is formed than a contributor to his physical or spiritual makeup (**Matthew** 1:18–25; **Luke 1**, 2:1–7). This comes from his Father, God. But even in this perspective, Jesus appears as a less perfect incarnation than the Aboriginal man and lawgiver Nambirrirrma (pages 31–32) who emerged directly from *Amawurrena* without either a human "mother" or father.

But in Scriptures Jesus alone is born through this process. Everyone else continues to be born "naturally" and must be *reborn* through Jesus by accepting his words as the son of God. In Renunciative cosmology, everyone is born of his or her own archetypal spiritForm on the "other side" as a personal spiritForm on "this side." Each human being is in a sense "renounced" or expelled over from the "other side" containing an inner spirit that renounces or expels "matter" from itself to others on "this side."

In Christian Scriptures there are only fleeting references to "spirit" and "soul" and they are not systematically distinguished or interrelated (see **Matthew** 10:28, 16:26 and **Mark** 8:36 on soul; also **Matthew** 26:41, 27:50, **Mark** 14:38, **John** 19:30). **Luke** 17:21 refers to the Kingdom of God that is within you but it is not clear whether this refers to spirit/soul, the Word, or the power of God.

"Soul" in Christian Scriptures is a translation of the Greek *psuche* which is, in turn, rooted in the Hebrew *nefesh*. *Nefesh* means a "diminutive image of the body" (McGregor in Sullivan 1989, p. 214). "Spirit" in Christian Scriptures is a translation of the Greek *pneuma* which is equated with the Hebrew *ruah* or "breath of life." We could, perhaps, equate the Hebrew concept of "soul-as-image-of-the-body" with the Aboriginal *Ama-wurrena* and equate the Hebrew "spirit-as-breath-of-life" with *alawuduwarra*. But, strictly speaking, in Aboriginal terms this image would be the outerForming aspect, and breath the innerForming.

The Gospels also contain references to people's experience of spirit and soul. Take **Matthew's** (3:16) account of Jesus' baptism (also **Mark** 1:9–11, **Luke** 3:21–22, **John** 1:28–34):

> Then Jesus, when He had been baptised, came up immediately from the water; and behold, the heavens were opened to Him, and He saw the Spirit of God descending like a dove and alighting on Him. And suddenly a voice came from heaven saying, "This is My beloved Son, in whom I am well pleased."

The shepherds have an experience of spirit when they hear the angel announcing Jesus' birth in **Luke** 2:8–13. Then there is Jesus' experience in the wilderness in **Matthew** 4:1–11 (also **Mark** 1:12–13 and **Luke** 4:1–13); the transfiguration of Jesus in **Matthew** 17:1–8 (also **Mark** 9:1–8 and **Luke** 9: 28–36); the women's experience of Jesus' tomb in **Matthew** 28: 2–4 (also **Luke** 24:4). All these accounts are, in Renunciative terms, "aesthetic/transcendent"—an experience of the Presence/ Form of something outside oneself.

In three accounts of the transfiguration of Jesus—**Matthew** (17:1–8), **Mark** and **Luke** (9:28–36)—the experience of spirit is *of* Jesus' *by* his disciples:

> Now after six days Jesus took Peter, James, and John his brother, and led them up on a high mountain apart by themselves; and He was transfigured before them. His clothes became shining, exceedingly white, like snow, such as no launderer on earth can whiten them. And Elijah appeared to them with Moses, and they were talking with Jesus. Then Peter answered and said to Jesus, "Rabbi, it is good for us to be here; and let us make three tabernacles: one for You, one for Moses and one for Elijah"—because he did not know what to say, for they were greatly afraid. And a cloud came and overshadowed them; and a voice came out of the cloud, saying, "This is My beloved Son. Hear him!" Suddenly, when they had looked around, they saw no one anymore, but only Jesus with themselves. (**Mark**: 9:1–8)

In **Luke** the prophets also appear "in glory," or enFormed, during the experience, Moses representing the Law, in turn representing God.

The really significant thing from a Renunciative point of view here is that the disciples draw "pluralist" implications from their experiences. They propose making three booths— three separate "homes," that is, one for each of the prophets, rather than, say, one booth for them all or two for the prophets and a separate one for Jesus.

The experience of angels in Scriptures can be taken as of something outside oneself, but only if we consider spirit-beings to be real and normally inaccessible to perception. In two accounts, **Matthew** and **Luke**, the angels are described as dazzling and shining, as was Jesus at the moment of his transfiguration. Likewise the angels who appeared to the shepherds announcing Jesus' impending birth.

But perhaps the most interesting account of "spirit" in Christian Scriptures is Jesus' after his crucifixion and resurrection. This "second birth" is a more "perfect" incarnation then the first, with Jesus emerging out of the empty but Formed space of a cave as distinct from a woman's womb. In **Mark** 16:12, the resurrected Jesus appears "in another form" from the one in which he had appeared earlier to Mary Magdalene. In **Luke** 24:16 Jesus appears to two of his disciples and they conversed, "But their eyes were restrained, so that they did not know him." It was only when Jesus sat down at the table and broke bread with the disciples in their village, recreating the familiar experience of the Last Supper, that their eyes were opened and they knew him. Then he "vanished from their sight" (24:31). Later (24:36–37), As they said these things, Jesus Himself stood in the midst of them, and said to them, "Peace to you." But they were terrified and frightened, and supposed they had seen a spirit.

As evidence of his "existence" after death, Jesus shows the disciples the holes in his hands and his feet, but still they do not believe him. Then he asks them for food and is given a piece of fish and some honey. In renunciative terms, Jesus *is* nothing, *has* nothing, and is therefore entitled to something from those who have and are everything. Still they are unconvinced, so Jesus instructs them to "Handle Me and see, for a spirit does not have flesh and bones as you see I have" (24:39). Then he is described as actually eating in the disciples' presence. From this we may be forced to conclude that Jesus' appearance was flesh, not spirit. But it all depends on where exactly on his body Jesus was "handled."

John 20:20 specifically states that Jesus is recognised by the holes in his hands and his side. Thomas who doubts seeks further confirmation by asking permission of Jesus to actually examine these holes. Jesus agrees and says, "Reach your finger here, and look at My hands; and reach your hand here, and put it in my side" (20:27). Touching "nothing" does not confirm that there is "something" such as a body there. The earlier instruction in **Luke** 24:39, then, may have been to handle only these holes. The eating could refer to Jesus simply having been given something because he has and is no-thing. In other words, there is little to suggest that Jesus was present in any other than *spiritual* form, although Jesus may have been trying to convince his disciples he was real.

In **John** 20:20 Jesus breathes the Holy Spirit onto the disciples; breath is synonymous with spirit. What follows from this is, appropriately, a renunciative relationship:

> 21:4–7 But when the morning had now come, Jesus stood on the shore; yet the disciples did not know that it was Jesus. Then Jesus said to them, "Children, have you any food?" They answered Him, "No." And He said to them, "Cast the net on the right side of the boat, and you will find some." So they cast, and now they were not able to draw it in because of the multitude of fish. Therefore that disciple whom Jesus loved said to Peter, "It is the Lord!"

In other words, Jesus is at first unrecognised (as spirit) and then is recognised by this teaching: he gives everything to those who have nothing. Another teaching follows:

> 21:8–14 But the other disciples came in the little boat . . . dragging the net with fish. Then, as soon as they had come to land, they saw a fire of coals there, and fish laid on it, and bread. Jesus said to them, "Bring some of the fish which you have just caught." Simon Peter went up and dragged the net to land, full of large fish, one hundred and fifty-three; and although there were so many, the net was not broken. Jesus said to them,

"Come and eat breakfast." Yet none of the disciples dared ask Him, "Who are You?"—knowing that it was the Lord. Jesus then came and took the bread and gave it to them, and likewise the fish. This is now the third time Jesus showed Himself to His disciples after He was raised from the dead.

Even up close, the disciples are still not sure it is Jesus, and if he is known from his renunciative teachings, this particular teaching is somewhat ambiguous and obscure. The other disciples are fishing and see a fire on shore with fish and bread. But Jesus asks them to catch more fish and come and eat breakfast. They are puzzled with good reason if Renunciation is the teaching here. There is already fish and bread on shore. Why are they being asked to bring more fish? But it appears that Jesus then gives them, not their own fish, but the fish and bread at the fire. Even here, though, he should give them only what he has that they have not—the bread. That this is a puzzle for the disciples is illustrated in the episode that follows involving Simon Peter, of whom Jesus asks "do you love Me more than these?" "Yes," Simon Peter replies. Then Jesus says "Feed my lambs" (21:15). Jesus asks the same question again and again Simon Peter answers that he loves him. Jesus replies, "Tend my sheep." Then Jesus asks a third time which grieves Simon Peter who replies in exasperation, "You know that I love you." Jesus responds, "Feed my sheep." It is obvious that Simon Peter is missing the point. But what point is being made?

First, we have a clear-cut Renunciative teaching, then an ambiguous one and now two solitudes talking past one another. Jesus seems to be saying, feed and care for those who cannot look after themselves and Simon Peter doesn't get it. Instead he thinks he should be providing for the one whom he loves, namely Jesus. But Jesus is Nothing and needs nothing. What is startling is that it is Simon Peter, the rock upon whom Jesus will build his church, who is singled out as perhaps the *least* able to understand his teachings.

In exploring spirit in the Synoptic Gospels and John we encounter renunciation and hints of Renunciation. Perhaps Jesus' promise to come again a third time is to clear up the ambiguities, be understood, and instruct disciples who will at last get it right.

2. ChurchForm

In the Synoptic Gospels and John there are no Places comparable to Aboriginal Lands/Peoples from which resources can be renounced; there is not even mention of the Hebrews' Promised Land. But there is a church. It is perhaps understandable why there is no mention of a Promised Land or God's promise to restore the Land of Canaan to the Israelites in Christian Scriptures. Their forebears'—the Hebrews—attempts to realise this as the solution to their problems had all ended in failure. Their history to the time of Jesus history had been one of dispossession and exile in the midst of their own unsuccessful attempts to conquer their neighbours. At the time of Jesus, the Israelites were in the Holy Land but suffering under the yoke of Roman occupation. Roman legions had been dispatched to conduct a census and exact tribute from the local population, and Emperor Augustus had inaugurated a policy of indirect rule by dividing King Herod's lands between his three sons Archelaus (as ethnarch), and Antipas and Philip (designated tetrarchs). Antipas governed the Provinces of Peraea and Galilee where Jesus was raised and where the radical Jewish movement known as the Zealots originated. Though the Zealots called for an armed insurrection against Rome, their aims were ultimately the realisation of God's Kingdom—God's Promise—in the Holy Land.

In sharp contrast to the Zealots was the old Hebrew aristocracy and their religious leaders, the Sadducees, who collaborated with the Romans to preserve what remained of their traditional authority over their own people. Then there were the less establishment-oriented Pharisees representing the mass of devout laity. Ironically, the Pharisee movement had emerged during the Maccabean revolt of 165 B.C. against the high priests but had itself become corrupted by wealth and power. They advocated accommodation with the Romans but only to preserve the integrity of the Jewish people through the occupation.

The Pharisees and Sadducees advocated strict observance of the laws and customs of the patriarchs and of the Torah or Hebrew Scriptures. But the Pharisees believed in a soul that survived death while the Sadducees held to the more traditional belief that the soul perished along with the body. The Pharisees believed in Providence—a God in control of events in the world who had given humankind the freedom to choose between good and evil. The Sadducees believed that God was only in control of good, not evil. Contemporary with these estates were the Essenes, a monastic order who held their property in common and generally did not marry (see Zeitlin 1988 for more detail).

The Jesus of Christian Scriptures was certainly a Jew. He was circumcised as a Jew, lived and prayed as a Jew, performed Jewish rites and preached in Aramaic to his fellow Jews in Palestine. At the age of 12 we find him sitting among teachers in Jerusalem. He observed the Law, celebrated Passover, taught at the Temple, paid the Temple tax, respected the Scribes and the Pharisees and directed his own message mainly to Jews. But, as far as promoting the traditional aspiration of his people—Sadducees, Pharisees, Scribes, Essenes, Zealots—no. Jesus makes no reference at all of the Land Promised by God to the Israelites as their eternal birthright. Instead he (or whoever authored Scriptures) conceived an institution that could exist in whatever State might be invented or imposed on the people. This was the church.

*   *   *   *

The word "church," appears only twice in the Synoptic Gospels and John and these are in **Matthew**:

> 16:18 "And also I say to you that you are Peter, and on this rock I will build My church . . ."
>
> 18:17 And if he refuses to hear them, tell it to the church. But if he refuses even to hear the church, let him be to you like a heathen and a tax collector.

In both cases the word used is the Greek *ekklēsia* which refer to a "congregation" or a group of people coming together for a religious purpose. But the Greek term *ekklēsia* is a cognate of *ek-klētoi* which means "citizens of the state who have been summoned by a herald." Such a confounding of religious and secular meanings was not uncommon in the Greco-Roman world—the Latin *religio* or "religion" also referred to the powers people were obliged to obey as a condition of citizenship in the state. The church of Scriptures may have been conceived not merely as a collection of people occupying a particular space (**Matthew** 18:20: "For where two or three are gathered in my name, there am I in the midst of them"), but also as a form of jurisdiction akin to citizenship in which membership did not depend on co-residence in space but was yours to enjoy and to which you could return no matter what other space you currently occupied. In other words, a kind of mini-Promised Land.

How is the church organised? We are not told. **Matthew** 18 merely says it is the ultimate arbiter in disputes when individual efforts fail. There is no mention of a church or churches bounding different resources or services prohibited to their owners and available to others elsewhere. No Law proclaims "you have nothing and everything we have is yours." The church appears to be a kind of holding company for the faithful until the Day of Judgement arrives and the Kingdom of God and Heaven is proclaimed. It is this Kingdom to come, not the church, which, if you seek, will provide—from nowhere—the material things of life;

> **Luke**: 12:29–31 "And do not seek what you should eat and what you should drink, nor have an anxious mind.

For all these things the nations of the world seek after, and your Father knows that you need these things. But seek the Kingdom of God, and all these things shall be added to you."

But the idea of "the Kingdom" as an institutional framework, abstract and transcendent, remains undeveloped in Scriptures. If there is renunciation, it is on an individual level, not on the level of institutions.

3. Renunciation

First to be considered as an example of renunciation is the parable of the hidden treasure and the pearl in **Matthew** 13:44–46: "Again, the kingdom of heaven is like treasure hidden in a field, which a man found and hid; and for joy over it he goes and sells all that he has and buys that field. Again, the kingdom of heaven is like a merchant seeking beautiful pearls, who, when he had found one pearl of great price, went and sold all that he had and bought it."

Why did the man not simply remove the treasure from the field under cover of night? Why did he sell all he had to buy the field? This makes little sense unless you look at the passage as a statement of renunciation: a man empties himself of all he has and receives all he has not. Similarly, a merchant first gives up all he has in order to make himself eligible to receive what he has not.

In **Matthew** 18:23–35 the Kingdom of Heaven is compared to a king who decides to settle his accounts with his servants. One of them is brought to him who cannot repay the ten thousand talents he owes, so the king orders that he and his family be sold. But the servant begs the king's patience and offers to pay back everything he owes. In renunciative terms, as the servant has nothing but offers everything, the king would be obliged to forgive the whole debt so that he himself in a sense now has "nothing" (and is therefore now entitled to everything from someone else). But when this servant demands repayment of a small debt to himself by someone else who had begged his patience as he had begged from the king, the king has the servant thrown into jail.

In **Matthew** 14:14–21 Jesus has come ashore to find a great crowd awaiting him and he teaches and heals all day until it is time for supper. But the crowd has no food. The disciples, however, have five loaves and two fishes. Jesus instructs them to feed the crowd with these and they do. Now they have nothing. But the loaves and fishes have multiplied to feed everyone including, we assume, the disciples.

In **Luke** 14:16–24 a man gives a great banquet and invites many guests. But they do not come, saying that they have to pay attention to their possessions. The man's house is now "empty" but full of food intended for others. So he invites in the poor, the maimed, the blind and the lame to consume it, that is, those who in these times had nothing. In renunciative terms they are entitled to the food. The invited guests—those with "everything"—demonstrate that they should not have been invited in the first place.

In **Luke** 7:41–43, a certain creditor has two debtors, one owing five hundred denari, the other fifty. When they could not pay the debt he forgave them both. The one who owed him more is said to love him more. In renunciative terms both debtors have nothing, but he owing more has less than nothing. He gives back more in love in turn.

Matthew 5:40 says that if anyone sues you and takes your coat, let him have your cloak as well. Give to him who begs from you and do not refuse him who would borrow from you. In other words, give until you have nothing; give to those who have nothing; lend to those in need. This is a renunciative passage. But **Luke** 3:11 on the same subject is not: he who has two coats, let him share with him who has none; and he who has food, let him do likewise (see also **Luke** 6:29–30).

Matthew 19:21 says, "If you want to be perfect, go, sell what you have and give to the poor, and you will have treasure in heaven" (see also **Mark** 10:21). One does not renounce indiscriminately but gives to those who have nothing; then one receives what one does not have from somewhere/one else (i.e., treasure in heaven, given that you may not be renounced *to* with treasure on earth).

The passage in **Mark** 4:24 (also **Luke** 12:48), "the measure you give will be the measure you get," seems to advocate equality in the value of an exchange. Renunciation, by contrast, neither requires repayment nor evaluates comparative value. But then the passage ends with, "and still more will be given to you," which implies that equality of value is not the issue.

Mark 12:43 recounts the story of the woman who contributes to the Temple out of her poverty whereas others only contribute out of their abundance: "Assuredly, I say to you that this poor widow has put in more than all those who have given to the treasury." This is for the renunciative reason that she now has nothing and is therefore entitled to everything. The Aborigines give from abundance, but they give up *all* of what they have in abundance.

But perhaps the most poignant example of renunciation in the Synoptic Gospels and John occurs at the Last Supper

> **Matthew** 26:26–29 And as they were eating, Jesus took bread, blessed it and broke it, and gave it to the disciples and said, "Take, eat; this is My body." Then He took the cup, and gave thanks and gave it to them, saying, "Drink from it, all of you. For this is My blood of the new covenant, which is shed for many for the remission of sins. But I say to you, I will not drink of this fruit of the vine from now on until that day when I drink it new with you in My Father's kingdom."

There is nothing to suggest that Jesus himself consumes some of the bread and some of the wine before the others (to do so would be Renunciative heresy—like consuming one's own "Dreaming"—if it symbolised his own body and blood). He blesses and gives thanks and gives them up—renounces them—to those who don't have them. The blessing can be seen as infusing the bread with spirit, that which "expels" it to others. Nor does Jesus renounce the bread as a whole or the wine by the whole bottle. He breaks the bread and pours the wine (into goblets). These are distributed, it would seem, as "two," not "one" (in contrast to the Forbidden Fruit in Eden which was consumed and distributed as one).

In **Luke** (22:17) Jesus takes a cup, and when he had given thanks said, "Take this, and divide it among yourselves." The point is underscored when Jesus breaks bread with the disciples after his resurrection (**Luke** 24:30). He will not drink the fruit of the vine, though, until he meets the disciples much later in the Kingdom of God. This completes what was begun at the Last Supper where Jesus, as far as we know, did not receive back the wine—and the bread—after "renouncing" it to the disciples, leaving himself with nothing.

If renunciation is what Jesus is really on about, to be empty, both materially and spiritually, in his eyes would be to be blessed. In the Beatitudes (**Luke** 6:20–25) blessed are the poor and those who hunger, but "woe to you who are rich, for you have received your consolation. Woe to you who are full, for you shall hunger," to which we can add: <<if you do not give up what you have>>. If you do, though, having nothing, you become blessed. This perspective throws light on the comment in **Mark** 14:7, "For you have the poor with you always, and whenever you wish you may do them good." In a Renunciative world, everyone is temporarily poor, or fullemptied, until they are fulfilled. Conversely, everyone full is not blessed until emptied, or as **Luke** 11:41 says, "but rather give alms of such things as you have; then indeed all things are clean to you." Moreover, in Renunciation one empties without being asked and one is filled without asking. This seems to be the sense of **Matthew** 10:8, "freely you have received, freely give."

Fasting can be interpreted as a renunciative mechanism wherein denying oneself food thereby makes it available to someone else. The only reference to fasting in the Synoptic Gospels and John is when Jesus suggests that one abstain after a wedding (**Matthew** 9:14–15, **Mark** 2:18–20), that is, when one is full.

4. Peace and Order versus Economic Development

From the Aboriginal evidence we are led to conclude that peaceful co-existence varies inversely with technological change and economic development (the more there is of one, the less there is of the other). The Aborigines remained hunters and gatherers throughout their pre-contact history, even though they knew of agriculture from New Guinea and Indonesia. Domesticable plants and animals were available, but the Aborigines chose not to utilise them. Why not? The lifeway of Renunciation is selflessness, a giving up of your own interest in something to make it available to someone else. A principal motivation for technological change and economic development is to decrease your reliance on others and achieve a greater degree of self-sufficiency as an individual or a group by extracting more from the environment so that you can increase your productivity and wealth. Competition both fosters this aim and is a result of its achievement. With Renunciation, the impetus to technological change and economic development vanishes because selfishness, the need to compete and accumulate, vanishes and so does the conflict between self and other on an individual-to-individual and group-to-group basis. If you have nothing there is no point in anyone coming to take anything away from you. Someone will give it to you anyway. The Gospels seem aware of the relationship between peace and order and economic development:

Matthew 6:19 "Do not lay up for yourselves treasures on earth, where moth and rust destroy and where thieves break in and steal,
6:20: but lay up for yourselves treasures in heaven, where neither moth nor rust destroy and where thieves do not break in and steal.
6:25 Therefore I say to you, do not worry about your life, what you will eat or what you will drink; nor about your body, what you will put on. Is not life more than food and the body more than clothing?

> 6:26 Look at the birds of the air, for they neither sow nor reap nor gather into barns; yet your heavenly Father feeds them.
> 6:31 Therefore do not worry, saying 'What shall we eat?' or 'What shall we drink?' or 'What shall we wear?'
> 6:32 For after all these things the Gentiles seek. For your heavenly Father knows that you need all these things.
> 6:33 But seek first the kingdom of God and His righteousness, and all these things shall be added to you."

The Gentiles seek these things; seeking reflects greed. Since the Gentiles will not provide for the Jews, the "Heavenly Father" will provide (i.e., out of Nowhere).

In **Luke** 12:13–15 the same passage is prefaced with this introduction:

> Then one from the crowd said to Him, "Teacher, tell my brother to divide the inheritance with me." But He said to him, "Man, who made Me a judge or arbitrator over you?" And he said to them, "Take heed, and beware of covetousness, for one's life does not consist in the abundance of the things he possesses."

In Renunciative society one's life consists of one's ability to give up all that one has, however much of it there is. Covetousness is the desire to have what belongs to another. The **Luke** passage ends (12:32–33),

> "Do not fear, little flock, for it is your Father's good pleasure to give you the kingdom. Sell what you have and give alms; provide yourselves money bags which do not grow old, a treasure in the heavens that does not fail, where no thief approaches nor moth destroys. For where your treasure is, there your heart will be also."

Treasure in the heavens is, of course, Spirit—in renunciative terms, a force for renouncing matter.

If Renunciation is not explicit here, its obverse is. Greed and covetousness are as abhorrent to Jesus as they are to the lifeway of Renunciation.

Luke 12 preaches against covetousness and laying up the treasures of this world for oneself. In **Mark** 10:25 we find the well-known passage: "It is easier for a camel to go through the eye of a needle than for a rich man to enter the kingdom of God." A rich man is one who has accumulated wealth, something one cannot do if one is continually giving up all that one has (or even half of what one has) to those who have not.

Jesus does not condemn the rich if they give up their riches—even half their riches—to others. In **Luke** 19:8 Jesus chooses to stay at the home of the rich tax collector, Zacchaeus, much to the chagrin of his disciples. But Zacchaeus is so taken by Jesus' teachings—so touched by the Holy Spirit—that he gives half his goods to the poor and repays fourfold those he has defrauded.

"Blessed are the poor in spirit, for theirs is the kingdom of heaven" (**Matthew** 5:3). This seems an odd phrase. Surely it should read "rich in spirit." But in Renunciative terms "poor in spirit" implies the "Emptiness" that is associated with spirit. This is precisely its renunciating power.

The story of Jesus' temptation by the devil in the wilderness (**Luke** 4:3) can be read as renunciative possibility being undermined by the forces of self-sufficiency and selfishness. The devil says to Jesus: "If You are the Son of God, command this stone to become bread." The wilderness is, of course, nothing but stones so that Jesus has nothing to eat. There is no one else in the wilderness to provide Jesus with what he has not. The devil challenges Jesus to change what he has (not-food) for what he has not (food), thereby becoming self-sufficient in his Garden and repeating the original sin of Adam and Eve in Eden. But Jesus is "full of the Holy Spirit" and has been "led by the Spirit." What he does not have must be provided by someone else, not himself.

5. The Not-So-Holy Family

In Renunciative society, ties of co-residence and kinship, being rooted in material reality, are ignored in favour of ties of a spiritual or transcendent nature. Aboriginal ties to land, for example, are based on abstract, eternal, jurisdiction as in the Promised Land notion of the early Hebrews and to some extent of the church of Jesus as we have examined it thus far. In Aboriginal society the mother is the receptacle within which the child is formed while the father opens a pathway in her for the entry of a spiritForm from the "other side." Jesus is born of the woman, Mary, fathered by The Holy Spirit, God. The pedigree traced in **Matthew** 1:2–16 which claims to connect Jesus to Abraham is, in fact, Joseph's, and he is explicitly not the father of Jesus but "the husband of Mary, of whom Jesus was born."

God's seed is the Word (**Luke** 8:11) and Jesus says (**John**: 8:31–32), "If you abide in My word, you are my disciples indeed. And you will know the truth and the truth shall make you free." The Jews he is addressing reply, "how can you say, 'You will be made free?'" Given the context, one answer could be, "free from the bonds of kinship and ethnicity."

According to Scripture, Jesus had brothers (**John** 2:12) and the people around him considered him to have a mother and father in a conventional sense. Yet **Matthew** 12:46–50 relates:

> While He was still speaking to the multitudes, behold, His mother and brothers stood outside, seeking to speak with Him. Then one said to Him, "Look, Your mother and Your brothers are standing outside, seeking to speak with You." But He answered and said to the one who told Him, "Who is My mother and who are My brothers?" And He stretched out His hand toward His disciples and said, "Here are My mother and My brothers! For whoever does the will of My Father in heaven, is My brother and sister and mother."

Even one's mother, then, is to be defined in non-kinship,

"spiritual," terms.

Matthew 10:34–39 continues with the anti-family theme: "For I come to set a man against his father, a daughter against her mother." And by **Matthew** 19:29 ties of co-residence have been included in with kinship as institutions to be rejected: "And everyone who has left houses or brothers or sisters or father or mother or wife or children or lands, for My name's sake, shall receive a hundredfold, and inherit everlasting life." This passage also carries renunciative overtones insofar as in giving up all of one thing, one gets all of something else.

Though one is to honour one's father and mother and not speak evil of them, one is to *love* one's enemies—those to whom one has no kinship ties.

Marriage in the form of unity between two people seems to receive Jesus' blessing when he reiterates the prescription in **Genesis** that "the two shall become one flesh. So they are no longer two but one flesh. What therefore God has joined together let no man put asunder." But this is marriage *after* the Fall and may be indicative of the kind of relationship— unity and oneness—to which humankind has been condemned and not an ideal at all. On the other hand, it may be a prescription incompatible with the principle of Renunciation.

6. Love and Other Miracles

"God so loved the world that He gave his only begotten Son, that whoever believes in Him should not perish but have everlasting life" (**John** 3:16). Is this love Renunciative? God giving his son to us would certainly meet our criterion; but giving up his son to *die* for us is sacrifice and sacrifice, however noble, is not Renunciation. To give up one's body in Renunciative terms would mean to give up one's abilities or gifts in service to *living* others. To give up one's body in the sense of giving up one's life is to become no-body at all and thereby relinquish one's life's purpose—which is the ability to renounce (suicide, for instance, was unknown in traditional Aboriginal society).

Jesus' teachings on love are often formulated around the concept of sacrifice, which is not surprising since he himself gave up his life for the forgiveness of humanity's sins. "Greater love," it says in **John** 15:13, "has no one than this, than to lay down one's life for his friends." But love need not involve sacrifice in this sense. **John** 15:12 says simply, "This is My commandment, that you love one another as I have loved you." And, "You shall love your neighbour as yourself" (**Matthew** 22:39), as well as, "But I say to you who hear: Love your enemies, do good to those who hate you" (**Luke** 6:27; also **Matthew** 5:44).

Jesus modelled his Love for others, theirs for each other, on his relationship with his Father and it may be instructive to examine this relationship in more detail. In **John** (3:35) he defines the relationship as this: "The Father loves the Son, and has given all things into His hand." This sounds renunciative—a giving up of everything from one to another. But does it result in part-of-one-in-the-other relationship?

14:10 "Do you not believe that I am in the Father, and the Father in Me? The words that I speak to you I do not speak on My own authority; but the Father who dwells in Me does the works. Believe Me that I am in the Father and the Father in Me . . ."

14:20 "At that day you will know that I am in My Father, and you in Me, and I in you."

There are many more references of like kind and almost all express Jesus' relationship to his Father in terms of overlap and concurrence—not quite "unity" (if unity were your intent, why separate "you" and "me" at all?), and yet not quite separation. One exception to this rule is revealing: John 15:7 "If you abide in Me, and My words abide in you, you will ask what you desire, and it shall be done for you." The passage is followed almost immediately by another of like kind: "These things I have spoken to you, that *My joy may remain in you, and that your joy may be full* (15:11)."

The italics are mine. Unlike the rest, these passages locate a type of relationship in which a part of one is placed in the other, as is the case with relationships in the Aboriginal lifeway of Renunciation. But in the Gospel passages there is no *vice versa*. No part of you or anyone else comes back to "me," Jesus; no part of the "you" comes to the "me" independently of Jesus. It is rather implied that you and the I merge together through common affiliation with Jesus. Not only is unity still implicit, then, but so is hierarchy. Is this meant to imply that relationships, love, involve or should involve an element of hierarchy, one partner over the other?: I am the way, the truth and the life. No one comes to the Father except through Me (14:6).

Again, as in the language of relationship, there is ambivalence here too: does *through me* mean me as a person or what I represent? It could be said that Jesus represents God and God is Trinity: Father, Son, and Holy Spirit. Trinity is plural and contains Holy Spirit. Could this mean that the path to redemption in Christian terms is through something like the Aboriginal *Amawurrena*, that is, Spirit in differentiated form? Again, there is a problem. The Christian Holy Spirit is writ in the singular and the Trinity itself runs backwards, from the Father through the Son to the Holy Spirit, as if still building Towers of Babel from the ground up in an effort to reach the transcendent. An Aboriginal Trinity might run Holy Spirit/Father-Son, indicating that Spirit is transmitted through one's father (and father's sister) to one's son (and daughter).

There is less renunciative ambiguity in the Synoptic Gospels and John in the case of the miracles performed by Jesus during his ministry. The miracles seem to defy the laws of nature, but they are almost perfect examples of the lifeway of Renunciation. That is, they code according to the formulation *anti-thesis* —> *thesis* —> *plurality* or Nothingness —> being —> relationship. This is the process of something emerging from Nothing and being twisted into something else to form a part-of-one-in-the-other relationship between them. The Aborigines call the process *gemalyanggerranema* which also means to create and is the essence of what I mean by Renunciation.

Whether the miracles in question actually occurred the way they are described is, in a sense, beside the point. The point is that they all code according to this formulation. Someone seems to be trying to tell us something about Renunciation—about it as a process transcending material determination. The significance of the miracles is underscored by Jesus who says he does them in his Father's name as witness to him (**John** 10:25).

The penultimate miracle is, of course, Jesus' resurrection, or Jesus' re-creation. He dies (*anti-thesis*), returns (*thesis*), and re-relates to his followers (*plurality*)—however imperfectly the relationship is realised (for example between Jesus and Simon Peter). Other miracles are of like kind and differ only in the degree to which they actually proceed from nothing. Most, in fact, proceed from something a little *more* than nothing. In the discussion that follows I will omit general accounts such as: Now Jesus went about all Galilee, teaching in their synagogues, preaching the gospel of the kingdom, and healing all kinds of sickness and all kinds of disease among the people (**Matthew** 4:23), and concentrate on those in which the details are recounted.

a) Those that Proceed, *Anti-thesis* —>: Some miracles are very close to the Jesus-event in form. These are those in which the dead are brought back to life. Lazarus, for instance (**John** 11:1–44), has been in the tomb for four days when Jesus arrives and orders the stone sealing the cave to be moved. After invoking his Father in Heaven he calls on Lazarus to rise and come out, which he does. We do not know of Lazarus' relationship to others after he has risen but it appears he was later killed on the orders of the chief priests lest he bear witness to Jesus' powers. If we are looking for a rational explanation of what happened here we are provided with one at the outset of the episode when we are told that the disciples believe that Lazarus is not dead but asleep. Although Jesus corrects them on this point, it is possible that Lazarus was in some kind of coma and Jesus merely took advantage of the situation to create the illusion of a resurrection. Another explanation is spiritual: it was Lazarus' ghost that appeared when Jesus opened the tomb. My point, though, is that the Lazarus-event proceeds according to a certain logic which implies Renunciation.

In **Matthew** 9:18 (**Luke** 8: 40–48, **Mark** 5:35–43) Jesus is called upon to restore to life the daughter of a ruler, but he tells him that she is only sleeping. Then he awakens her. In **John** 4:50 Jesus brings a child near death back to health.

The famous feeding of the multitudes in **Matthew** 14:13–21, **Mark** 6:30–44, **Luke** 9:10–17 and **John** 6:1–14, follows the *anti-thesis —> thesis —> plurality* formula, though here proceeding from almost nothing rather than from nothing as such. We begin with five loaves and two fishes and some 5,000 hungry people. But after Jesus blesses the food and breaks the bread, all of a sudden there is more than enough for everyone. In renunciative terms we find one person (in **John**) or a few people (in **Matthew** and **Luke**) who have everything while everyone else has nothing. The latter, then, have a right to what the former possess. The real miracle is not the multiplication of the food but Jesus' success in persuading those with everything to give it up. But once they do, others follow suit and soon the food is redistributed so there is enough for everyone. In **Luke** the multitude first separate out into different groups—as befits those in a renunciative relationship—before receiving their food.

In **Matthew** 15:29–39, seven loaves and a few fish are all that is available for a crowd of some 4,000, but the same redistribution occurs.

Fish are also the focus of attention in two other miracles, both of which code according to the same *anti-thesis —>,* logic. In **Luke** 5:1–11 Simon, James, and John abandon fishing because there seem to be no fish in the sea. Jesus sends them out again and this time they cast their nets and they are filled to overflowing. In **Matthew** 17:24–27 Jesus instructs Peter to cast his hook into the sea and tells him that when he catches a fish and opens its mouth he will find a shekel with which to pay the temple tax on behalf of himself and of Jesus. Here something comes from nothing and a relationship is established—not only between Jesus and Peter, and between both of them and the authorities, but also by implication between the authorities and the Jewish people as a whole. The message is << find ways to raise money for taxes other than by exploiting one another as the authorities are exploiting you>>.

"Nothing" becomes "something" when Jesus heals the lepers in **Matthew** 8:1, **Mark** 1:40, **Luke** 5:12 and elsewhere. Leprosy has caused holes, wounds, in the victims' flesh which Jesus fills in. In the miracle of the withered hand Jesus restores something to it that is not currently there (**Mark** 3:1 and **Luke** 6:6). The miracle of "water-into-wine" in **John** 2:1–11 is of the "almost-nothing-into-something-more-substantial" variety. Water is "near-nothing" in the sense that it was the first thing to emerge from the void at creation in **Genesis**. Water is also associated with the healing miracle in **John** 5:2–9 where Jesus brings a sick man out of a pool in which he has been lying for a very long time and makes him walk—become something more than he was. In effecting the miracle of walking on water in **John** 6:16–19 (**Matthew** 14:22–33) Jesus takes this "almost-nothing water" and turns it into "something more substantial" on which he can now walk (or, he appears on the water in spiritual form and doesn't change anything at all).

The healing of the paralysed servant in **Matthew** 8:5 effectively uses Form (Nothingness) to release content (being), or at least releases the means of releasing content —the fully-functioning body (see also 9:6; **Mark** 2:3, **Luke** 7:2; **Luke** 5:18). The stilling of the wind and the water in **Mark** 4:35–41 and **Luke** 8:22–25 is, in a sense, the reverse of this—i.e., "paralysing" in order to establish Form.

Finally, there is Jesus' healing of the blind and the mute (see **Matthew** 9:27, 10:51, 12:22, 15:31, **Mark** 10:51, **Luke** 9:39, **John** 9) which effects "something from nothing," though the method usually involves expelling something else such as "demons" before the cure is effected. This brings us to the "expelling-to-create-emptiness" miracles.

b) Those that Proceed, —> *Anti-thesis*: The most obvious examples of this process are those in which Jesus touches or is touched, speaks or is spoken to, and as a consequence a disease or a "demon" is expelled from the body (for instance, **Matthew** 8:14, 14:35, 17:14, 20:29, 15: 21, **Mark** 1:27, 32, 3:11, 5:1, 5:11, 7:25, 9:17, Luke 4:33, 4:39, 8:33). The miracle of expelling "demons" and transferring them over into swine (**Mark** 5:1–13) is of a similar type, though far from kind to the poor swine.

Perhaps the most interesting of the miracles of this type, though, is the fig tree which Jesus, for no apparent reason, causes to whither (**Matthew** 21:18–21). This would seem to be a case of something-into-nothing, —> *anti-thesis*. But in withering, the tree's fruit presumably fall to the ground and re-generate, taking us into a nothing-into-something, *anti-thesis* —>, "healing" sequence. The death of the tree, the shedding of its fruit, could also be interpreted as "content-released-from-Form" and could be compared to the soul being released from the body on death.

A miracle that sits somewhere between the *anti-thesis* —>, and the —> *anti-thesis*, scenarios is the case of the haemorrhaging woman (**Matthew** 9:20–22, **Mark** 5:25–29 and **Luke** 8:43–48). Jesus stops her over-outflow by "the power gone forth from me," that is, by in-Forming her with spirit in preparation for further healing

In sum, what the miracles of the Synoptic Gospels and John suggest to us is awareness not only of the process of small-r renunciation but also its significance as a means of healing and re-creation.

7. The Logic of Separation-Withdrawal

Persons in a Renunciative mode operate according to a logic of thought which proceeds analytically rather than analogically to break down the status quo into its component parts and then imagine the consequences of altering any one of the parts that maintain the whole. Anticipating the disastrous consequences, they are moved to separate and withdraw from the problem before it arises.

We see evidence of this logic at work in two critical periods of Jesus' life. First is his initial refusal at the time of his initial teaching to come in from the periphery and confront his enemies directly in Jerusalem, anticipating that if he does he will be killed (**Mark** 1:40–45; 8:27–31; 9:30–32; 10:32–34); second is after the resurrection when after at first being ignored and then, apparently much misunderstood by his disciples, he departs for Heaven.

While these episodes do not define Jesus' overall response to dealing with problems, which was to confront them directly, they do in a sense frame the confrontational approach as a kind of lesson of a "see I told you so" kind illustrating that if one does engage the enemy directly in a confrontational way, then conflict and violence is likely to be the result.

8. Anomalies?

Examples of capital R Renunciation seem present in the Synoptic Gospels and John, though they are not explicitly defined as such, although in the form of the miracles they are highlighted as pivotal. If they really are intended to be pivotal, then nothing in the way of Jesus' prescriptions should contradict the Renunciative principle.

In **Matthew** 25:14–20 a householder goes on a journey and entrusts his property to his servants. To one he gives five talents, to another two, and to a third, one—each according to his abilities. The one with five, trades with them and makes five talents more; the one with two makes two talents more; but the one with one talent hides it in the ground until his master returns for fear of losing it. When the master does return he rewards the one who increased his property and admonishes the one who did not, saying, "you ought to have deposited my money with the bankers, and at my coming I would have received back my own with interest." The master then takes the talent from him who has one and gives it to the one who now has ten, saying, "For to everyone who has, will more be given, and he will have abundance; but from him who does not have, even what he has will be taken away."

This seems like a clear-cut case of what Renunciation is not—profit-taking, accumulation, even greed. But it could be an allegory referring not to material but to spiritual gain; and it could be something else again: to give each according to his ability in unequal amounts does not contradict the renunciative principle. The awkward point is the master giving to the one who has, rather than to the one who has not. But then he who acquired more than what he had been given, gave it back to the master (everything to nothing). He who did not acquire more had his taken away from him (leaving him with nothing). Now master and servants are in a potentially renunciative relationship, but the story ends here so that we do not know what transpired thereafter. Perhaps the servant was punished because he did not grasp what the master was really trying to do. He says of him, "Master, I knew you to be a hard man, reaping where you did not sow [i.e., obtaining something from nothing], and gathering where you did not winnow." However, if I am right, the master is actually a "soft man."

In **Matthew** 20:1–16 a householder goes into the market-place to hire labourers for his vineyard and offers them a denarius a day. He returns four times during the day for more labourers and at the end of the day when the time comes to pay their wages, gives those hired in the 11th hour the same as those hired in the first hour. They complain and he replies: "Is my eye evil because I am good?" In renunciative terms, the last to work will work the shortest hours and end up with almost nothing, so he is due everything.

In **Matthew** 21:33–43 a householder plants a vineyard and sets a hedge as a boundary about it, letting it out to tenants while he visits another country. When the harvesting season draws near he sends his servants home for the fruit but the tenants beat one of them, kill another, and stone a third. The master then sends other servants who suffer the same fate. Finally he sends his son and they kill him too. Jesus asks the chief priests and scribes listening to his Parable what should the owner do to his tenants? They say that he should put them to death. For this answer Jesus says that the Kingdom of God shall be taken away from them. But why?

It is actually the householder who is at fault. He owns the garden in the manner of a Promised Land, continuing to retain jurisdiction, even though he is absent. But he wishes the fruit of his garden for his own use. In a Renunciative world the resources you own are not for you but for others outside your garden who hold jurisdiction elsewhere. The tenants actually have a right to the produce. If the tenants were basing a claim to these resources by right of occupancy of the garden they would be in the wrong. It is certainly wrong for them to kill the servants. But it is even more wrong for them to be killed. The priests and scribes not only don't understand the moral of the story, they advocate revenge which only reproduces the mistake of the tenants.

There is however, a passage that seems to go completely against the spirit of Renunciation and cannot be redeemed by a renunciative reading. This is Jesus' call to arms in **Matthew** 12:30 that "He who is not with Me is against Me, and he who does not gather with Me scatters abroad." This seems to mean "whoever speaks against the Holy Spirit" which in our terms would be to speak against the power of renunciation. But even this reading does not save the passage. Renunciation recognises no such absolute divisions into "us" and "them." Each is (to be) a part of the other irrespective (indeed because of) their differences.

Hand in hand with this division into "us" and "them" is Jesus' instruction to the disciples to proselytise or convert in

Matthew 28:19 and **Mark** 16:15–20, though these are passages that biblical scholars now believe were added on by the early church for their own purposes. It is to the writings of the early church that we now turn.

Acts of the Apostles and Epistles

It is even more problematic than with the Synoptic Gospels and **John** to try and approach **Acts** and/or **Epistles** as coherent wholes. Though I am lumping them together and apart from the Synoptic Gospels and **John** for purposes of thematic analysis, **Acts** in fact seems to be a continuation of **Luke** whereas the **Epistles** are mainly attributed to Paul. There is no story line and no consistent philosophy to integrate the texts. Jesus is now gone and the authors are going about the business of organising a church and communicating with each other about the problems of doing so. **Acts**, however, does open with a passage that, in a sense, sets a "renunciative" tone for what is to follow 1:9–11: "Now when He [Jesus] had spoken these things, while they watched, He was taken up, and a cloud received Him out of their sight. And while they looked steadfastly toward heaven as He went up, behold, two men stood by them in white apparel." The two men tell those present that Jesus will return in the same manner as he has just departed, namely descend from a cloud to two witnesses (interestingly, the same way Nambirrirrma came to the Aborigines of Bickerton Island to reiterate the Law in the pre-contact past; see pages 31–32). Together with the women and Jesus' brothers, the disciples then return to Jerusalem, and "when the Day of Pentecost had fully come, they were all with one accord in one place" (2:2–4). But

> . . . suddenly there came a sound from heaven, as of a rushing mighty wind, and it filled the whole house where they were sitting. Then there appeared to them divided tongues, as of fire, and one sat upon each of them. And they were all filled with the Holy Spirit and began to speak with other tongues, as the Spirit gave

them utterance. (2:2–4)

The move to unity, then, is undermined and differentiation proceeds on the basis of languages, as at Babel in **Genesis**. The remainder of **Acts** and of **Epistles** can be seen as a working out of the two tendencies at issue here: one toward unity and the other toward plurality within the early church and between the church and non-believers.

1. SpiritForm

Ephesians 5:18–19 introduces a renunciative element missing from the Synoptic Gospels and John, the association of Spirit with music—even melody: ". . . but be filled with the Spirit, speaking to one another in psalms and hymns and spiritual songs, singing and making melody in your heart to the Lord."

Consistent with Renunciative cosmology is the statement in **1Corinthians** 15:49–50 that we are born both in the image of the man of dust (Adam) and in the image of the man of heaven (Jesus)—but the important image is that of "the man of heaven." "Your body," says 5:19, "is the temple of the Holy Spirit who is in you, whom you have from God, you are not your own" And, **2Corinthians** 4:16, 18; 5:1:

> Even though our outward man is perishing, yet the inward man is being renewed day by day . . . while we do not look at the things which are seen, but at the things which are not seen. For the things which are seen are temporary, but the things which are not seen are eternal.

> For we know that if our earthly house, this tent, is destroyed, we have a building from God, a house not made with hands, eternal in the heavens.

Not only are we humans inFormed and enFormed, but so is each "species" of nature:

1Corinthians: 15:38–41: But God gives it a body as He pleases, and to each seed its own body. All flesh is not the same flesh, but there is one kind of flesh of men, another flesh of beasts, another of fish, and another of birds. There are also celestial bodies and terrestrial bodies; but the glory of the celestial is one, and the glory of the terrestrial is another. There is one glory of the sun, another glory of the moon, and another glory of the stars; for one star differs from another star in glory.

If we eliminate God from the picture, the scene could not be more Aboriginal/Renunciative. Each material form is defined by its Glory or illuminated Presence—its outerForm. So too are the lands assigned to the peoples of the world insofar as they are "bounded habitations":

And He has made from one blood every nation of men to dwell on all the face of the earth, and he has determined their preapportioned times and the boundaries of their habitation. (**Acts** 17:26)

Bounded habitations are Promised Lands writ in the plural.

Perhaps the most dramatic experience of Glory (albeit of someone on the "other side") in all of Scriptures is Paul's of Jesus on the road to Damascus (**Acts** 9:1–9):

Then Saul, still breathing threats and murder against the disciples of the Lord, went to the high priest and asked letters from him to the synagogues of Damascus, so that if he found any who were of the Way, whether men or women, he might bring them bound to Jerusalem. And as he journeyed he came near Damascus, and suddenly a light shone around him from heaven. Then he fell to the ground, and heard a voice saying to him, "Saul, Saul, why are you persecuting Me?" And he said, "Who are You, Lord?" And the Lord said, "I am Jesus, whom you are persecuting. It is hard for you to kick against the goads." So he, trembling and astonished, said, "Lord, what do You want me to do?" And the Lord said to him, "Arise and go into the city, and you will be told what you must do." And the men who journeyed with him stood speechless, hearing a voice but seeing no one. Then Saul arose from the ground, and when his eyes were opened he saw no one. But they led him by the hand and brought him into Damascus. And he was three days without sight, and neither ate nor drank.

Saul, the self-serving persecutor and murderer (**Galatians** 1:13) is suddenly cleansed by a blinding light—the glory of Jesus—regains his identity but in relationship to others who provide him with what he does not have—sight. In other words, out of an encounter with enFormed Presence, Saul "re-incarnates" in a renunciative relation to "other." Saul then appropriately fasts, in principle giving to others that which he has now refused to consume.

Paul says that when Jesus comes again he "will transform our lowly body that it may be conformed to His glorious body, according to the working by which He is able even to subdue all things to Himself" (**Philippeans** 3:21).

"So also is the resurrection of the dead. The body is sown in corruption, it is raised in incorruption. It is sown in dishonour, it is raised in glory. It is sown in weakness, it is raised in power. It is sown a natural body, it is raised a spiritual body." (**1Corinthians** 15:42–44)

In Aboriginal cosmology enForming Glory is *Amawurrena*, its activating power, *alawuduwarra*.

Though Paul mentions the soul he uses the Greek *pneuma* in all cases, referring in turn to the soul as such (**2Corinthians** 2:13), to the soul as the seat of consciousness (**1Corinthians** 7:34), and to the soul as the spiritual realm where it is situated after being permitted access through Jesus (i.e., the Kingdom of Heaven).

Paul's writings appear to be the earliest in Christian Scriptures. At least one scholar, G. A. Wells in his *The Historical Evidence for Jesus*, thinks that Jesus and Christianity were the invention of Paul based on his visionary, mystical, experience on the road to Damascus. The story of Jesus, he thinks, was invented to give credibility to this revelation and the Gospel writers skilfully drew on the predictions in Hebrew Scriptures of the-Messiah-to-come to construct a tale that would be credible to the Jews.

2. ChurchForm

Some passages of **Acts** and **Epistles** indicate that church organisation tends toward unity: "Now all who believed were together, and had all things in common, and sold their possessions and goods, and divided them among all, as anyone had need" (**Acts** 2:44–45).

Communalism and sharing are not Renunciation. They are characteristic of people banding together for their own common good, not reaching out to others who have nothing in an ever-expanding chain of interdependence. But in **1Corinthians** 16:1 Paul speaks of "the churches of Galatia" in the plural and in 16:19 of "the churches of Asia . . . together with the church in their [Aquila's and Prisca's] house." In **2Corinthians** 8:1 Paul mentions "the churches of Macedonia."

The picture we get in **Acts** of Paul travelling from church to church along the preordained path of conversion is reminiscent of the Creative Beings in Aboriginal culture travelling along their songLines, reconfirming the partnership of those in the separate, enFormed, spaces within. What makes the analogy even more poignant is the linking of membership in the church to the concept of citizenship:

Ephesians 2:19–22 Now, therefore, you are no longer strangers and foreigners, but fellow citizens with the saints and members of the household of God, having been built on the foundation of the apostles and the prophets, Jesus Christ Himself being the chief cornerstone, in whom the whole building, being joined together, grows into a holy temple in the Lord, in whom you also are being built together for a habitation of God in the Spirit.

The passage, though, has overtones of unity or oneness and it is not clear if citizenship applies indiscriminately to all who follow Jesus or to individuals as members of lesser "dwelling places." The point about citizenship, however, is that it allows individuals to carry their membership around with them even when they leave the bounds of their own jurisdiction.

Elsewhere (**Acts** 21:39) Paul says he is "a Jew, from Tarsus, in Cilicia, a citizen of no mean city." Paul was also a Roman citizen. It seems the term "citizenship" can apply to membership in bounded jurisdictions at a number of levels, the domestic, the urban and the national or imperial. In terms of a church this could be equated with the congregation, the diocese, and the universal church.

Whether these jurisdictions were Renunciative or not, that is, whether the resources and services contained and embodied within one were there to be made available to those in another—is difficult to determine. We have already seen that "all who believed were together and had all things in common" (**Acts 2**:44–45), a statement of communalism. But then the "all" in the passage could refer to believers in, say, a congregation, and the selling off and giving to others that follows in the passage *could* be to other Christians in other congregations elsewhere.

There is something of renunciation in the metaphor of the church as the Body of Christ. Though Aboriginal Renunciative society puts the emphasis on the Land/People rather than the People/Land (or just on People) as the basic building blocks of the Renunciative way of life, it all depends on where you choose to begin in the cycle of (musically Formed) Spirit moving from the "other side" out of the L/land and into humanForm and back to the land and then the Land again on death. Nevertheless, in Aboriginal Renunciative society, the Land relation would be more likely to be chosen as a metaphor for the Body relation than the other way around. The metaphor, however, would not be based on but one Land but on Lands' interrelations. Choosing the Body metaphor as the point of departure displays a human-centric focus that separates us from, and situates us above, the rest of nature.

In **Romans** 12:4–5 Paul states, "For as we have many members in one body, and all the members do not have the same function, so we, being many, are one body in Christ, and individually members of one another."

Having then gifts differing according to the grace that is given to us, let us use them; if prophecy, let us prophesy in proportion to our faith; or ministry, let us use it in our ministering; he who teaches, in his teaching; he who exhorts, in exhortation; he who gives, with liberality; he who leads, with diligence; he who shows mercy, with cheerfulness. (12:6–8)

In **1Corinthians** 12, to one person is given the word of wisdom; to another the word of knowledge; to another faith; to another the gift of healing; to yet another the working of miracles; to another the ability to discern spirits; to another the ability to speak different languages, to another the ability to understand them.

For in fact the body is not one member but many. If the foot should say, "Because I am not a hand, I am not of the body," is it therefore not of the body? (12:14)

But God composed the body, having given greater honor to that part which lacks it, that there should be no schism in the body, but that the members should have the same care for one another. And if one member

suffers, all the members suffer with it; or if one member
is honoured, all the members rejoice with it. (12:24–26)

Here is an interdependent world, each providing what he or
she has for what another does not, a principle which also
applies between churches. In **2Corinthians** 8:1 the churches of
Macedonia are said to give beyond their means even when they
are poor. But here are some problems with this "fit." The head
(Jesus) rules over the body (the church) (**Ephesians** 2:21–23),
and the church rules over its congregations through bishops,
deacons and elders (**ITimothy** 3:1–13, 5:17–22). Moreover, the
head rules to unite the many into one:

> For He Himself is our peace, who has made both one, and
> has broken down the middle wall of division between us,
> having abolished in His flesh the enmity, that is the laws
> of commandments contained in ordinances, so as to
> create in Himself one new man from the two, thus
> making peace, and that He might reconcile them both to
> God in one body through the cross, thereby putting to
> death the enmity. (**Ephesians** 2:14–16)

The "gifts" one has in the interdependent world that is to be
the membership of the church, moreover, are rather static
things which, once "inherited," may condemn one to a life of
subordination. **1Corinthians** 7:20–24 instructs, "Let each one
remain in the same calling in which he was called. Were you
called while a slave? Do not be concerned about it." The passage
goes go on to say that if you can regain your freedom you
should, but if not, your real freedom is with the Lord. **1Peter** 2:
13–14, 18 says:

> Therefore submit yourselves to every ordinance of man
> for the Lord's sake, whether to the king as supreme, or
> to governors, as to those who are sent by him . . .
> Servants, be submissive to your masters with all fear,
> not only to the good and gentle, but also to the harsh.

For this is commendable, because of conscience toward
God, one endures grief, suffering wrongfully.

The seemingly hierarchical element in the organisation of
the church and this deferential, unRenunciative, attitude
toward authority may be endemic to the faith; alternatively, it
may reflect a practical strategy for survival—a "unite against
the enemy" approach, and a "render unto Caesar's what is
Caesar's" strategy in the face of overwhelming secular power
outside the faith that would crush and destroy it.

Any Renunciative society facing a predatory, incorporating,
power that would subordinate and consume it is faced with an
agonising dilemma. To retaliate and fight back would be to
destroy its own integrity and risk annihilation; to accept
domination would risk assimilation. The Renunciative
response, in the face of impending conflict, is to separate and
withdraw a safe distance until the threat passes or an
accommodation is reached. Accepting a subordinate position
within a larger order that one objects to, is a form of
accommodation. But it only works in the long term if the
superior power in question either destroys itself or is
destroyed by another power of superior strength. Little
wonder that Christians were instructed to seek their reward
not on earth but in Heaven.

*   *   *   *

The real problem with the Body metaphor is that the body
is a bounded whole and Renunciation does not allow for
bounded, would be all-encompassing, wholes, particularly
those which set themselves up in opposition to other bounded,
would be all-encompassing, wholes (as in **1Peter** 2:7–10).

3. Renunciation
A fairly clear-cut statement of renunciation occurs in
2Corinthians 8:13–15:

For you know the grace of our Lord Jesus Christ, that though He was rich, yet for your sakes He became poor, that you through His poverty might become rich . . . For I do not mean that others should be eased and you burdened; but by an equality, that now at this time your abundance may supply their lack, that their abundance also may supply your lack—that there may be equality. And it is written, "He who gathered much had nothing left over, and he who gathered little had no lack."

The equality at issue here seems not to be of outcome, that is, equal of quantity or value, which would be sharing, but equality in the sense that both parties are equally giving up everything to have nothing—renunciation. A weaker version of the same principle is found in **Ephesians** 4:28: "Let him who stole steal no longer, but rather let him labour, working with his hands what is good, that he may have something to give him who has need." The thief is not urged to labour to provide for his own needs but to labour for those in need (i.e., with nothing). In **Romans** 12:20 we find: "Therefore if your enemy hungers, feed him; if he thirsts, give him drink."

Acts and **Epistles** seems to abandon the idea of food prohibitions which, at least by implication, leaves the unconsumed foods "therefore available to someone else." If anything, **Acts** and **Epistles** seem to advocate consuming anything that is available:

Romans 14:2–3: For one believes he may eat all things, but he who is weak eats only vegetables. Let not him who eats despise him who does not eat, and let not him who does not eat judge him who eats;
He who eats, eats to the Lord, for he gives God thanks; and he who does not eat, to the Lord he does not eat, and gives God thanks. (14:6)

1Corinthians 10:25 Eat whatever is sold in the meat market, asking no question for conscience' sake; for

"The earth is the Lord's, and all its fullness." (see also
1Timothy 4:4–5)

4. Peace and Order versus Economic Development

In **Acts** and **Epistles** there is no explicit statement to the
effect that peace and order vary inversely with economic
development, but there is condemnation of the engine that
fuels the latter:

> **1Timothy** 6:6–10 But godliness with contentment is
> great gain. For we brought nothing into this world, and
> it is certain we can carry nothing out. And having food
> and clothing, with these we shall be content. But those
> who desire to be rich fall into temptation and a snare,
> and into many foolish and harmful lusts which drown
> men in destruction and perdition. For the love of money
> is a root of all kinds of evil, for which some have strayed
> from the faith in their greediness, and pierced
> themselves through with many sorrows.

Self-gratification, greed, the desire to be rich—all these
pursuits lead to self-destruction. But money itself—even
riches—is not condemned. It is rather the *love* of money and
the *desire* to be rich that is the problem. In a Renunciative
world one has money and one has riches to make them
available to those who have them not. Love of "other" in
Renunciative society is the engine that "expels" money and
riches from one person to another. The result is their peaceful
co-existence. If **Acts** and **Epistles** do not quite make this
connection, they at least link the *absence* of accumulation to
peace:

> **James** 4:1–3 Where do wars and fights come from
> among you? Do they not come from your desires for
> pleasure that war in your members? You lust and do not
> have. You murder and covet and cannot obtain. You fight
> and war. Yet you do not have because you do not ask.

You ask and do not receive, because you ask amiss, that
you may spend it on your pleasures.

In a Renunciative world, to ask rightly is to ask for
something you need because you have it not. What you have
you must be willing to give to others in need. It is in this sense
that the poor are chosen as heirs to the Kingdom of God (2:5–
7)—as the Hebrews were chosen to receive the Promised Land.
They have nothing and are therefore entitled to everything.

5. The Somewhat-Holier-Family-than-in-the-Canonical-
   Gospels
The "chosen people" of Paul are not a group bound by ties of
kinship or ethnicity but a "faith community."

[you] have put on the new man who is renewed in
knowledge according to the image of Him who created
him, where there is neither Greek nor Jew, circumcised
nor uncircumcised, barbarian, Scythian, slave nor free,
but Christ is all and in all. (**Colossians** 3:10–11)

Nevertheless a kinship idiom is employed in discussions of
love which seems to imply the former is a model for the latter,
rather than the other way around, as was implied in Jesus'
teachings. **Romans** 12:10 says to "love one another with
brotherly affection," and **1Timothy** 5:1–2 says to exhort an
older man *as if* he were a father, younger men *as if* they were
brothers, older women *as* mothers and younger women *as*
sisters.
The institution of marriage is confirmed in **Acts** and
Epistles, but relations between husbands and wives seem to be
blatantly hierarchical and authoritarian.

1Peter 3:1–2 Likewise you wives, be submissive to your
husbands, that even if some do not obey the word, they,
without a word, may be won by the conduct of their
wives, when they observe your chaste conduct

accompanied by fear.

Though this passage seems to advocate wives' submissiveness in the interests of the conversion of the husband, other passages suggest the same submissiveness within Christian marriages:

1Timothy 2:8–15 Therefore I desire that the men pray everywhere, lifting up holy hands, without wrath and doubting; in like manner also, that the women adorn themselves in modest apparel, with propriety and moderation, not with braided hair or gold or pearls or costly clothing, but, which is proper for women professing godliness, with good works. Let a woman learn in silence with all submission. And I do not permit a woman to teach or to have authority over a man, but to be in silence. For Adam was formed first, then Eve. And Adam was not deceived, but the woman being deceived, fell into transgression. Nevertheless she will be saved in childbearing if they continue in faith, love, and holiness with self-control.

In a Renunciative order, men and women would *both* pray and cease quarrelling; men and women would both avoid ostentation indicative of the pursuit of wealth; men and women would both learn in silence and submissiveness; women would teach what they know and learn what they know not, as would men; neither men nor women would have authority over each other; each would realise there is a time to remain silent and listen to the other; Adam completed the Fall by eating of the same apple as Eve and *both* were expelled from Eden; woman partly redeems man by giving him something he cannot produce himself—children.

In renunciative terms, Paul goes from bad to worse in **1Corinthians** 11:3, 7–10 when he states, "the head of every man is Christ, the head of a woman is man, and the head of Christ is God. For a man indeed ought not to cover his head, since he is the image and glory of God; but woman is the glory of man. For man is not from woman, but woman from man. Nor was man created for woman, but woman for the man." But Paul is being selective here. **Genesis** 5:2 says, "He created them male and female, and blessed them and called them Mankind in the day they were created."

Paul redeems himself somewhat in renunciative terms in 11:11 when he says, "Nevertheless, neither is man independent of woman, nor woman independent of man, in the Lord." In **1Corinthians** 7:4 he redeems himself even more: "The wife does not have authority over her own body, but the husband does. And likewise the husband does not have authority over his own body, but the wife does." In the lifeway of Renunciation, my maleness is for you, your femaleness for me. **Peter** 3:1–7 tells wives to be submissive to their husbands but instructs husbands to live considerately with their wives and bestow honour upon them.

What is odd about all this is not so much that Paul's pronouncements on gender relations are often at odds with the lifeway of Renunciation, but that they seem to go against the grain of Jesus' relations with women as recounted in the Synoptic Gospels and John. It was the women in Jesus' life who stuck by him more than the men. Present at the crucifixion were "many women . . . among whom were Mary Magdalene, Mary the mother of James and Joses, and the mother of Zebedee's sons" (**Matthew** 27:55–56). Jesus' disciples—all males—by contrast, abandoned him. Women are the first to see him after the resurrection (27:61, 28:17) and the angel present tells these woman, not the men, where to find him: "And go quickly and tell His disciples that He is risen from the dead, and indeed He is going before you into Galilee; there you will see Him . . . Jesus met them, saying, 'Rejoice!' And they came and held Him by the feet and worshipped Him." By contrast, when the men saw him, "some doubted" (27:17).

The Book of Revelation

The **Book of Revelation**, which ends Christian Scriptures, closes on this word of warning—enough to scare off any would-be re-interpreter:

> 22:18 For I testify to everyone who hears the words of the prophecy of this book: If anyone adds to these things, God will add to him the plagues that are written in this book; and if anyone takes away from the words of the book of this prophecy, God shall take away his part from the Book of Life, from the holy city, and from the things which are written in this book.

To me, **Revelation** is written by someone who realises the limitations of Scriptures but who lacks adequate concepts to express their "hidden meaning." In his search he looks back to the origins of his own tradition—the **Book of Genesis**—for guidelines only to find the same limitations there. The result is a world of fantasy and imagination as the author searches for concepts that will resolve the dilemma. But without knowledge of the lifeway of Renunciation he is doomed to fail. If **Genesis** is the "book of commencement" of the Bible, **Revelation**, is indeed, "the book of consummation" (Strauss 1964:17). But it is a consummation devoutly to be wished. **Revelation** may merely be a rewrite of the **Book of Genesis** on the way to fathoming the lifeway of Renunciation.

*   *   *   *

In the opening chapters of **Genesis,** Paradise is lost. In the closing chapters of **Revelation**, it is regained—and with the same flaws as the original.

Revelation concludes (21:1–2) "And I saw a new heaven and a new earth, for the first heaven and the first earth had passed away, Also there was no more sea [*anti-thesis* or nothingness]. Then I, John, saw the holy city, New Jerusalem, coming out of heaven from God, prepared as a bride adorned for her husband [*thesis* or being]." What kind of *relationships*, then, does this city herald?

This New Jerusalem seems not to be a church as such ("And I saw no temple in the city"), nor is it the Promised Land, its boundaries failing to correspond to the land of Palestine. While it may not be a Land on the ground, it is definitely a "sacred space," described as transcendent, three-dimensional and four-square, pure gold and clear as glass, adorned with every jewel, the "glory of God" being its light. It is intended to be an agent of reconciliation for "By its light shall all the nations walk." At first glance the "nations" appear to be the 12 tribes of Israel. The new Jerusalem has twelve gates, one for each of the twelve tribes, three on each of the four sides; the wall of the city has twelve foundations and on them are written the names of the twelve apostles of Jesus. The implication is that Jesus' teachings through the apostles transform the twelve tribes so as to situate them in the new Jerusalem and fulfil God's covenant with the Jews, not as an ethnic or kinship group, but as converted Christians.

Running through the middle of the city is the river of the waters of life. On either side of the river is the Tree(s) of Life, which here is apparently an agent of differentiation and an agent of healing. There is more than one tree and each has twelve kinds of fruit whose leaves are for "the healing of nations." The leaves, like the fruit, are a detachable part of the Tree(s) and at least raise the possibility that they could be the "part of the one" that could be renounced to "the other." The metaphor of the New Jerusalem as a bride prepared for her husband is also to anticipate (if I may be so crude) a part of him in her and, eventually, a part of her—a child—for him. That the City as such is the bride also implies another City—the husband's—elsewhere. What we have here, then, is a new start from a renunciatively-based "two."

But, in the end, **Revelation**, like **Genesis**, ends in a separation, not a plurality.

In **Genesis,** Adam and Eve are separated from the Garden, evil is separated from good; in the New Jerusalem the righteous are separated from the unrighteous who are consigned to another "city"—a fiery lake of sulphur. The "two" that is established here is an antagonistic one between opposites with no part-of-one-in-the-other, Renunciative, implications. In **Genesis**, Adam and Eve embark on their historical course of isolated self-sufficiency, autonomy, and self-determination; in **Revelation** the redeemed likewise set out on their own independent course. In both cases the problem of relationship is left unaddressed.

In the New Jerusalem there is no night and day, "And the city has no need of the sun or of the moon to shine in it, for the glory of God illuminates it, and the Lamb (Jesus) is its light" (21:23). But if there are no oppositions in the City, neither are there the weaker evening and morning that mark the end of each day of Creation (except the last) in **Genesis**. In the New Jerusalem there is only the oneness of the glory of God and the oneness of the redeemed once the unrighteous have been "imprisoned." Division has been overwhelmed, not eliminated. Accommodation has failed.

The book of **Revelation** is replete with images borrowed from **Genesis**, as we would expect if it is a rewrite: the waters (of Creation), the stars, the sword, the sun (1:12); the tree of life, paradise (2:7), the morning star (2:28), the rainbow (4:3), the creatures of the heavens, of the earth, under the earth and in the sea (5:13), as well as the river Euphrates (9:14). **Revelation** is also replete with reference to things in sevens. Almost all are associated with the end of Creation (16:1) in anticipation of a new one (21:1). Examples are the seven churches, seven lampstands, seven stars (1:12), the seven torches and spirits of God (4:3), the seven seals (6:1)—the seventh seal marking the beginning of the end (8:1)—the seven thunders (10:4), and the seventh angel announcing the new creation that emerges in the wake of destruction (10:7). Seven angels and seven plagues mark the endpoint itself (15:1). Seven is the number of days of Creation in **Genesis**. But Creation remained incomplete and its incompleteness is reproduced in **Revelation**. As I pointed out, there is no evening or morning in the New Jerusalem as there was none on the seventh day of Creation in **Genesis**. There is only light—and a solitary morning star.

The book of **Revelation**, like most of what transpires after genesis in **Genesis**, is the story of the undoing of Creation, or at least the undoing of a potential inherent in Creation. A door in heaven opens and John stands in the Spirit, and the seven seals are revealed to him in the presence of 24 elders and four living creatures. One is like a lion, another like an ox, a third has the face of a man, and a fourth is like an eagle.

In the beginning of this tale, then, we discern the differentiation of intelligent life along the lines of **Genesis** into bird, wild animals, domesticated animals, and humankind in-the-image-of-God. It is, however, the supposedly highest form of intelligent life—man—(not woman) who opens the seven seals and initiates the destruction of Creation. In the final analysis man is destroyer, not Creator.

Opening the first four seals releases the Four Horsemen of the Apocalypse to ravage the earth. Opening the fifth seal resurrects the souls of those slain for the word of God who are to host the souls of those yet to be slain. With the opening of the sixth seal the stars fall out of heaven, representing the undoing of what there was of "part-of-one-in-the-other" interdependence in **Genesis**. There the stars were part of the light of day placed in the darkness of night at the outset of Creation.

The opening of the seventh seal continues the process of destruction. A great star falls from heaven to pollute a third of the rivers and fountains of water on earth. The waters were the very medium of Creation. As the end of Creation draws near, still more stars fall from the sky (8:10, 9:1).

Then, suddenly, in a vision of redemption, the stars reappear in the form of a crown on the head of a woman with child. She is clothed with the sun, the moon is under her feet. The moon, like the stars, is part of the light that was placed in the darkness of Creation. Perhaps more significantly, "woman with child" represents "part-of-one-in-the-other" logic. Woman here is re-Creation. The child of Woman in a form transcendent is the part of her that would, in theory, go to man to complete the part-of-one-in-the-other potential inherent in original Creation when Eve was made from a part of Adam. But a dragon, the Devil, appears with the intention of devouring the woman's child as soon as it is born. With his tail he sweeps a third of the stars of heaven down to earth. But the child is born and is immediately taken up by God for protection. Thus is the incorporation of the child by the Devil prevented and the possibility left open for the child to be a part-of-one-in-the-other instigator. The Woman now flees to the desert to escape the Devil where God makes a safe place for her.

In the war that follows between the Devil and God's representative, the archangel Michael, the latter triumphs and the Devil returns to earth to again pursue the Woman. But God gives her wings that enable her to transcend her earthly existence and escape. Indeed, earthly existence as such is transcended as the earth literally comes alive and opens its mouth to swallow the flood that the Devil has created to sweep Woman away. (This "transcendence" could be an assertion of Form over and above content, Spirit over and above matter.)

Elsewhere in the tale, the battle between God and the Devil continues with the Devil conjuring up beasts (false prophets) to seduce the earthly children of God. The first is a sea beast resembling a leopard but with feet like a bear's and a mouth like a lion's. Insofar as the beast is evil, this would seem to imply a critique of a "three-in-one" Trinitarian concept of God and relationship as Father-Son-Holy Spirit. The second beast is a land beast with horns like a lamb but speaks like a dragon and causes all to bear the same mark on their right hand and forehead. The number of this beast is 666. This implies a critique of a more sophisticated notion of the "three-in-one" Trinitarian conception. In the representation 666 we find three separate expressions of the same form, 6, but without the picturing of an ultimate one 6 from which they emerge. If this is implied by the representation it would be a critique of the notion of God! If it is not implied it would be a critique of a quasi-Renunciative mode of representation which depicts a multiplicity of Forms (like "laughing waves"). But a genuine

Renunciative representation would have to include another plane in its formulation:

<u>666</u>

999

This is a "transcendent-imminent" representation that sees each person as an incarnation of him or her self on "this side" in mirrored image of him or her self on the "other side." This formulation **Revelation** does not critique. But then nor does it assert it. (It must be said at this point that the Orthodox reading of 666 is that it is 2 [the two natures of Jesus: divine and human] X 3[Father-Son-Spirit] repeated three times).

At this point in **Revelation** Jesus arrives to "sing a new song" to the hundred and forty-four thousand persons who alone are redeemed (the 12 tribes of Israel X 2 X 1,000, the Jewish number of completion). All the redeemed seem to be men. All are said to be chaste. None have "defiled themselves with woman." In consequence, "in their mouth no lie was found, for they are spotless." At this point in the text there is a switch in perspective from the previous image of Woman-with-child as an agent of re-Creation and Redemption to an image of Woman as defiler, that is, the "Whore of Babylon." The "good news" is now proclaimed to every nation, tribe, people, and tongue. The earth and its evil inhabitants are to be destroyed and with them the last vestiges of original Creation in **Genesis**. The river Euphrates, the waters, dry up.

What is happening here? Has some man revised the previous notion of Woman and her exalted place in Creation? Has some man glimpsed her true significance as two-in-one, with one renouncing the other within, without (as God renounced Jesus to the world), judged her a threat, and is denigrating her out of jealousy and fear, all the while appropriating her significance for himself? Or is the "Whore" epithet less a judgement of woman and more a critique of sex-for-sale rather than a loving act leading to procreation? We have no way of knowing.

What is evident here is that someone has rejected the

original form of Creation in **Genesis**, but is also dissatisfied with the re-Creation attempted in Christian Scriptures. But this someone is unable to reach the truth—the secret of the Tree of Life—himself and so he backslides into the old vision of truth carrying a sword to subdue its enemies and rule with an iron hand, seemingly resigned to the final victory of the forces of conflict and destruction over the forces of love and reconciliation—to "eye-for-an-eye and tooth-for-a-tooth solutions."

The "two" now emerge in **Revelation** as God and the Devil in mortal combat. Satan is defeated but not destroyed. He and those humans whose names are not found in the book of life are thrown into the lake of fire where they will be tormented day and night for ever and ever. Then, suddenly, out of nowhere a new Creation, a new Jerusalem, appears. But, as we have seen, this final apocalyptic vision is also flawed. As if realising this, and suffering from insecurity, **Revelation** ends with a warning as if to discourage further questioning which might discover its inadequacies. But what is the prophecy that we must not tamper with? Is it the misunderstanding of the secret of the Tree of Life that is apparent here? Is it the flawed vision of the New Jerusalem? No. The prophecy is that further clarification of all that is contained in the book of **Revelation** is necessary. In the final, *final*, analysis, Jesus is to reappear:

"Surely I am coming quickly." Amen. Even so, come. Lord Jesus!

A man called Nambirrirrma appeared to the Aborigines of Bickerton Island in Australia long before the appearance of Europeans there to reiterate the Law who met the criteria of Jesus' reappearance as set down in Scriptures (from a cloud to two witnesses). But it was to *reiterate* a Law already known to Aborigines. In a sense he was redundant, as was the Jesus brought by the Missionaries to the Aborigines.

The Gospel of Thomas

Suppose we have missed something. Suppose Scriptures are not the only source on the lives of Jesus and Paul. Perhaps other sources will be discovered which will explicitly locate the lifeway of Renunciation in principle and practice as the central teaching of the faith. Some claim these sources already exist. These are the Gnostic Gospels discovered near Nag-Hamadi in Egypt in 1945. In her book on the texts, *The Gnostic Gospels*, Elaine Pagels calls them "banned documents." (p. xvii) omitted from Christian Scriptures because they did not accord with the teachings of the early church. The Gospels include *The Gospel of Thomas*, *The Gospel of Truth*, *The Gospel of the Egyptians*, *The Apocrypha* and date from 350 to 400 A.D. But the originals from which they stem probably date between 120 and 150 A.D. In Pagels' words (p. xvi), they form

> The diverse texts range, then, from secret gospels, poems, and quasi-philosophic description of the origin of the universe, to myths, magic, and instructions for mystical practice . . . some of the texts tell the origin of the human race in terms very different from the usual reading of Genesis: the *Testimony of Truth*, for example . . .

They are not the work of a single mind and exhibit little overall consistence and coherence.

According to Pagels, the Gnostic texts were declared heretical by orthodox Christians in the mid-2nd century who were interested in consolidating a church under the rule of bishops, priests, and deacons and selected texts to reflect that interest.

Some passages in the Gnostic texts, claims Pagels (p. xx), imply that all people—not just Jesus—are an incarnation of the same spiritual source—God—in contradistinction to Christian Scriptures which designate only Jesus as God's spirit-child. Even if we grant this, it only brings us a half-step closer to the cosmology of Renunciation which sees each person as a spiritual incarnation of him or her self on the "other side" (though it does put the Gnostic texts squarely within contemporary New Age spirituality).

To explore this question further I would like to examine perhaps the most widely publicised of the Gnostic texts, *The Gospel of Thomas*, originally compiled in Greek about 140 A.D. The Thomas of this Gospel is supposedly the disciple Thomas—doubting Thomas.

*   *   *   *

What is striking about *The Gospel of Thomas* is how close it is to Christian Scriptures when evaluated against the lifeway of Renunciation. Some passages appear to support a renunciative interpretation, while others are ambiguous:

Verse 81/16 asks how to pray, questions whether one should give alms and observe dietary restrictions and instructs one not to lie or do what one hates. 83/16 reiterates that one should not fast, or give alms. But 86/16 says that one should fast and keep the Sabbath.

81/24 contains the curious pronouncement: "blessed is the lion the man eats but cursed is the man whom the lion eats." The blessing on the man seems to be because he conquers and devours, the curse because the man in question submits and loses. This is hardly a "renunciative" blessing and cursing.

81/32 says, "amongst a catch of small fish a man finds one large fish and throws the small ones back." This could reflect greed on his part or it could reflect concern for conservation.

82/3 says, "On the day when you were one you became two. But when you became two, what will you do?" The question is not answered here but 85/24 seems to indicate that one into two is a problem: "when you make the two one, when you make the male and female one, you will enter the Kingdom." 98/19 says that when you make the two, one, you shall become the sons of Man. Two into one is not the lifeway of Renunciation, it is the lifeway of unity and incorporation.

But we find some ambiguity here in 94/2 when Jesus asks, "Who made me a divider? I am not a divider, am I?" Is he?

In 83/4 Jesus says to Thomas, "I am not thy Master because thou hast drunk from the bubbling spring which I have measured out." This could mean that Jesus and Thomas both originate from the same (spiritual) source, which, however, is still not a renunciative notion.

84/10 says, "Where the beginning is, there shall be the end. Blessed is he who stands at the beginning and he shall know the end." At the beginning of the Bible is **Genesis** and at the end is **Revelation**. Perhaps here is evidence that someone else, closer to the source, considered the latter to be a rewrite of the former.

In 85/16 a man comes and cuts his fruit when it is ripened. But the passage doesn't say whether he consumed it himself or gave it to others.

95/22 says that God's image is concealed by light; your images came into existence before you and neither die nor become manifest. This does seem to imply that you are also your Self on the "other side." Light implies enFormed Presence. On the other hand, Jesus is described as "God the All and is said to be both inside and outside everything" (94/24). This does not leave much room for one's own spiritual being.

In 81/11–14 "Jesus said: Know what is in thy sight, and what is hidden from thee shall be revealed to thee. For there is nothing hidden which will not be manifest." This seems to refer to Presence.

Dead against the lifeway of Renunciation is 85/2: Some children come into a field which is not theirs and are asked by the owners to leave. In renunciative terms they should be allowed to stay as guests. They are merely innocent children not there to steal.

86/26 says that empty you have come into the world and empty you seek to go out, which is certainly a renunciative perspective. 90/4 says that the Father is both a movement and a rest. The Aboriginal *alawuduwarra* is the activating aspect of spirit, *Amawurrena*, the "substantive." This interpretation helps to make sense of the apparently strange statement in 88/24 that the Jews love the tree and hate the fruit, and love the fruit and hate the tree. In renunciative terms this is actually a compliment. One should be attached to the Form (the tree) and give up the content (the fruit), though I suppose one could equally be attached to the fruit and give away the tree.

90/24 says that you must hate your father and your mother, your brothers and your sisters in order to follow Jesus, seemingly taking a much stronger line on the "evils" of kinship than Christian Scriptures. But 98/32 does say, hate your father and mother *my way*, that is, Jesus' way. But Scriptures tell us that Jesus only loves.

In 92/6 a man who uses his money to sow, reap, and plant, as well as fill his storehouse so that he will lack nothing, suddenly dies. In the lifeway of Renunciation one's purpose is to lack everything. Accumulation is an anathema.

In 97/1 one is instructed not to lend money at interest but give to him who *won't* give it back. This is renunciation.

99/1 is a variation on the "hidden treasure in the field" parable of Scriptures. Here a man inherits the field unaware of the treasure and when he finds it he gives it away. This too is renunciation.

Perhaps the most unRenunciative words of *The Gospel of Thomas* are those of the final stanza which declare that woman is not worthy of the Life and that to be worthy she must become male, "that she too may become a living spirit, resembling you males." I say "seemingly" because the previous passage says that "the Kingdom of the Father is spread upon the earth and men do not see it." Why, then, also prevent women from seeing it by making them men? (even if "men" is used in a generic sense it does not alter the point). Perhaps this expresses the exasperation of the author of **Thomas**, who, like the author of **Revelation**, has reviewed Scriptures, felt an incompleteness—something lacking—but himself remains imprisoned within words and meanings established by the **Genesis** text and the Hebrew and Christian Scriptures that follow.

The Gnostic texts emerged in the wake of the destruction of the Jewish Temple in Jerusalem by the Romans in 70 C.E. —as did the early Christian church and Rabbinical Judaism. It was a period of Hellenization and Romanization, of doubt and messianic anticipation, of sectarianism, as new ideas and insights emerged and were discarded or accepted. It was a time of spiritual enlightenment as traditional Jewish formalism gave way to mystic explorations in a renewed effort to reach God and invoke him to alter the course of events. It was a time for looking back and reviewing the legacy of the past but with a reverence for the Word which maintained the bounds of "newness" within established limits.

Our contemporary knowledge of the first Australians and their lifeway of Renunciation expands these limits—the limits of the possible and perhaps completes and clarifies the picture of life before **Genesis** and heralded by **Revelation**.

Theoretical Reflection

I began by asking if there really was hermeneutical evidence of the Aboriginal lifeway of Renunciation in Hebrew and Christian Scriptures or was I in danger of reading such evidence into the text from my theoretical/Aboriginal perspective? I think that the passages I have examined are indeed examples of Renunciation, but since there is no abstract statement of such a principle in the text, I cannot claim confirmation within the framework of the text itself. But if I *am* right, a new point of articulation is thereby established between the Aboriginal, Hebrew, and Christian religions.

Indeed, the lifeway of Renunciation is a framework of, and for, reconciliation—for diffusing opposites and accommodating them one to the other by placing a part of one permanently in the other to prevent them from re-emerging again as opposites. The Aborigines observe and activate Renunciation as a process on two articulated planes, transcendent Form and imminent matter. The Renunciation of matter from Form or Presence—Person to Person, Land/People to Land/People— links everything and everyone in an open-ended, ever-connecting, great chain of being.

According to Aborigines—and this is a fundamental tenet of their Renunciative awareness—we leave or expel parts of ourselves wherever we go in life and with whomever we encounter along the way, leaving more in places we visit more frequently and more with the people with whom we most frequently interact. On one level what we leave is the invisible "stuff" of original Creation—Spirit. On another level we leave impressions and things in our wake such as gifts, services, or more casual everyday interactions. Awareness of this and its implications realises Renunciation. To Aborigines we are by nature Renouncers, then, whether we are aware of it or not. They simply build on this "fact" and construct a way of life around it.

We have no idea how the Aboriginal lifeway of Renunciation originated or where. Was it carried by migrants to Australia from somewhere else many thousands of years ago. Did it develop in Australia? The Aborigines, as far as I know, have no tradition or theory answering this question. To them, the Renunciative lifeway always was Eternally Uncreated.

For insight into this issue of "origins" we have much to learn from the Judeo-Christian tradition with its promise of salvation through suffering. In the circumstances of threat and suffering—the anticipation of literally becoming Nothing as Spirit-devoid-of-body—would seem to lie the very foundations for realising alternatives to selfishness and greed.

Suffering under oppression is a circumstance in which many *have* nothing and *are* nothing in the eyes of their oppressors. In anticipating their annihilation at the hands of their oppressors, a Renunciative starting point is reached. Out of the Nothingness of material-less-ness expectation (*anti-thesis*), we affirm our identity (*thesis*)—but with others in similar circumstances—and accommodate accordingly (*plurality*). What's more, in pain and suffering the mind is stripped of its habitual categories of thought and for a moment we see, hear, and feel Nothingness (in the active sense) at a more fundamental level (see Smith-Eivemark 1995; Sullivan 1988: 364; Ueno 1995). We now enter the Renunciative stream of history at least until such time as we are destroyed by our "creators" or attempt to unify ourselves in order to destroy this enemy, ironically now taking on the very attributes of those who oppressed us and moved us for a moment out of the Renunciative stream.

Apart from the episodes in Hebrew/Christian Scriptures already identified as r/Renunciative, I think I have found other expressions of the terms of Renunciation—or at least the potential for it—in the Upanishadic texts of the Hindu tradition, in aspects of Buddhism in a Zen Buddhist monastery in Japan, and in passages of the *Qur'an* as I encountered them in prayer among Gujar Muslim nomads in the Indian Himalayas. And seemingly outside the religious sphere I think I have found aspects of Renunciation in the terms of Canadian Confederation as set down in the British North America Act and in a social setting within a jurisdiction established by the terms of this Act, namely Lanark County Ontario. This is the game of Sunday Morning Hockey we play in my hometown of Perth. I think I can explain these latter occurrences in particular as a response to the threat of becoming "Nothing" as explained above.

In the accounts that follow, styles of presentation will vary according to the material under discussion and range from text-based analysis to descriptions of personal experience.

In the first case study below I detect aspects of Renunciative cosmology in Hindu metaphysics of the Upanishadic period and in the structure of the *varna* system. While the caste system as we know it today is hierarchical, it is also a system of functional interdependencies and may have once been without the hierarchical aspect. The Brahmans provide religious services for the benefit of the others, the Kshatriya land holding and military services, the Vaishya craft productions and the Sudra agricultural and animal husbanding services. Debate continues as to whether Brahman, the ultimate force in their universe, is Personal or Impersonal, One or a Multiplicity.

In recounting my experiences at Kokokuji Zen temple in Japan I describe an instance of accessing the "Spiritual/ aesthetic realm" as critical to the Hindu-Buddhist tradition as it is to the Aboriginal insofar as what is learned from this experience confirms to them the foundations of their respective lifeways. This methodology at issue is what I call "Nothinging" (1995). This is to systematically eliminate thought and category from one's sensory apparatus to more directly apprehend reality. The Aborigines do this primarily through music, Hindu ascetics through "seeing," Zen monks through *zazen* meditation. In the course of meditating at Kokokuji, I entered into dialogue with the Abbot of the Temple and discovered some interesting parallels between Aboriginal and Buddhist cosmologies.

The Gujar people of northern Himachal Pradesh in India seem to have developed a Renunciative culture similar in outline to that of the Australian Aborigines, and a theology— really a *realisation*—to go with it. The society likely emerged at a time in the past when the Gujar were Hindu and under threat from Muslim invaders, consolidating later when they were a Muslim minority in the midst of a Hindu majority. The problem of "God" in obfuscating the realisation of the lifeway of Renunciation is handled by the Gujar by turning him into a truly transcendent being, far removed from their own experienced reality. There is precedent for this and Renunciation in the *Qur'an*.

I have also located potentially Renunciative Forms in 19th century Canadian political space which developed largely in response to the threat of the American revolution and was the creation of people oppressed by that revolution as well as people oppressed in their homeland, Britain. Canada, I argue, was originally conceived, and partially realised as a grid of abstract, eternal jurisdictions bounded as Town/ships, Counties, and Provinces arranged in a mutually inter-dependent way and regarded with almost religious reverence by the people who originally came to occupy these jurisdictions and establish citizenship there. In their boundedness they represented something akin to Aboriginal Lands/Peoples or Promised Lands.

One of these "Promised Lands" is Perth in Lanark County, Ontario (Plate 7), and Perth is where Sunday Morning Hockey is played with the same respect for difference, the same will to accommodate, and the same lack of "warfare," as in Australian Aboriginal society. Formed in response to the threat of competitive N.H.L.-style hockey, the game is played through the two Red and Green Sweaters of the competing teams (functioning rather like illuminated Forms or Presences). When one Sweater starts winning too many games some of the players inside one of them are temporarily renounced to the other as guests and remain in them on the other Sweater-team as guests until things even up on the scoreboard.

The Sunday Morning Hockey example is included here because it is a contemporary expression of all the principles embedded in the concept of Renunciation, including the tit-for-tat humour that keeps one appropriately humble in such a lifeway. Being more familiar to most readers than is the Aboriginal, Sunday Morning is perhaps a more comprehensible example of how Renunciation can be lived in our own society today.

Nowhere in the cases I am about to relate—except for Sunday Morning Hockey—do we find Renunciation full-blown. At best the other examples are only partial expressions of the principles of Renunciative relationships. My own view is that, except among the Australian Aborigines, Renunciative forms are kind of slip-streams within non-Renunciative—mainly incorporative and hegemonic—mainstreams. But even these slip-stream examples in combination with the evidence from Australia do indicate that something other than selfishness and greed (the lifeway of accumulation)—a different human nature—*is* possible.

V

Renunciation in Other Religious Traditions?

Renunciation in the Hindu Tradition

The Upanishads

The Indian Hindu tradition (Plate 4) looks back to the writings of the *Rig-Veda* and anticipates both the emergence of Buddhism and Jainism. An important nexus in its history is the *Upanishads*, a collection of texts compiled in the seventh and sixth centuries BCE and marking the end of the Vedic period and the beginnings of a metaphysical development which perceived an identity between Brahman as "universal soul" and *atman*, as "individual soul" (Renou 1963: 66). As Narayanan (1996: 29) observes, these *Upanishads* emerged during a period of social upheaval and theological controversy:

> The mood of critical thinking was characteristic of the seventh and sixth centuries BCE. It was a time of questioning and rejecting authoritarian structures: the religious leadership of the priestly class (the brahmins), the caste system itself, and the revealed or 'trans-human' status of the *Vedas*.

It is precisely under these conditions that we would predict that notions of Renunciation would emerge. It is well to keep in mind in this connection that the *Upanishads* were composed and transmitted orally before they were written down, and constitute the work of ascetic seers. As Radhakrishnan (1953: 22, 23) puts it,

> As part of the Veda, the *Upanishads* belong to *sruti* or revealed literature . . . . They are not reached by ordinary perception, inference or reflection, but seen by the seers, even as we see, and not infer, the wealth and riot of colours in the summer sky . . . . Though the knowledge is

an experience of the seer it is an experience of an independent reality which impinges on consciousness.

He goes on to say (p. 54), that "the thinkers of the *Upanishads* attempt to establish the reality of God from an analysis of the facts of nature and the facts of inner life." Apart from the notion of God, this approach in itself is sufficient to place the Upanishadic tradition within the experiential ambience of the Australian Aboriginal/Renunciative lifeway. I have arranged the following quotations in thematic order, along the lines of the previous biblical analysis, in order to facilitate comparison with the Aboriginal lifeway. All quotations from the *Upanishads* are from Olivelle's 1996 translation and draw heavily on the Brhadaranyaka and Chandogya *Upanishads*, thought to be the two earliest (Olivelle 1996: xxxvi–xxxvii).

(a) BrahmanForm

In the Aboriginal/Renunciative tradition, in the beginning was Emptiness(es) and soundForm(s). In the *Upanishads*,

'Where does this world lead to?'
'Space,' he replied. 'Clearly, it is from space that all these beings arise, and into space that they are finally absorbed; for space indeed existed before them and in space they ultimately end.'
Chandogya Upanishad
1.9.1

Brahman is OM. This whole world is OM. When one says OM it indicates compliance.
Taittiriya Upanishad **1**.8

A man who meditates on that highest person by means of this very syllable OM with all three of its phonemes [AUM] . . . . enters into the effulgence in the sun. He becomes released from evil, just like a snake from his slough. He is led to the world of *brahman* by the Saman chants and beholds the fort-dwelling person far beyond this entire mass of living beings.

Prasna Upanishad **5**.5

In the Aboriginal/Renunciative tradition, in the beginning was Emptiness(es) and soundForm(s) from which incarnated the real. In the *Upanishads*,

In the beginning this world was simply what is non-existing; and what is existing was that. It then developed and formed into an egg. It lay there for a full year and then it hatched, splitting in two, one half becoming silver and the other half gold. The silver half is this earth, while the golden half is the sky. The outer membrane is the mountains; the inner membrane, the clouds and the mist; the veins, the rivers; and the amniotic fluid, the ocean.

Chandogya Upanishad
3.19.1–3

In the beginning only the waters were here. Those waters created the real (*satyam*), the real created *brahman*, that is, Prajapati, and Prajapati created the Gods.

Brhadaranyaka Upanishad
5.5.1

In the beginning there was nothing here at all. Death alone covered this completely, as did hunger; for what is hunger but death? The death made up his mind: 'Let me equip myself with a body (*atman*).' So he undertook a liturgical recitation (*arc*), and as he was engaged in liturgical recitation water sprang from him. And he thought: 'While I was engaged in liturgical recitation (*arc*), water (*ka*) sprang up for me.' This is what gave the name to and discloses the true nature of recitation (*arka*). Water undoubtedly springs for him who knows the name and nature of recitation in this way. So, recitation is water.

Then the foam that had gathered on the water solidified and became the earth. Death toiled upon her. When he had become worn out by toil and hot with exertion, his heat—his essence—turned into fire.

Brhadaranyaka Upanishad
1.1.2

In the Aboriginal/Renunciative tradition, in the beginning was Emptiness(es) and soundForm(s) from which incarnated the real in illuminated inner and outer Form(s)/Presence(s). In the *Upanishads*,

Now, far above here the light that shines from heaven on the backs of everything, on the backs of all things, in the very highest of the high worlds—it is clearly this very same light here within a man. We see it when, on touching the body, we feel the warmth within it. We hear it when, as we press our ears shut, we hear something like the hum and the noise of a blazing fire.

Chandogya Upanishad
3.13.7

And take what people call '*brahmin*'—clearly, it is nothing but this space here outside a person. And this space here outside a person—clearly, it is the same as this space here within a person. And this space here within a person—clearly, it is the same as this space here within the heart; it is full and non-depleting.

Chandogya Upanishad
3.12.7

As the single fire, entering living beings, adapts its appearance (shape) to match that (form) of each, so the single self within every being, adapts its appearance (shape) to match that (form) of each, yet remains quite distinct.

As the single wind, entering living beings, adapts its appearance (shape) to match that (form) of each; So the single self within every being, adapts its appearance (shape) to match that (form) of each, yet remains quite distinct.

Katha Upanishad **5**.9–10

This self (*atman*) of mine that lies deep within my heart —it is made up of mind; the vital functions (*prana*) are its physical form; luminous is its appearance; the real is its intention; space is its essence (*atman*); it contains all actions, all desires, all smells, and all tastes; it has captured this whole world; it neither speaks nor pays any heed . . .
It is *brahman*. On departing from here after death, I will become that.

Chandogya Upanishad
3.14,2–3,4

There are, indeed, two visible appearances (*rupa*) of *brahman*—the one has a fixed shape, and the other is without a fixed shape; the one is mortal and the other is immortal; the one is stationary, and the other is in motion; the one is Sat, and the other is Tyam.

The one with a fixed shape consists of everything other than air and the intermediate regions; it is mortal and stationary; and it is Sat. That which gives warmth and is the essence of the one that has a fixed shape, that is mortal and stationary, and that is Sat—for it is the essence of Sat.

The one without a fixed shape, on the other hand, consists of air and the intermediate region; it is immortal and in motion; and it is Tyam. The person within the sun's orb is the essence of the one that is without a fixed shape, that is immortal and in motion, and that is Tyam—for he is the essence of Tyam . . . .

Now, the visible appearance of this person is like a golden cloth, or white wool, or a red bug, or a flame, or a white lotus, or a sudden flash of lightening. And when a man knows this, his splendour unfolds like a sudden flash of lightening.

Here, then, is the rule of substitution: 'not—, not—', for there is nothing beyond this 'not'. And this is the name—'the real behind the real', for the real consists of the vital functions, and he is the real behind the vital functions.

Brhadaranyaka Upanishad
2.3.1–4, 6

Then he told them (the deities): 'Enter, each into your respective dwelling.'

So, the fire became speech and entered the mouth; the wind became breath and entered the nostrils; the sun became sight and entered the eyes; the quarters became hearing and entered the ears; the plants and trees became body hairs and entered the skin; the moon became mind and entered the heart; death became the in-breath and entered the navel; the waters became semen and entered the penis . . . He told them: 'I give you a share in what belongs to these very deities, and I make you a sharer with them.'

Aitareya Upanishad **1**.2.3–5

Like *Amawurrena-alawuduwarra* in the Aboriginal tradition, Brahman is often envisioned as an impersonal Absolute. But *Amawurrena-alawuduwarra* is plural and composed of Forms interconnected by lesser forms—an "incarnation" of Forms from a higher level and as interconnected Forms on the same level. Brahman is conceived as one, though form(s) is implicit (*saguna*). In Aboriginal, Renunciative, cosmology there is no final form or, rather, Final

Form, One, would be interpreted as a mental construct, an inference from the reality of forms perceived in nature and the Forms or Presences around and within them (i.e., waveForm over and above the form of each and every wave).

A "question that assumed special importance for the early Indian metaphysicians was as to how the One became the many" (Singh 1986: vii). The Aboriginal/Renunciative answer would be that it didn't. The One was always many, if the question makes any sense at all in an Aboriginal/Renunciative context. In their cosmology the many were always the many, though an interdependent many. In general, though, Hinduism is ambiguous on the point.

In Hindu metaphysics, then, there has always been at least some hesitation in affording "reality" status to a single Final Form and drawing from it the theological conclusion of monotheism. For instance, there is no cult or institutional incarnation attached to Brahman and some schools of Hinduism like the Vedanta affirm an Ultimate One, while others posit a dualist view, and still others a pluralist.

The difference in perspective between the Aboriginal/ Renunciative and the Hindu here may very well have something to do with what may be the origins of the Brahmanic system in the perception of humanForm rather than natureForms, though natural representations do figure prominently in the tradition. Though the basic principles of the Universe are equated with naturalistic elements like water and fire, the Rig Veda posits ultimate origins in a Cosmic Giant from whose head sprang not only the elements but also the Brahmin caste, from whose shoulders the warriors emerged, from whose thighs the folk emerged and from whose feet the Sudra emerged. Some *Upanishads* do assert that "In the beginning, this world was just a single body (*atman*), shaped (form) like a man" (*Brhad-Aranyaka* **1**.4.1).

The implications of drawing one's inspiration from human-Form is that it retains the subjective, individual, focus, despite the perceived "objectivity" of humanForm in the world outside the self. HumanForm as the basis of a cosmology, then, is prone to reduction to "One"—the self-reflective individual—as well as to seeing "mind" or consciousness as "real" and all-encom-passing in a cosmological sense. The same tendency would occur if the inspiration originated in an inner, subjective, experience of the transcendent.

Regarding levels of Form in Hinduism, Brahman manifests itself as Brahman the Creator as well as lesser Gods on lower levels comparable to those differentiated by Aborigines in their perception of nature:

Brahman

|

the higher Gods

|

the lesser Gods

|

viva/atman

|

samsara

While there is an element of hierarchy as we move from less inclusive forms to more exclusive forms, a relation of interdependence does exist between them in the Indian system. On each level is a *plurality* of same-status Forms each of which encloses Spirit, defined symbolically on the level of the higher Gods as Shiva (the Destroyer), Shakti (the Great Goddess) and Vishnu (the Preserver). These on level two assume many more forms on level three: Shakti as Shiva's bride, as bloodthirsty Kali and as Durga, while Vishnu becomes the 10 Avatars. At the base we find that these Gods, or the spiritual substance they enForm, finally assume material or human form, that is, *samsara*. Vishnu makes the transition between the levels in both animal and human form as, for example, Fish, Tortoise, Boar, and Man-lion, on the one hand, and as Dwarf, Rama-in-two-forms, Krishna, Buddha, and Kalkin, on the other.

As in the Aboriginal/Renunciative religion, Hinduism can also be termed, "transcendent/imminent" positing (as many of its schools school do), the non-manifest (*duyakta*) and the manifest (*wyakta*) in a relation of co-determination and interconnectedness.

(b) Renunciation and Sacrifice

In the Aboriginal/Renunciative tradition, a pre-condition for Renunciation is detachment from attachment to the things of the world so as to be willing to give them up to others who have them not. In the *Upanishads*,

> Then Kahola Kausitakeya began to question him. "Yajnavalkya," he said, "explain to me the *brahman* that is plain and not cryptic, the self that is within all."
> "The self within all is this self of yours."
> "Which one is the self within all. Yajnavalkya?"
> "He is the one who is beyond hunger and thirst, sorrow and delusion, old age and death. It is when they come to know this self that Brahmins give up the desire for sons, the desire for wealth, and the desire for worlds, and undertake the mendicant life. The desire for sons, after all, is the same as the desire for wealth, and the desire for wealth is the same as the desire for worlds—both are simply desires. Therefore a Brahmin should stop being a pundit and try to live like a child. When he has stopped living like a child or a pundit, he becomes a sage. And when he has stopped living like a sage or the way he was before he became a sage, he becomes a Brahmin. He remains just such a Brahmin, no matter how he may live. All besides this is grief."
> *Brhadaranyaka Upanishad*
> **3**.5.

"Now, a man who does not desire—who is without desires, who is freed from desires, whose desires are fulfilled, whose only desire is his self—his vital functions (*prana*) do not depart. *Brahman* he is, and to *brahman* he goes."

Brhadaranyaka Upanishad
4.6

"This immense, unborn self . . . is he that Brahmins seek to know by Vedic recitation, sacrifice, gift-giving, austerity, and fasting. It is he, on knowing whom, a man becomes a sage. It is when they desire him as their world that wandering ascetics undertake the ascetic life of wandering."

Brhadaranyaka Upanishad
4.4.22

Thunder, that divine voice, repeats the very same syllable: "*Da! Da! Da!*"—Demonstrate restraint! Demonstrate bounty! Demonstrate compassion!. One should observe the same triad—restraint, bounty, and compassion.

Brhadaranyaka Upanishad
5.2.3

Maitreyi asked in reply: "If I were to posses the entire world filled with wealth, sir, would it, or would it not, make me immortal?" "No," said Yajnavalkya, "it will only permit you to live the life of a wealthy person. Through wealth one cannot expect immortality."

Brhadaranyaka Upanishad
4.5.3

This whole world is to be dwelt in by the Lord,
  whatever living being there is in the world.
So you should eat what has been abandoned;
and do not covet anyone's wealth.

Isa Upanishad 1–2

The people who win heavenly worlds, on the other hand, by offering sacrifices, by giving gifts, and by performing austerities—they pass into the smoke, from the smoke into the night, from the night into the fortnight of the waning moon . . . Reaching the moon they become food. There the gods feed on them . . . When that ends they pass into this very sky, from the sky into the wind, from the wind into the rain, and from the rain into the earth. Reaching the earth they become food. They are again offered in the fire of man and then take birth in the fire of woman.

Brhadaranyaka Upanishad
6.2.16

Then the breath within the mouth procured a supply of food for itself by singing, for it alone eats whatever food is eaten and stands firm in this world. But the other deities said to it: "This whole world is nothing but food! And you have procured it for yourself by singing. Give us a share of that food." It told them, "Come and gather around me." They said, "Very well," and gathered around it on all sides. Therefore, whatever food one eats through it satisfies also these others.

Brhadaranyaka Upanishad
1.3.17–18

The first morsels of food that one takes, therefore, are to be offered in sacrifice. The first offering he makes, he should offer with the words: "to the out-breath, svaha!" Thus the out-breath becomes satisfied.

> The world there is full;
> The world here is full;
> Fullness from fullness proceeds.
> After taking fully from the full,

> It still remains completely full.
> *Brhadaranyak Upanishad*
> **5**.1

Renunciation does indeed require full-emptying in order to be full-filled.

We find calls for detachment and prescriptions for giving in the *Upanishads* but not to the degree of giving everything of something to those who have none of it. However, Renunciation would explain how, in this last poem something could remain completely full after being emptied. In Renunciation as soon as one is emptied one is entitled to be filled.

Is sacrifice a form of Renunciation? According to the *Rig Veda*, the First Sacrifice was *of* the Cosmic Giant out of whose immolation non-being originated spirituality and all things. This original act of sacrificial creation was henceforth re-enacted by ritual sacrifices by humans to Brahman, the Gods, spirits and living people in the form of food and water, burnt offerings, grain, and, between people, the fruits of hospitality. In return should come prosperity and progeny. Through good deeds of a sacrificial nature one could, to a degree, speed up the cycle of birth and rebirth and enter into union with Brahman. Aboriginal/Renunciative cosmology is neutral on the question of humans' ability to influence the process of rebirth and there is no final enlightenment. One merely continues to pass back and forth between the realm of the living and that of the spirits of the dead. However, one must proceed through initiation into adulthood before moving through the whole cycle.

Here one does give up or renounce what one has or owns to somebody, or something, else, but by turning it into nothing—by destroying it. In the Aboriginal lifeway of Renunciation there is no sacrifice in this sense (though some of the possessions of a deceased person are burned to send their spiritual essence over to the "other side" to join him or her). Sacrifice, then, is really a form of "double renunciation" based on the rather paradoxical premise that in order to create you must first destroy. In traditions practising animal or even human sacrifice the paradoxical aspect is even more pronounced.

In Aboriginal Renunciation one renounces to others the material contents of the Form to which one is attached; in the Indian context, sacrifice is not so much *from* as *to* spiritual Presence—a deity—outside oneself which stands to one in a relationship mediated by the Presence of the sacrifice after its destruction. In cases where what is sacrificed is not destroyed but is redistributed after being purified, we come closer to the Aboriginal form.

There is renunciation in Hinduism in the more conventional sense of giving up worldly pursuits to attain spiritual enlightenment but this is not an aspect of the Aboriginal/Renunciative tradition, though there is an aspect of the Aboriginal form that follows from it. Asceticism is a way of living apart from the world to the extent that one is completely dependent on others for one's sustenance. And, indeed, in the Hindu tradition. the ascetic, having nothing, is thought to be due something from others, if not all of that something. But it is a one-way renunciation from others to you. In the Indian tradition the ascetic extreme, the ascetic on the final step to enlightenment, is seen as a "human-in-pure-Form"—a person so devoid of "content" that he is regarded as a "living dead."

The Dharma-sutras and Dharma-shastras set down the rules of inner sacrifice for the ascetic and for people generally: avoid injuring living things, be truthful, abstain from appropriating the property of others, be continent and liberal. Having nothing, when you receive something apportion some of it to living beings.

This all has an Aboriginal/Renunciative ring to it, except that in Aboriginal/Renunciative society everyone is, in effect, an ascetic, but he or she must actually produce or procure something to renounce to others. There is no class of idealists engaged in a one-way dependency on others for material sustenance.

156

(c) Caste

In the Aboriginal/Renunciative tradition, society is co-equivalence of status and interdependence of function. In the *Upanishads*,

In the beginning this world was only *brahman*, only one. Because it was only one, *brahman* had not fully developed. It then created the ruling power, a form superior to and surpassing itself, that is, the ruling powers among the gods—Indra, Varuna, Soma, Rudra, Parjanya, Yama, Mrtyu, and Isana. Accordingly, at a royal anointing a Brahmin pays homage to a Ksatriya by prostrating himself. He extends this honour only to the ruling power. Now, the priestly power (*brahmin*) is the womb of the ruling power. Now the priestly power. Therefore, even if a king should rise to the summit of power, it is to the priestly power that he returns in the end as to his own womb. So, one who hurts the latter harms his own womb . . . .

Brahman still did not become fully developed. So it created the Vaisa class, that is, the types of gods who are listed in groups—Vasus, Rudras, Adityas, All-gods, and Maruts.

It still did not become fully developed. So it created the Sudra class, that is, Pusan. Now, Pusan is this very earth, for it nourishes this whole world, it nourishes all that exists.

Brhadaranyaka Upanishad
1.4.11–13

What a man turns out to be depends on how he acts and how he conducts himself. If his actions are good, he will turn into something good. If his actions are bad he will turn into something bad. A man turns into something good by good action and into something bad by bad action.

Brhadaranyaka Upanishad
4.4.5

'Now, people here whose behaviour is pleasant can expect to enter a pleasant womb, like that of a woman of the Brahmin, the Ksatriya, or the Vaisya class. But people of foul behaviour can expect to enter a foul womb, like that of a dog, a pig, or an outcaste woman.

Then there are those proceeding on neither of these two paths—they become the tiny creatures revolving here ceaselessly. "Be born! Die!"—that is a third state.'

Chandogya Upanishad
5.10.7–8

Caste can be defined as a hierarchy of status with an interdependence of function. As Kolenda (1978: 3) says, Western observers have emphasised the inequities and what they perceive as the injustice of the caste system. Quoting Dumont, though, she points out that in contrast to the Western system which emphasises individual competitiveness, "the caste system involves a holism, an orientation toward the welfare of all." The theoretical basis of the caste system as set down in the *Rig-Veda* and other texts and traditions is the four Varna division of society into Brahmins as wielders of spiritual power, Kshatriya as holders of secular power, Vaishya as artisans and cultivators, and Sudras as the servants of the first three.

Aboriginal/Renunciative society can be defined as co-equivalence of status with interdependence of function. In both cases there is a Renunciation of what one has (a service in the Hindu case) to those who have it not. But in the Hindu case services, along with those who perform them are ranked as to degree of purity or meritoriousness. It is as if something has intervened in an Australian Aboriginal-like scheme of things to render its component parts hierarchical. This, I hypothesise, was the Aryan invasions into north India in the second millennium B.C. In other words, the Aryans, as victors, would have come in at the "top" of the new order (as a Land/People and Company of Lands/Peoples or their equivalent), and then rearranged the conquered Lands/Peoples and their respective Companies beneath them. Hence the one pure caste at the top, two other "twice born" castes below them, and, finally, the Sudra at the bottom. Implicit here is an economic ranking whereby the Aryans become "overseers" of pastoralism, over agriculture over craft production over labouring, respectively. The Untouchables at the very bottom who are not part of the Varna scheme might have been the hunter-gatherers the Aryans encountered, or they may have been tribals contacted after the Varna system had been established and consolidated.

In the caste system in its ideal form each caste is endogamous with respect to marriage (and the taking of meals) but exogamous with respect to function. Thus is each caste's own degree of spiritual purity guaranteed. But considerations of racial purity may well be a by-product and not a fundamental attribute of this system. Indeed, according to the philosophy of the *Upanishads*, spirituality seems to be what is transmitted in the act of procreation as is biological matter.

By contrast, among the Australian Aborigines each Land/People within each Company of Lands/Peoples is exogamous in terms of marriage and there is no attempt to monopolise the degree of purity one's own division possesses. This is because "purification" is a quality shared to the same degree by all. Also by contrast, in terms of function Aboriginal society is differentiated by Form and content, each Land/PeopleForm "expelling" to the other what is has that the other does not, whether this be a resource or a service. What the caste system seems to have done is differentiate the *dimensions* that constitute a Land/People in a Company of Lands/Peoples and assign one dimension as the "function" of each of the four strata of Lands/Peoples, now castes. To the now Brahman caste, then, goes jurisdiction over the *Form* of the Land, to the Kshatriya ownership and control over the *contents* of Land, to the Vaishya responsibility for creation of the *products* of the land, and to the Sudra responsibility for labouring. Thus a mutually-renunciative interdependence is retained, though a concept of degree of purity is introduced as well as an element of endogamy and hierarchy. That is, purity has been concentrated, if not exclusively situated, on one stratum to which the rest aspire through rebirth.

In this respect, the relation of spirit to matter assumes a new form compared to the Australian case. Spirit and matter are now *ranked* as to the degree of purity in the one and the degree of pollution in the other domain such that the more one is removed from *contact* with matter, especially waste matter, the more one is pure *in* spirit. Hence the function assigned each caste in the hierarchy proceeding from the Brahmans whose function is purely religious, down to the Sudra whose hands and feet are firmly planted in the soil (not to mention the Untouchables whose job it is to clean up the waste left by the four castes above them).

Whether caste represents a movement from an Australian-like Renunciative lifeway or whether it emerged under particular historical conditions without regard to tradition, I do not know. Was hierarchy an Aryan imposition, was it already there (as the Indus Valley evidence seems to indicate), or did it emerge for reasons intrinsic to the nature of the transformation? Perhaps caste was an accommodation between the Aryans and the indigenes which at least precluded their annihilation.

It is interesting, though, that in the Vedic period the Gods were regionally distributed as well as differentiated by function as War God, the God of Commerce and so on. But even if we presume a development from an Australian-like base for caste, only a movement to a more Australian-like future could correct its present deficiency, that is, its "Fall" into hierarchy. What would be required from an Australian point of view is some form of equality in interdependence of its component parts.

(d) Cosmological Determination

In the Aboriginal/Renunciative tradition, life is lived through transcendent Forms Renouncing matter from one to the other. In the *Upanishads*,

It (*brahman*) still did not become fully developed. So it created the Law (*dharma*), a form superior to and surpassing itself. And the Law is here the ruling power standing above the ruling power. Hence there is nothing higher than the Law. Therefore, a weaker man makes demands of a stronger man by appealing to the Law . . . .
Brhadaranyaka Upanishad
1.4.14

There are three types of persons whose torso is the Law (*dharma*).
The first is one who pursues sacrifice, vedic recitation, and gift-giving.
The second is one who is devoted solely to austerity.
The third is a celibate student of the Veda living at his teacher's house; that is, a student who settles himself permanently at his teacher's house.
Chandogya Upanishad
2.23.1

The question of cosmological determination is critical and the most difficult to answer from evidence in the *Upanishads*. We ask to what extent in the Upanishadic period of the Vedic-Hindu tradition, relative to the Aboriginal, was material existence and the substance of socio-economic relations, determined by experientially based, transcendent, "categories/experiences" (of an inner and/or outer-Formed nature)? For one thing, the Varna system, like the Aboriginal ground plan of Lands/Peoples interrelated by intermarriage and songLine ties, was all-encompassing. It was similarly conceived as universal in Form(s) with particular manifestations, spanned a continent, and permitted strangers to interact and function in unfamiliar areas among unfamiliar people, giving stability and predictability to the social life. And it was founded in religion (see Dumont 1970).

Proceeding deductively from what we know of the effect of determination by a Renunciative order from the Australian evidence, we can deduce certain facts and then test them against the Indian, if not the Upanishadic, evidence. The following comments should be taken as suggestive areas for further enquiry.

First, in a Renunciative order consideration of peace and order would take precedence over technological change and economic development. While we cannot glean much from the *Upanishads* on this issue, we can from Indian history. Relative to European civilisation over a comparable period of its history (that is over the millennia and up to the present day) India has been technologically less developed, but has enjoyed a greater degree of stability and order on a continent-wide basis. India is also over-populated relative to Europe, as Australia was over-populated relative to other parts of the hunter-gatherer world—a consequence of spacing or situating relatively large populations in relatively small bounded jurisdictions of territory to prevent self-sufficiency on their part.

Next, if Renunciative cosmological considerations did determine basic social relations on the ground, then in the domain of so-called kinship, the connection between sexual intercourse, procreation, and genetic, substantive, connectedness should have been weakly defined in the Indian case. Primacy would have been given instead to the transmission of abstract or spiritual factors. This is evidenced in some passages from the *Upanishads* (where qualities rather than blood are transmitted through procreation) but is contradicted by the extreme emphasis on racial purity on an intra-caste basis in the Hindu system. In short, in this domain we encounter paradox if not contradiction.

Third, we should find matter as resources, goods, and services, being moved out of and between institutionally imminent Forms to interrelate people in a mutually inter-dependent way. Evidence of this idea rests in the structure of the caste and *jati* system, where one category of persons, at least ideally, expels its specialised service or product to another both within and between castes. The statistical frequency of practice here, however, is problematic (see Kolenda 1978). Another interesting example is the Indian sacred cow. Here the cow is a Form worshipped which expels matter in the way of by-products such as milk and dung to humans who give what the cow needs for sustenance in turn.

As I said, these deductions from Renunciative first principles require further testing against the facts of history and contemporary society as well as against the evidence of other Hindu sacred texts such as the *Bhagavad Gita*.

*　　*　　*　　*

Renunciation at Kokokuji Zen Buddhist Temple

Kokokuji Zen temple was founded in 1227 near Wakayama in Japan by Katsurayama no Gore Kagetomo as a place to repose the soul of Minamato no Sanetomo, the third Kamakura Shogun. Originally the temple was called Saihoji and belonged to the Shingon sect of Buddhism. In 1258 Kagetomo invited Shinchi Kakushin to become the temple's head priest. Kakushin changed the temple's sect affiliation, switching from the Shingon to the Rinzai sect of Zen. In 1340 Emperor Gomurakami honoured the temple with the new name of Kokokuji.

It was at Kokokuji Temple during a trip to Japan in 1992 to visit my PhD student Yuji Ueno and his family in Wakayama that I experienced "contentless Form" or "Presence" as I had amongst the Australian Aborigines (see pages 31–32), during Zen meditation. It was also where I entered into a dialogue on the implications of this with the abbot, Sougen Yamakawa.

Perhaps the best way to carry out this comparison between Aboriginal religion and Zen, then, is to take you with me through that learning experience. After all, to *do* it rather than talk about it, is the Zen—not to mention the Aboriginal—way. This section, then, simply recounts "what happened" in this brief period at Kokokuji without an attempt to relate it to a body of literature and scholarship on the nature of Zen Buddhism. I do, however, assume some familiarity with the basic precepts of Buddhism and Zen. My justification for this approach is not only that it is consistent with an Aboriginal/Zen line of inquiry but also that an actual encounter between traditions—even if momentary—may reveal possible points of articulation between them that are not always apparent when reading about them separately as texts.

Sitting *Zazen,* Painfully

It was about half-past six and the shadows were lengthening as the setting sun disappeared behind the mountain tops to the west. Cobblestone steps rose before us and disappeared into the darkness as they swung to the left under a canopy of deciduous trees. We headed up and moved around the bend and onto a landing where a path led to another set of steps leading up to the main gate. The gate was locked so we made our way around to a building adjacent to the walled courtyard. We knocked on the door and were met by a monk dressed in a simple gray cotton tunic who bade us enter. We removed our shoes and followed him to an ante-chamber adjacent to a room furnished with a low Japanese table, a few mats and a very, to me, arresting vase of flowers on a shelf just off the floor to our left. There was something "right" about it, yet something "not right." I wasn't sure what, but it kept drawing me back.

From the ante-room we could look out onto the courtyard, a sweeping sandScape of narrow parallel furrows partitioned into squares and rectangles by stone pathways and in each patch of sand the odd tree here, the odd tree there. It was the trees that threw me off, one towards the back of one partition, another toward the front and off to the side as if deliberately trying to disturb the impression of geometrical symmetry fostered by the sand furrows. It was the same thing with the flowers in the vase. They looked as if they needed balancing on the right-hand side to complete some kind of symmetry potential or implicit in the arrangement on the left-hand side of the vertical plane.

As I looked out on the scene, now growing dim in the twilight, I imagined two now non-existent trees in the same relative positions as the ones that were there, but reversed— toward the front of the compartment. I suddenly realised I had not only completed the symmetry potential in the scene but also recreated the Aboriginal view of the cosmos: if the compartment as a whole were folded over on the diagonal, one side would mirror the other. In Aboriginal cosmology this is the relationship of life on "this side" of Creation to afterlife on "the other side" of Creation (the so-called Dreamtime). The two are actually a sensed and non-sensed (under normal circumstances) dimension of the same Creation space.

Sougen Yamakawa (Plate 5) entered the main room to our right, knelt and bowed. We reciprocated and introduced ourselves. His smile was enigmatic. He wished to know if I preferred being called "David" or "Turner." I laughed, not quite knowing why. "David," I replied. He smiled back as if "Turner" would have done just as well. Then he and Yuji fell into Japanese to discuss the arrangements for our visit. Tonight we would sit *zazen* with the monks and then *we* would decide if we wished to spend the whole weekend in the monastery. If we could bear it, we were welcome.

We removed our socks and left them in the ante-room and followed Sougen through the outer room and down a hall to our left, pausing as we passed a mediation hall on our right where Sougen stopped and placed his hands together in the praying position and bowed before a statue of the Buddha. We did likewise before moving on. At the end of the hall was another courtyard with a building directly in front of us and another to its right. Sougen motioned us to put on sandals—wooden platforms with rope bindings—and follow him. As we were walking he turned and explained the proper way to walk. The hands should be clasped in front with the head erect and the back straight. We were always to be mindful that we were in a holy place.

The building on the far right was the main meditation hall. We left our wooden sandals at the door, bowed, and entered. Inside was a platform constructed like a shelf around perimeter along the walls. On the platform were prayer mats. In the middle of the room was another platform and more prayer mats so that the overall impression of the room was of two rectangles of prayer mats, one inside the other. We would sit side-by-side with another meditator (as Aborigines did when they sang during mortuary ceremonies, each performer concentrating on his/her own personal connection to the "other side" of Creation space as he/she entered into a kind of musical meditation). But in the meditation hall we would also face a meditator on the other side. The Aborigines did not, though they did face dancers enacting the events of the songs they sung.

Stepping immediately into leather slippers at the door we moved to the platform on our right where we stood before our prayer mats and arranged them into a cushion by folding the length back on itself from back to front leaving what would have been the final fold to extend down in front to form another cushion for the feet. Then we discarded our slippers and climbed onto the mat, sitting with our legs folded and awaiting instructions. We noticed that we were the only people there.

There were three aspects critical to meditation, Sougen said before we started. First was posture, second breathing, and third a clear mind. The tradition used to require the full lotus sitting position with both legs crossed and the feet up on opposite thighs, but this has been relaxed to allow the half-lotus. The lotus posture is necessary to achieve good balance as it realises equal pressure on all points in the body. To achieve this the back must be straight, the head erect, and the gaze slightly down. The hands are clasped in front, left in right, and rest just below the navel. At a later stage they may be left open and rest independently on the thighs. To straighten the back one bends forward from the lotus sitting position and stretches out to raise the buttocks slightly and then leans back into position with the back erect. This description reminded me of the way the old Aboriginal songmen sat when they sung, backs erect and tapping sticks held in the lap.

During meditation one breathes in and out through the nose and concentrates on the exhalation, not the inhalation. Just before the out-breath expires one inhales but only briefly and when one exhales one does so from the energy point or *ki* point below one's navel. One should be able to feel the energy move down along one's legs and out one's toes, circling up the outside of one's body to a point just above and to the back of one's head. Then one draws it down and in on the in-breath by pushing down from one's diaphragm at the energy point. The important thing now is to establish a constant rhythm in one's breathing. One does this by counting to one's self in one's mind until one gets into a rhythm; then one stops counting.

As you sit, Sougen said to me, thoughts will pop into your mind. Don't let them. Say "stop" to yourself and keep them out. Focus instead on a scene in front of you, perhaps the mat across from you on the other platform. Don't focus too long on just one point, though. Instead, relax and expand your gaze. The whole point in meditation is to relax and keep those thoughts out.

Now we began. I shifted into half lotus but found I first had to rearrange my mat to accomplish it, raising the sitting cushion by increasing the number of folds so that I could bring my legs underneath me and take the pressure off my hips. I had never sat like this before and my muscles weren't ready for it. I managed the half lotus, but not to the extent of placing my left foot on my right thigh. I had to settle for tucking my foot between my thigh and calf. It was reasonably comfortable and Sougen came over to have a look, but not before peering down at my sandals on the floor in front of me, bending down and straightening them out. Just another little lesson before we began.

Sougen took his position about half a dozen mats away to

my right, and I am suddenly startled by the sharp clap of two wooden sticks. Then comes the ringing of a struck bell which seems to go on forever. I know I'm not supposed to be thinking but I do. I think of the way Aboriginal singing begins, first with the sticks and then with the didjereedoo, their hollow log instrument, and then with the song. Except here there's no song—just sitting and gazing. I start well enough and get into some kind of rhythm with my breathing, though I can't quite get that "down through one's legs, out one's toes and back in through one's head" feeling. Despite myself I seem to be breathing more with my lungs than my diaphragm. At least now I don't seem to be thinking about much else and I have managed to fix my gaze on a mat on the platform at the far side of the hall as Sougen suggested. I begin to feel a bit dreamy, though there are no dreams. I don't know how long this goes on, but all of a sudden I begin to feel off-balance, like I'm going to fall over backwards. This distracts me for a time, but I manage to regain my balance and concentration.

The light is changing on the surface of the mat I'm watching as the room begins to grow dark. My gaze begins to widen so that I see the whole room in front of me, almost to the point of being able to see Sougen to my right and Yuji to my left. Then I hear a movement to my left and the sound of the sticks startles me again. The bell rings in my ear. Twenty minutes have passed. It hadn't seemed that long.

We undid our legs. Apart from being a bit stiff, they seemed all right. They hadn't gone to sleep. Sougen said to relax for a few minutes and then we would sit again. We did but I didn't really get back into the same position or mood I had achieved after regaining my balance during the first session. At the end of our second 20 minutes my feet were numb and my legs, lower back, and hip ached. It is very important, I thought, to get comfortable right from the start because once one is in position one is stuck with it.

After shuffling our way out of the meditation hall we retraced our steps to the main building and went back to the ante-room. Sougen said that we were to return on Saturday about 7 p.m. and sit with the monks and the other guests. There would be three periods of meditation of 35 minutes each with five minute breaks between them. On Sunday morning we would rise with the monks at 4 a.m. and meditate after which we would help them in their labours around the monastery, then have breakfast. This would be followed by calligraphy— copying a Buddhist *sutra* written in Japanese characters— and lunch during which time we would be required to sit *seiza* for about 45 minutes and 35 minutes, respectively. This, I reflected, was *not* going to be easy!

Sougen said that he could spend more time explaining all this but it was better to just *do* it. "See you on Saturday."

Back at Yuji's I practised sitting for 40 minutes at a time in preparation for our return to Kokokuji on Saturday evening.

Arriving at the monastery we entered the administrative building, as before, shed our shoes, and proceeded to the ante-room where we were greeted by one of the monks and led directly to the main meditation hall. This was to be the three-periods-of-35-minutes-each session—after we sat in position for ten minutes waiting for Sougen to arrive. I was reasonably comfortable at the outset but the under-parts of my legs below the knees were not touching the mat and were kind of suspended above my feet. I could feel some pressure in my groin and lower back. The sticks and bell signalled the opening of the session, and I established an easy rhythm in my breathing and concentrated on the same mat as I had before, except that this time there was a layperson sitting on it.

It must have been toward the end of the period as the light was growing dim with the setting sun that I began to see the plank on the wall behind the person I was gazing at. I mean *behind* him, right through him. It came and went, but I was certain of what I saw. And then I noticed there was a whitish light along the left side of his body (my point of view) which slowly moved behind him like a shadow. This impression lasted until the clap of the sticks and the ring of the bell startled me out of my concentration. It was the end of the period.

We undid our feet and rested for five minutes then started again. This time, though, I didn't achieve a balanced position and my legs ached throughout. I had a brief glimpse early on of what I had seen before, but it went as my muscles began to throb and my legs shake from the tension. It seemed an eternity until the period ended and I was able to undo myself. Sougen had said that we could leave after any of the periods if it was getting too much for us, but I was determined to see it through to the bitter end.

Right from the start of the third period my legs were shaking. It was painful to the point of agony and I thought it would never end. I vowed when this was over I'd never sit *zazen* again. I couldn't concentrate at all and decided the only way out was to take a whack on the shoulders from Sougen on one of his patrols around the meditation hall with his wooden whacker (*kyosaku*). If a monk felt himself dozing off or unable to concentrate it was his duty to signal the abbot to strike him. Some had been struck in earlier sessions and it looked and sounded very painful with Sougen hitting down with both hands firmly gripping his whacker which did indeed make a sharp "whack" when it connected with the person's shoulder. But it was the only way to find an excuse to get my legs out of the half lotus. To be whacked you had to bend forward so that you were hit just behind your shoulders and I couldn't do that in my present position. I would have a legitimate excuse to shift to a cross-footed position. So, as Sougen was passing silently by, I put my hands in the praying position and bowed slightly forward. He stopped and faced me and bowed in return, "apologising" for what he was about to do. But somehow I didn't think this was going to hurt him as much as it was going to hurt me.

I undid my legs and sat cross-ankled and bent forward, my hands still praying. But instead of immediately whacking me as he had the others, he reached forward and felt my shoulder, locating the muscle. Then he stood back and whacked me there. The pain left my legs but didn't come into my shoulders. The effect lasted for about five minutes. After that I was able to return to the half lotus position without much difficulty and at least sit without pain for the rest of the session.

Then, during the prayers at the end of the session, as I sat there with my legs unlocked in a more relaxed position, something remarkable happened. Sougen's voice deepened as he chanted the *sutras* and all of a sudden I was hearing a high-pitched overtone inside my head. I didn't so much hear it as *feel* it "pingggging" away in my head and then right through my body. This had happened to me on occasion before as I listened to the didjereedoo being played by Aborigines during mortuary ceremonies. Their hollow log instrument is capable of simultaneously producing a fundamental note and an overtone.

After the session, Yuji and I bathed in the wooden tub in the bathhouse with our fellow guests and I began to feel much better as the ache started to go away from my legs. Then we went to sleep on our mats, being careful to close the door of the guest house after Yuji read the sign outside warning visitors to beware of poisonous snakes which might slip in during the night to keep us company. Well, my adopted Aboriginal people's surname, Lalara, meant "dangerous snakes" and I reckoned that if I wasn't supposed to harm them they weren't supposed to harm me. I fell into a deep sleep.

At 4 a.m. we were awakened and taken back into the main building to the room where we had first bowed before the Buddha for morning prayers. The problem was, there were no mats and I had to sit half lotus on the floor without being able to raise my torso above my legs. The ache in my legs vanished as Sougen was chanting and that same overtone "pingggg" reverberated in my head and through my body. This did nothing, though, to dull the pain of the two 35 meditation *zazen* sessions that followed in the main hall. When they finished I was more than relieved to get to work cleaning the monastery.

With one of the monks we gathered up our buckets and brushes and proceeded to the building in front of the main meditation hall. This building is normally forbidden to the public. Two things strike one's attention once one is inside. One is a set of stairs at the rear leading up to what looks from a distance to be the mummified body of a man in monks' habit. The other is a very large dragon painted across the ceiling of the main chamber.

The stairs, as we found out when we had to climb them to wash the woodwork, led to a wooden statue of the founder of Zen at Kokokuji, namely Kokushi, though even up close one is still not sure it isn't a mummy. It was an honour to be asked to wash the woodwork around the statue and down the stairs and we treated it as such backing down carefully as we cleaned, making sure not to turn our backs on the statue at any point. Our overseer seemed pleased. Then it was on to scrubbing the stone floor. As we made our way toward the centre of the room our overseer stopped us and looked up to the ceiling to the dragon and clapped his hands. Out of the dragon's mouth came this eerie whining vibration, a kind of "wranggggg," which reverberated through the room. The monk smiled. This was the dragon crying he said. It would only do so if you stood directly underneath and clapped your hands. Another "overtone" effect.

Finally it was time for breakfast—a bowl of rice and a few vegetables. For this it was required to sit *seiza*, kneeling with the buttocks resting on the heels, which proved much less difficult for me than I had feared. We were instructed not to eat directly from our vegetable bowl but to lift the bowl with our left hand and, with our right hand and chopsticks, transfer some vegetables to our rice bowl and eat from it. In other words, the integrity of each utensil and dish is respected and not allowed to "merge" with another. To put it in Aboriginal terms, each bowl "renounces" its contents to an "other." We were also instructed to leave one pickle in our vegetable bowl and when we had finished pour tea into our rice bowl, then with our chopsticks use the pickle to clean the bowl as we would the vegetable bowl after that. Then we would drink the tea and eat the pickle. Nothing was to be wasted.

After breakfast we did more cleaning in this the main

building and then broke for lunch—much like breakfast except more of it—before proceeding to our calligraphy exercise. Sougen prepared the ink by rubbing a solid ink stick on the base of a stone dish as he mixed in small amounts of water (it reminded me of the way Aborigines prepare paint for bark paintings). He then poured it out into the small containers provided for us and we proceeded. Sougen had copied out a line from a *sutra* and gave it to me to copy. He hadn't given any instructions except that I should sit *seiza* in order to bring my torso up over the table.

Almost instinctively I held the bamboo brush erect with my wrist elevated, up off the table. I tried to capture the sweep of each of his brush strokes as I saw them revealed in his work, assuming that his hand had moved in the same direction as the thinning ink. I soon became wholly absorbed in the exercise and copied my line not once but twice. Then I noticed Sougen was standing behind me, watching. He didn't say anything but returned to his position at the end (not the head) of the table. After everyone had finished he came over and, through Yuji, talked to me. He said what I had done was very good and had I done this before. I said, no, I had made a number of mistakes, and pointed them out to him. He replied neither confirming nor denying what I had said, pointing out that each character had a right order of strokes in the sense that if the various components of the character were drawn in a certain sequence, the character would assume its best appearance. Some strokes had to be reversed without lifting the brush from the paper and to do this the brush had to be held almost upright. The arm and hand moved as one but with a certain flexibility, the stroke usually flowing outward, away from the body. What he was describing to me was precisely how Aborigines execute bark paintings!

After calligraphy Sougen beckoned Yuji and me over and led us to the ante-room of his own chambers. He wanted to talk to us about my work with the Aborigines. First he served tea and a few sweets and then we talked, with Yuji translating,

Sougen had seen a cartoon of some kind depicting

Aborigines as a primitive stone age people who fished and hunted and cooked their food without any preparation. This actually appealed to him. But he wondered if there was more to them than this. Did they have a spiritual side? I tried to explain their notion of Creation the "Dreamtime." Yuji couldn't translate in a way that Sougen could understand which wasn't Yuji's fault. English was failing me.

Then I got an idea from breakfast and lunch. I took two of the tea cups on the table and placed a small sweet in each, then took out one sweet and placed it in the other cup. Then I took both from the other cup and placed them in the first. It was simple but Sougen instantly grasped in it the Aboriginal notion of Renunciation—that the containing Forms remained fixed while all the variable contents passed between them. Through Yuji Sougen drew a parallel with the Buddhist saying that "to have nothing is to have everything." In fact he said that this demonstration clarified the paradox for him. It was ironic considering that I had borrowed the demonstration from his instructions during our meals.

I told Sougen of my experience of the enForming light around the person sitting opposite me during meditation in the hall. He said the light was *ki*, a reflection of the Great Ego or Self connected to the universal Buddha. There was, however, a little ego or self—the source of selfishness—which had to be eliminated through self-discipline and meditation before one could reach the Great Ego. The Great Ego, then, was both one's own self and part of a larger cosmic reality expressed metaphorically as the Universal Buddha. I knew this Universal Buddha was not God nor any personified Form and I knew that this Universal Buddha was not a mediator between some God and humankind. The actual person of Gautama the Enlightened One, unlike Jesus in the Christian tradition, is completely irrelevant to, well, anything. Buddhas come and go in history, their role being to shed light on the nature of ultimate reality ("role" is not the best word here; they simply do what they do). The statues you see in Buddhist temples must not be mistaken for representations of Gautama, that particular Enlightened One. Rather they represent all the Enlightened Ones ever to appear in history and in meditating on their Form one is carried to another plane of existence which is empty of any appearance at all. Hence "the Universal Buddha which is not-Buddha."

A parallel can be drawn here with the artistic representations of Creation Beings one sees on Aboriginal bark paintings as well as the statues that are carved for the sacred Amunduwurrarria ceremony. These too must not be taken as real but as representations of something more fundamental whose nature can be revealed by contemplation of their Forms—as they are contemplated by adults and initiates during ceremonies. But they do not reduce to One. I tried to explain this to Sougen through Yuji.

What the Aborigines call *Amawurrena-alawuduwarra* is not a Form but a *force for forming* spiritual substance into *classes* of substances. These substances constitute the prototypical Selves which are simultaneously on the "other side" and "this side" of existence as well as which constitute the personal Selves "incarnated" within the human person on "this side." That is, the created prototypical Self incarnates individual selves within the parameters of a limited Universe of a certain archetypal Form in parallel with other limited Universes of different archetypal Forms. There is no One from which these Forms and Selves derive nor a One that expresses itself in all forms.

To me there is an implicit Oneness or All-encompassing-ness lingering in the background of Buddhist teachings, whether this be Buddha, Buddha Qualities, Buddhahood, or even *sunyata* or Emptiness. Ultimately in Buddhism, reality is One something—or One nothing. This is not the case in Aboriginal religion and I attempted a demonstration by way of my experience of "laughing waves."

Sougen's reply surprised me.

Gautama the Buddha, he said, didn't have the whole story. Had the Aborigines been taught their way of life by someone, or was it just there? He had taken my point—my demonstration with the tea cups and sweets and of the "laughing waves"—and was looking for evidence of a previous Buddha-incarnation among the Aborigines to explain how they knew what I told him. I didn't know, though the Aboriginal people of Groote Eylandt and Bickerton Island do tell the story of Nambirrirrma who descended from the sky in the pre-European past to reconfirm the Law (see pages 31-32).

I thought I had better back-track a bit. "Aboriginal society wasn't perfect," I said. "While organised warfare was absent, they did kill people for religious transgressions. They have a lot to learn from Buddhism about not killing any living things." His reply threw me for a loop. He said you could look at that as sending someone away to come back "corrected" in a later life as someone or some*thing* else. I realised that this was the way some Aborigines might look at it. If someone died before they were fully initiated, they would come back and try again before moving on. It was but one step from here to killing them if they *couldn't* be initiated. I didn't like this line of argument, though, and told Sougen so. It could be used to justify killing for all kinds of reasons. He smiled back at me and I knew this was the answer he, as a Buddhist monk, was really looking for. Buddhism really did have something to offer Aborigines as Aborigines had something to offer Buddhism.

Sougen said he thought I had been to Japan before—in a previous life. He felt we had once "brushed sleeves," though not necessarily as human beings. We had, he said, one profoundly important thing in common. We both were trying to keep something very important alive for future generations until the crisis occurred which would make its relevance apparent.

I mentioned to Sougen about that overtone sound I heard in myself when he chanted. Yuji hadn't been aware of it. Sougen said that something happened to his voice during chanting that he couldn't explain. It sort of dropped and deepened and he could feel an echoing in it. I said that it sounded like Tibetan harmonic chanting and didjereedoo playing and somehow connected us together. "I told you we'd brushed sleeves before," he said.

Sitting there talking I realised that the pain in the sciatic area of my back had vanished. I had pinched a nerve a few months before leaving Canada and after physiotherapy had failed to heal it my doctor had declared it chronic. I told Sougen about this and he simply nodded and said that the pain would stay away so long as I sat properly in the *zazen* position. Then he laughed. He had seen how I was sitting in the main hall and realised I must have been in a lot of pain. "If it's pain you want, we have lots of it here," he said, laughing "You must come back for another visit."

Sitting *Zazen*, Comfortably

We accepted Sougen's invitation to return again and on July 30th arrived at Kokokuji to sit with the monks. It seemed, though, that Sougen was more in the mood to talk. We arrived at 7 p.m. but instead of going immediately to the meditation hall, he led us to the ante-room of his chambers, served us tea and picked up the conversation where it had left off on our first visit. The subject, of course, was again Zen and Aboriginal religion. At 9 we were to break for 45 minutes of *zazen* and prayers.

During our conversations Sougen wanted me to recapitulate what I had said—really demonstrated—about Aboriginal cosmology on my last visit. This time I used the metaphor of a cloud.

Creation is like a vast cloud. Here and there you can see different patches of light and shade and almost make out recognisable shapes and forms. Then rain falls, not all at once, but here and there from different parts of the cloud, splashing into the ocean below. The rain stops and the waves roll across the ocean connecting all the "places" in the water where each droplet has made an impression. Finally the sun appears and the water begins to evaporate, drawing the droplets from their respective "places" back up into the sky to reform a cloud. The patches of light and the shapes and forms implicit therein, are the archetypal Forms, the rains are incarnatings and the droplets are incarnations as such. The waves effect the Form-expelling-content process.

Sougen picked this up immediately. He told me how people could be separated but still connected *by* space. It wasn't conventional space he was thinking of but *ma* space or "spiritual" space (also the space between shakuhachi flute notes that continues them one silently from one note to the next). You could be connected without directly communicating. For instance, one person is in Japan, another in Italy. One steps into the Pacific, the other into the Mediterranean and the moment they do, they're connected. Both feel warm. That's how they know they're connected. They don't become "one"; they don't "share" anything, but they're not separate. He added that Zen has another saying to express right relationship: "we share the same mat." But it's still each sharing a part of one thing rather than something of each other, I said. I went back to the "sweets in the cup" demonstration I had used earlier to illustrate what I was trying to communicate. He thought for a moment and then responded: "We have a saying for that in Zen. In order to fill you first have to empty."

Zen, though, isn't concerned with debating apparent inconsistencies in dogma or even with translating its teachings into a secular blueprint for living. Once you have experienced enlightenment you simply behave in the appropriate manner. That's it. Zen has no interest in constructing institutions.

"But a monastery is an institution," I replied.

"Zen is just a method of attaining Enlightenment," was Sougen's final word, bringing us back to what we were here for.

I had a very good sit after our conversation. Sougen opened the shutters in the hall and the wind wafted in bringing the scent of pines and sounds of frogs and crickets. I quickly entered into a restful state and my vision began to widen and take in the whole of the room in front of me. I began by gazing at the mats on the platform on the far side but soon began to see only the spaces *between* the mats. Sort of a "no-matForm" experience. But as soon as I was conscious of this I lost it. Still, I was startled when the bell rang to end the session and felt I could have sat much longer. Afterward, during prayers, I heard that overtone ringing in my head again. This time I could almost *see* it, but it didn't quite materialise (if that is the right word).

Sougen mentioned how meditation can be used in healing. If you are ill with fever you meditate and imagine you have something like a block of melting butter on your head. It is very warm and it starts to drip all around your body to the tips of your toes until you are enveloped in it. Then it begins to move down off your head and upper body until only your lower body is covered. That's when you start to sweat and after sweating you are well. Sougen uses the technique in winter to keep warm in the meditation hall when there's snow on the ground outside and it is freezing cold. I told him I thought he was cheating. Zen monks are supposed to put up with such discomforts . . . .

I reflected that Aboriginal musical meditation is a form of healing too: it dissolves the pain of grief experienced on the death of a loved one.

At one point in our conversation Sougen and I both found ourselves explaining to Yuji something we were trying to explain to each other. We suddenly realised that we had understood each other perfectly well without the use of language. That "said" it all.

Sougen said that Buddha and Jesus both gave intellectual expression to the Truth so that it could be taught. He said that if I could do that for what I knew of Aboriginal culture, it would be equivalent to what Buddha and Jesus had done. I laughed. No, I retorted, what it would mean is that all the Aborigines are Buddhas and Jesuses and that I had been well taught. Anyway, if what Jesus and Buddha and the Aborigines know *is* really different from what was known in their times, how would anyone recognise it? Language bounds and organises experience for us and we immediately put accounts of new experiences into old categories. In fact, the accounts of the new experiences *have* to be expressed in terms of the same old categories. So how can the newness be communicated? The Zen way, said Sougen, was by a direct experience, by demonstration and example. This was the way the Aborigines had taught me.

I really felt at ease at Kokokuji. Not *déjà vu*, but at peace with myself. About 11:30 p.m. we left, promising to return again.

Back at Yuji's I mentioned that it would be nice to have the experience of a Japanese tea ceremony before I left for Australia. Yuji smiled: "You already have," he replied, "each time we visited Kokokuji." The Japanese tea ceremony was Sougen serving us tea. I hadn't clicked in, thinking it to be something ritualised, compartmentalised, separate from "just drinking tea." I read up on the ceremony and then thought back to our tea times at Kokokuji.

The tea room is a special room, usually "four-and-a-half mats" in size, separate from but connected to the main dwelling. Outside is usually a small garden and a fountain or pond where the guests assemble, wash and chat before the fragrance of incense wafting from the room beckons them enter. Entrance is by a small panel about three feet square in the wall. A painting, a scroll containing a *haku* poem, and a flower arrangement face the guests on the opposite side as they enter. These they discuss until they hear the kettle boil and sing and tea is served. Each of the guests is served in turn and each drains his or her cup in three gulps, the host being the last to do so. The host then places the tea-making equipment before the guests for their inspection. He then offers each of them an item but retains the mixing bowl, breaking it at the conclusion of the ceremony. The point of the tea ceremony is to cleanse one's senses from contamination. The painting cleanse the sight, the flowers (or incense) the smell, the water boiling and being poured the hearing, and the tea itself the taste.

Basically the above description is what happened each time we had tea with Sougen.

When we entered Sougen's ante-room he invited us to sit at

the table in *seiza* if possible but if this was too difficult, then to sit cross-legged. Then Sougen left the room and Yuji and I chatted about our experiences at the monastery and about the objects in the room—a pen and ink drawing of bamboo in black and white, a large urn on its right and a small flower arrangement on its left, behind which was a cylindrical vase, behind which again propped up in the left-hand corner of the alcove was a stringed instrument called a *shamisen*. We wondered about the age of the painting and commented on the simplicity of its style. My gaze was then drawn from the painting down to the flower arrangement (which seemed to complement the mural but in a way I couldn't quite pin down), then up to the vase and *shamisen* and finally to the urn and the scene as a whole, including the framed paper window on the far wall of the alcove which seemed to expand the space beyond itself.

Then Sougen re-entered the room with a bowl, a small bamboo whisk and a caddy containing powdered green tea. These he placed beside his mat and turned to what I now realised was an electric water boiler behind him to his right. He left the room and returned again with a large bowl, some jellied sweets and three drinking bowls. As we chatted and ate our sweets Sougen took the tea from the caddy and put it in a large bowl and then turned and poured in the hot water and began mixing the contents with the whisk, whipping it into a froth. All the while we carried on the conversation almost oblivious to what he was doing. Then he placed the bowl on the table and poured the contents in turn into my drinking bowl, then into Yuji's and then into his own. We drank at leisure thereafter, though I noticed that Sougen drained his cup at one gulp.

The Aboriginal Renunciative logic in this is too obvious to be missed. There is this last example of the pouring of the tea from one who has all the tea in turn to those who have none. But there something more profound that, in fact, structures the whole ceremony. The guests enter the room with nothing then become Nothing with subsequent purification; they are now entitled to everything in a material sense and so receive.

The host, by contrast, begins with everything and, appropriately, ends with nothing.

On August 7th Yuji and I returned to Kokokuji. Sougen was away in a nearby town officiating a funeral and he had left instruction for us to sit with one of the other monks. This we did for about 40 minutes. When Sougen returned we sat with him for another hour but in two half-hour sessions. In between he took us for a brisk walk around the adjacent temple building to loosen up. Sougen was determined to make our sittings as easy as possible so that we would be encouraged to continue on our own.

Toward the end of the first session with the other monk, I was concentrating on the space between two mats just below a low light. The meditation hall as a whole began to grow dim and the mats began to disappear. The same thing happened about half-way through the next session as I sat with Sougen, but now there were parallel bars of light running right across the room. During the third session the bars of light became one-dimensional and they too faded away, leaving a blank room except for a dim spot of light. Yet I felt alert and awake, more so than in any other session. But when the bell sounded to end the final session my body gave a start as if it had been dozing.

This was the first time that the experience at the end of one session carried through immediately into the experience at the beginning of the next despite the break. Was it the effect of *ma*? When I asked Yuji about this he said, yes, you didn't withdraw your *ki* during the break but were actually continuing your meditation.

Afterwards we retired to Sougen's ante-room where we drank tea and chatted until about midnight. I had brought with me an article I had written on the Aboriginal view of Creation which contained photographs of two bark paintings which I asked Sougen to interpret. I identified the animal forms depicted on one of the barks for him as Dove and Rainbow Serpent belonging to the Wurramarrba and Wurramara people, respectively. I told him that I had always wondered why in Aboriginal culture a particular species of animal or plant was attached to a particular people and another to another.

Anthropologists had lots of theories to explain why Aborigines had "totems," but no one had succeeded in explaining why particular "totems" were attached to particular groups. Sougen thought that it didn't matter. If "spiritual nothingness" was behind each of these incarnations, including human ones, then each was really the same. In other words, to him the question was meaningless. I could almost see his point, but to my Aboriginal way of thinking and perceiving, the "spiritual nothingness" of a species or a group had a particular identity or archetypal Form and I could not see why the Shape of the Snake connected to the Shape of the Wurramara people. On the other hand, if both Snakes and people originated in the same spiritual substance, whatever form it took, it only became two perceivably *different* forms at a later stage of incarnation, and Sougen was right.

It was now midnight and time to say goodnight and good-bye. On the 10th of August I was flying to Brisbane Australia.

Back at Yuji's I continued meditating each morning, but it was never quite the same as at Kokokuji. It was much harder to keep thoughts from creeping in and distracting me. My legs seemed to ache even more, though I was sitting for shorter periods. But I did see things in illuminated, outlined, Form and I did lose parts of the room from time to time, though the experiences did not last long. And the therapeutic physical effects persisted: no more sciatic and back problems, no more ache in my Achilles tendon, no more stress in my shoulders, no more pain of grief in the space in my solar plexus which now seemed somehow filled, no more troubling thoughts from the past and my energy level was higher. Though alone I did not feel lonely. I sensed that the Aborigines I know and the Zen monks I met feel the same way in the same circumstances. And if they do, and if their experiences of the non-discursive are the same under similar circumstances (silent meditation in one case, musical meditation in the other), does this not constitute a validation of the claims of their respective "faiths"?

Was the Zen experience the Aboriginal experience? Was the Zen experience, Buddha's experience as he gained enlightenment? What was he enlightened about? Could it have been the event that immediately preceded the experience? After six years in the forest Buddha rejected asceticism as the path to enlightnment and came to a river where he bathed (purifying himself) and accepted a bowl of milk from the hand of Sujata, a maiden, who lived in the neighboring village. In other words, having nothing of something he received (perhaps) everything of it from someone else (pure like himself). The Renunciative significance of this may be what the whole tradition is really all about. It is recorded that the disciples who left him *because* he took the milk from the maiden returned to him after he talked to them following his enlightenment. There was indeed much to ponder.

*   *   *   *

Renunciation in Gujar Society and in the Qur'an

The Gujar

The *Anthropological Survey of India* (K. S. Singh ed., 1991) lists the Muslim Gujar as one of India's Scheduled Tribes and estimates their numbers in the Scheduled Areas of Himachal Pradesh at 28,121. Muslim Gujar are also found in Jammu-Kashmir in the vicinity of Punch, Rajauri, and Doda in the south-western part of the state as well as in the foothills of Arantang and Baramula to the north and the east, respectively. Gujar are also found in Punjab, Haryana, Rajasthan, Madhya Pradesh, Uttar Pradesh and the city of Delhi. There are also Hindu Gujar in north India, but they will not concern us here.

Muslim Gujar trace their conversion to the Sunni sect of Islam during the reign of the Mughul ruler Aurangzeb (1658–1707). According to the Anthropological Survey the Gujar were originally one of the Scythian tribes who conquered Kabul about 100 B.C. and established the Gujara Kingdom in north India where they integrated with the indigenous cultures. By the end of the thirteenth century the Gujara empire began to collapse at the hands of Mahmud Ghazi, then the Pathans and finally the Mughuls. During these conquests the Gujar were pushed eastward into Jammu and the Punjab and then into the foothills of the Himalayas in Himachal Pradesh. In the process some converted to Islam, others did not.

The Survey describes the Muslim Gujar as lean in physique, tall-statured, large and round headed, of oblong facial profile with long, narrow noses conforming to the Mediterranean type. They lead a pastoral life, moving with their cattle (or buffalo) from the higher altitudes in the summer and fall to the lower hills and plains in winter in anticipation of the snow. Their staple diet is maize and pulse complemented by milk products such as curd and buttermilk. Gujar basically lead a subsistence existence but earn some cash from the sale of milk products in the plains during the winter months.

Gujar social organisation is characterised by exogamous *gotras* or clans, community exogamy, cross but not parallel cousin marriage (which is allowed in Muslim law), sister exchange, junior levirate and sororate and the virtual absence of divorce.

According to the Anthropological Survey, their neighbours the Gaddis also came originally from the plains and were driven into the hills by Muslim invaders. However, they remained Hindu, though without a strong sense of caste. The Gaddis venerate Lord Shiva and his consort who, they believe, created the Himalayas and continue to dwell there along with a host of other deities. In the vicinity of Brahmaur to the east of Chamba, the Gaddis are nomadic herders of goats and sheep, but elsewhere in the state they are semi-nomadic, devoting most of their time to the cultivation of maize and pulse and to the spinning and weaving of cloth. They earn some cash by the sale of these products in the villages and by hiring out as porters in the summer months when the passes are open to traffic. In physical appearance the Gaddis are generally shorter and more slightly built than the Gujar and the two people do not intermarry except when one converts to the faith of the other.

The Gujar I visited in the Kalaban Valley on the approach to the Sach Pass distinguish three kinds of "eternal places," those of the plain (*dabarrda*) from which they originated, those of the mountains (*dhar*) where they pasture their cattle during summer, and those associated with their religion at its place of origin, Saudi Arabia. All are interconnected.

One can see *dhar* at a glance. These are the ridges that mark the Kalaban Valley as viewed from any one of them. It is these rather than the valleys between them, or the valley as a whole, that are the Gujar's point of reference. Indeed, I could locate no word for "valley" in the Gujari language. Ridges are *punjal*. Each *punjal* upslope and downslope is named. The spaces—or valleys—between them are generally named on the downslope of the ridge as one proceeds up from the bottom of the valley. The Gujar view of the world, then, is figuratively this, /\, while their neighbours', the agriculturist Gaddis', is this, \/. The Gaddis name the valleys on both upslopes, the ridges on the upslope as one proceeds up the valley. The two visions, then, mirror each other, as do their respective lifestyles.

The Gaddis are sedentary, producing staple foods consumed by the Gujar; the Gujar are nomadic, producing milk products consumed by the Gaddis. The two peoples have lived side-by-side for centuries, yet each retains their own language, communication being through bilingualism and, more recently, common knowledge of Hindi.

Each ridge in the Kalaban Valley is associated with a particular Gujar *gotra* or *jaat* or a branch of a *jaat*. This is their "eternal pastureland" to which they return each season accompanied, perhaps, by the members of an in-marrying *jaat*. Eleven *jaats* are represented in the Valley: Chechi, Lodah, Kartana, Paswal, Pambara, Bajar, Baniya, Batliya, Katariya, Kaals, and Sayeed. These *jaats* might be considered clans in the conventional sense insofar as they are patrilineal descent groups. However, in only three cases did informants locate the origin of one of these *jaats* in a common ancestor, and even in these cases the place of origin of the ancestor in question was considered equally important.

Jaats are rather groupings of people linked to the same place or origin. Whether "origin" means "in the beginning" or at the point of conversion to Islam is not clear. I suspect the latter. Some *jaats* were said to have once been associated with particular occupations. For instance, the Tikria were once potmakers from Ragura near Chuardi, southeast of Jammu. It seems that at the time of conversion to Islam the Gujar abandoned the caste or *jati* system, and adopted instead the local community in which they were resident at the time as their point of reference.

In all, 17 *jaats* were known to my Kalaban collaborators. In addition to those listed above are Chard, Tikriya, Bartiya, Didrr, Kasana, and Gorsi. They say there are many more in Jammu-Kashmir, but they do not know much about them. The 17 are ones with places of origin in the south-western part of that state. Of the 17, I located places of origin for 14, though not without considerable discussion and disagreement among my collaborators. One reason is that most of these places are no longer frequented by the Gujar as most of the Kalaban people now live in the vicinity of Pathankot during the winter months where they have access to a market for their products. While place names may be known, exact locations are being forgotten (they are country places) and most often they were identified by the name of the closest town. Baniya, for instance, was located near Surff, northwest of the town of Udumpur in Jammu-Kashmir. Lodah was at Baridabar near Udumpur in Jammu-Kashmir; Bajar at Bajar near the town of Jammu; Paswal at Gaunyardi near Jammu; Chechi at Gaunyardi near Jammu; Pambara at Seri near Tissa in Himachal Pradesh; Chard at Mujajak near Samba in Jammu-Kashmir; Tikriya and Baffiya at Ragura near Chuardi near Jammu; and Didrr at Aknurr west of Jammu. The places of origin of Katariya, Kaals and Sayeed were not known. All are associated with small, remote, ridges in the Valley. Batlia is a "foreign" *jaat* from Kashmir. Kasana and Gorsi are said to originate in Saudi Arabia.

The case of Kasana and Gorsi is instructive. Tradition holds that two Gujar came originally from the Holy Land to settle near Jammu and established two separate *jaats* there whose names my collaborators translated as "brass pot" and "mother's milk," respectively. Since their point of origin as Muslims was Saudi Arabia this is their recognised homeland, not the place where they settled in Jammu. Though the two brothers established *jaats* with two separate names, the normal procedure when such fissioning takes place is for each to retain the same place of origin name but prefix it with the name of the sub-branch founder. Hence, Subia Chechi and Trebia Chechi.

There is in Gujar society little sense of common ancestry from a common founding father and no sense that any one *jaat* or grouping of *jaats* was the original founder of them all. Genealogical memories extend back only to the grandparent level.

The Gujar world, then, like the Aboriginal/Renunciative world, proceeds from a *plurality* of "eternal places" linked through common religious affiliation and the bonds of inter-marriage, a world that emerged out of the circumstances of persecution and conversion some 300 years ago.

The importance of place among the Gujar is reflected in the (so-called) kinship and marriage system. The only marriage rule is that one cannot marry into one's own *jaat*, no matter how genealogically distant the relationship. Hence the prohibition on father's brother's son or father's brother's daughter marriage. There is a strong preference for marriage with a *jaat* of one's own Valley and this is reflected in the situation of the Ranikot Chechi with whom I stayed. In 12 recorded marriages over three generations, five were with Lodah, four with Baniya and one each with Bajar, Kartana, and Bazard. My friend Abdul's father and grandfather both married Baniyas and there was one case of sister exchange but no polygamy, although it is allowed in Islamic law. In a wider sample of 30 non-Chechi marriages I found eight cases of marriage with the same *jaat* in consecutive (five), alternate (two) and over three (one) generations.

On marriage the father of the husband pays the family of the bride a small sum of money which they, in turn, must repay two-fold the following year. This then must be paid back two-fold again the next year and so on until a bargain is eventually struck equalising the situation. My collaborators said that if a man dies, his wife goes to an elder brother if he is not married. If he is, or refuses, the woman then goes to a younger brother whether he is married or not. But I found no instances of this among the people sampled. Divorce is said to be rare and I found one exception which proved the rule. A man whose wife had died took first one teenage wife, then another, then a third, divorcing the previous two while they were pregnant. My collaborators regarded this as morally reprehensible, though legally possible. The women he left with children would have no option but to return to their families and have few prospects thereafter.

Place or *jaat* has a profound influence on the so-called kinship terminology. Four cognates are distinguished on the grandparent level and the terms applied to those cognates are also applied to anyone in the same *jaat* as the cognate. Two cognates are distinguished in the parent level and the terms applied to them are also applied to anyone in the same *jaat*. But in one's own level everyone related through these cognates and their respective *jaats* is called *bhay* (males) and *biybu* (females). This "brother/sisterhood" of intermarrying *jaat* members is explicitly linked to the "brotherhood of Islam." But despite this incorporative feature, one's *jaat* membership does not change with marriage. This is reflected in the differentiations in "kinship" terminology in the second ascending and first ascending generations.

While the terminology on one's own generation suggested that merging has taken place, then, difference reasserts itself on subsequent levels from the point of view of the next generation. Whether the incorporative feature was grafted onto a more consistently federative form emphasising exclusive *jaat* membership, or whether an originally incorporative arrangement is becoming more federative, is impossible to determine.

The anomaly here reflects another which runs deep in Gujar society. A Gujar put it to me almost apologetically, "Though we have many *jaats*, we are really all one people." Said another: "One God, but many *gotras*." I translate these comments as, "we are supposed to be Muslim where the One subsumes the many, but . . ."

Older Gujar ask younger Gujar who no longer wish to make the annual trek to the mountains with the cattle, "Why don't you come with us because that's where your fathers' and mothers' spirits are?" The Gujar believe that one's soul remains or returns to the mountains after he or she dies. The Muslim faith teaches that the soul goes to God. These Gujar believe that the water and the trees contain spirits and that a spirit-woman roams the hills at night with a torch in search of cattle to kill and eat. Many claim to have seen her light moving about on the slopes, and cattle do sometimes inexplicably disappear.

When a Gujar dies the family make an offering to the spirit of the deceased in the belief that it is starving. The body is then washed and wrapped in a white cloth and taken to a burial ground in the mountains shared by a number of interrelated families. After seven days a *malbye* or religious man joins mourners and reads hymns from the *Qur'an*. This is repeated for 40 days after the burial.

The Gujar generally pray in the morning at sunrise in the traditional Muslim manner—after washing and seated on a mat or *musalaa* wearing a prayer cap or *topi* or with the head covered by a shawl, and facing west to Mecca. While at Ranikot I developed a special bond with Sakhi, Abdul's younger brother, whom I found seated on a stone platform in front of our stone hut or *ghoti* chanting from the *Qur'an* the first morning I awoke (Plate 6). Thereafter I joined him in my own version of prayer—concentration on the form of the landScape in order to empty myself of presuppositions and preoccupations and open myself to whatever the day would bring. Though Sakhi never questioned me, Abdul did. Why didn't I pray? he asked. I said I did in my own way but he wasn't satisfied. The Gujar, he said, pray to invoke God's blessing for family and humankind in general. During prayer the spirit of the words flies to God and he sends angels down to give one spiritual strength for the day. The readings from the *Qur'an* also remind one to treat people kindly, not covet their possessions and work hard and honestly. Praying five times a day is for those whose behaviour needs correcting, he said. Repetition makes the message sink in.

As an honoured guest I was served three times more food than anyone else and not permitted to do any work, not even my own washing. Six *chapatis*, *dal*, curd, a glass of buttermilk and a glass of milk three times a day is more than I can handle and I learned to hand back the bulk of my portion as soon as it was handed to me so that it could be made available to someone else. I then learned that this was what I was *expected* to do.

It would be fair to say that the Gujar religion is a more gentle form of Islam than we have been accustomed to reading about elsewhere today. On principle the Gujar are non-violent. They eat little or no meat—certainly no beef—out of respect, they say, for the surrounding Hindu community (although I sensed an element of self-preservation in this). The one God to whom they pray, said my collaborators, could not possibly sanction violence among his own children. What matter if one prayed in a Muslim mosque, a Hindu temple, a Buddhist *gompa* or a Christian church? All led to the same source. On the other hand, these Muslim Gujar do not regard their Hindu counterparts as "brothers" and apply no relationship terms to them. Nor do they have much sympathy for the Hindu belief that deities like Shiva created the mountains and other natural phenomena, though they do equate Brahman with their own

God, Allah.

In a chance encounter with a *malbye* or Muslim preacher during our visit to another ridge and *jaat*, Abdul and he engaged in a heated debate over the presumed absolute truth of the *Qur'an* in comparison with other religions, particularly Christianity. Later Abdul told me that teachings such as this *malbye's* only led to intolerance and killing and went against the spirit of Gujar beliefs. The *malbye* thought that I must be there as a Christian missionary.

The first word I learned in the Gujari language was *gai* or buffalo. The second was *gobarr* or buffalo dung. The Gujar live easily with both. At first I did not. The cattle that are not up on the slopes live indoors with the Gujar. Where there are cattle there is dung and where there is dung there are flies and where there are flies there is disease. But, as I discovered, the cattle are turned out of the house at daybreak and all of the dung collected at night is cleaned up by hand and deposited outside in a pile away from the dwelling. The theory is that "If we give the flies a nice place to feed outside, they won't feed on us inside." The interior of the house is then thoroughly cleaned and washed, then everyone washes themselves as they do again in the evening and before and after every meal. The smoke that fills the house from the cooking fire is usually sweet-smelling cedar which keeps the flies and mosquitoes away at night.

Most of the Gujar's cattle are up on the mountainside, some three to five kilometres away. The Gujar tend them according to a strict daily routine. They wake up at daybreak and the women prepare the food for the men who wash, dress, and pray before leaving for the slopes. The men wear the traditional *damadk* or long cloth, the *kurta* or shirt and the *page* or turban and carry a *duparta* or shawl which serves as a cloak, a raincoat, a pillow or a cushion to buffer the weight of loads carried on the head. Reaching the slopes, they muster the herd, milk the cows, and return to base camp in the early afternoon. There they eat a meal and then sleep, returning to the slopes in mid-afternoon to again muster the cattle and settle them down for the night. They do not return to base camp until all the cattle have been accounted for.

Gujar classify slopes according to the kind of grazing land found there. By the time I reached the fourteenth type in my listing I realised that it would not end until every type of vegetation known to the Gujar and eaten by their cattle had been recounted. For instance, *nakro* is any kind of grazing land at the base of a small ridge; *karndlualo* is any kind of land containing trees with edible leaves; *biarnalo* is any grassy area; *panialo* is a grassy area with a stream running through it; *korlalogatu,* is a flat area with no trees; *goad* is a flat area with small bushes; *bardialo* is any bushy area; *kardialo* is a bushy area with short trees, *chawarlo* is an area with small plants but no bushes; *korrwalo* is land containing any type of deciduous tree whose leaves are edible; *sarbwalo* is any area with spruce trees; and so on.

The emphasis on edible bushes and trees as well as grass raises the issue of deforestation and soil conservation. The state government claims that the Gujar's cattle overgraze and kill trees. This causes soil erosion and landslides with a consequent loss of topsoil and forest. I asked the Gujar I was staying with about this. When they arrive at the beginning of the season, they said, there is very little grass so they sometimes climb certain deciduous trees and gather their leaves to feed the cattle. But they never cut down a tree or take too many leaves from one branch. When the grass becomes plentiful they move their cattle through different kinds of vegetation at different altitudes so as not to overgraze any one area. They say the deforestation and soil erosion is caused by the illegal cutting of timber by villagers for firewood and by commercial loggers. They say the government is simply looking for an excuse to stop them from migrating during the summer. The government prefers to see them settled on the plain where it can keep track of them. To this end, they say, the government has increased the levy on cattle moving to the mountains from 25 pence to 8 rupees per head over the past

10 years.

The Ranikot people estimate that about half of the Gujar who could be in the Valley with their cattle (because they have ridges here), are here, and with only about half their cattle. The others remain on the plain. In many cases a family will split in two, taking half their cattle to the mountains and leaving half on the plain. There are seven houses at Ranikot, four of which belong to Chechi *jaat*, three to in-marrying *jaat* only one of which, Lodah, is regarded as having long-term rights there. Only three are currently occupied and that only by some family members and their cattle. The owner of one of the empty houses had died and the owners of two others live permanently on the plain.

Those who come do so in mid-May and return in early September. The walk from Pathankot to Ranikot takes about two weeks by "short-cut" (which to a Gujar usually means "straight up" rather than "round about"), and an extra week on the main roads. On the way they sell milk to the local *dhabbas*, as they do when they arrive. These tea stalls service the porters as they travel back and forth between the Kalaban and Pangi Valleys over the Sach Pass. In the mountains the Gujar live mainly on *chapati, roti,* and *dal* which they obtain from the Gaddis, as well as their own milk products. While the men do most of the herding there is no strict division of labour, and women sometimes herd while men sometimes cook and wash. But the person who does the most work is *amijar* or "mother." She is first up in the morning and last to bed at night and is almost always to be found in the house cleaning and cooking. She is responsible for seeing that everyone has enough food to see them through the day.

Abdul's family—his parents, seven brothers, three wives and children—earn about 3,000 rupees a month from the sale of milk products in their winter quarters in Pathankot. The best market for their product is the army base which pays 6 rupees per kilo but require a consistent supply. Abdul's family's production is anywhere from 20 to 70 kilos of milk per day and little effort is made to rationalise it in economic terms, for instance, by co-ordinating the cow's cycles, in order to maximise profits. This is partly because the idea of maximisation is foreign to the Gujar and partly because of tradition. Tradition is geared to a subsistence, not a market, economy. The elders will not allow unproductive cows to be sold, nor will they allow borrowing to finance capital investment. It will take at least another generation, says Hanif, just to make few changes. Until then they must be patient out of respect for their fathers.

Another major problem is the lack of available pasture-land in the vicinity of Pathankot. Abdul's family have a few hectares of land some seven kilometres away from which they take grass and transport it back to their homestead for the cattle. But this is both time-consuming and expensive. There is vacant land right across the road from their homestead, but it is being held for speculative purposes by absentee landlords. Under the circumstances their domestic economy cannot support the whole family and there is pressure on the younger, single men to seek employment elsewhere (as one brother has already done). Nevertheless, the family has an obligation to support them until they are independent. Under their law the eldest son inherits the land and cattle but on behalf of the family as a whole.

The Gujar are between two worlds—the world of the settled dairy farmer and that of the nomad. One world is focused on Ranikot and the mountains and includes the mildly Hindu Gaddis, the other on Pathankot and the plain and the more fundamentalist Hindus. In Pathankot they have a market for their products and the prospect of improving their material standard of living, but they are spat at and reviled as potential allies of separatist Muslims in Jammu-Kashmir. Part of one of their mosques in Pathankot has been appropriated against their will by local Hindus and is now used by them as a shop. In the mountains, by contrast, the Gujar have, as they put it, "the enjoyment of nature," and have worked out a symbiotic relationship with the Gaddis. But here they must live at a subsistence level. However Pathankot and Ranikot continue to be their homes and they do not want to leave. So they commute between both.

"We are Gujar," says Hanif. "We will always be Gujar."

In its aspect of mutually respected jurisdictions (eternal homelands and eternal pasturelands), its out-marrying *jaats*, its *jaat*-defined rather than kinship-defined relationship terminology, its infinitely accommodating stance in relation to one's neighbours, its hospitality to strangers, and its spiritual pluralism, Gujar culture bears a striking resemblance to Australian Aboriginal Renunciative culture. Theoretically we can understand these aspects of their culture as an historical outgrowth of the response to threat posed first by the Mughuls and then by the larger Hindu society. This, perhaps, accounts for the under emphasis on the more monist aspects of mainstream Islamic theology and socio-political organisation. On the other hand, a tolerance for pluralism *under the umbrella* of monism has always been a part of Islamic theology and society, as is a renunciative obligation to strangers and a reverence for the Law, indeed as is a Renunciative creator of it all—Allah himself:

Renunciation in the Qur'an

The *Qur'an* is accepted by Muslims as the eternal speech of Allah as revealed to his prophet Mohammed early in the 7th century A.D. Tradition holds that the words, transported on the sound of a loud, ringing bell, were spoken into Mohammed's ear by an angelic messenger (Adams 1971: 397). As with Gautama the Buddha in Buddhism the person of Mohammed himself is of little significance in this process. He received the texts in a series of trance states and considered himself merely a receptacle for transmission of the word of Allah. The revelations to Mohammed, however, are seen by his followers as the culmination of a prophetic tradition which includes the *Torah* of Moses, the *Zabur* or Pslams of David and the *Testament* of Jesus.

In the discussion of the Renunciative aspects of the *Qur'an* that follows I will be working from the "Tahrike Tarsile Qur'an" edition translated by M. H. Shakir, with respect to the original Arabic.

At first glance it might seem that nothing could be farther removed from the Aboriginal *Amawurrena-alawuduwarra* than the Muslim conception of Allah. Allah is One and undifferentiated; *Amawurrena-alawuduwarra* is pre-differentiated into Forms. *Amawurrena-alawuduwarra* is a kind of spiritual substance that manifests itself on both "sides" of existence. Allah is on the "other side" only. Allah is personal; *Amawurrena-alawuduwarra* is not.

But if we examine the being and nature of Allah in the *Qur'an*, we discover something very interesting. Allah alone in the *Qur'an* is Renunciator, and he alone embodies the necessary prerequisites for Renunciation. He is pure, illuminated, Form. He is transcendent and his creations are immanent. He gives everything to nothing: :

a) Allah as Form or Presence

The seven heavens declare His glory and the earth (too), and those who are in them; and there is not a single thing but glorifies Him with His praise, but you do not understand their glorification, surely He is Forbearing, Forgiving.

Surah XVII, 44

Allah is the light of the heavens and the earth; a likeness of His light is as a niche in which is a lamp, the lamp is in a glass, (and) the glass is as it were a brightly shining star, lit from a blessed olive tree, neither eastern nor western, the oil whereof almost gives light, though fire touch it not—light upon light—Allah guides to his light whom He pleases, and Allah sets forth parables for me, and Allah is cognizant of all things.

Surah XXIV, 35

b) Allah as transcendent, his creations imminent

His is what is in the heavens and what is in the earth and what is between them two and what is beneath the ground.

Surah XX, 6

And whatever is in the heavens and whatever is in the earth is Allah's; and Allah encompasses all things.

Surah IV, 126

Allah, (there is) no god but He, the Everliving, the Self-subsisting by Whom all things subsist.

Surah III, 2

Surely your Lord is Allah, Who created the heavens and the earth in six periods, and He is firm in power, regulating the affair; there is no intercessor except after His permission; this is Allah, your Lord, therefore serve Him;

Surah X, 3

c) Allah as giver of everything from and to Nothing

. . . Allah, the Originator of the heavens and the earth, and He feeds (others) and is not (Himself) fed.

Surah VI, 14

And it is He who sends the winds as good news before His mercy; and We send down pure water from the cloud,
That We may give life thereby to a dead land and give it for drink, out of what we have created, to cattle and many people.

Surah XXV, 48–49

d) Allah as Forming and illuminating his creations:

He it is Who made the sun a shining brightness and the moon a light, and ordained for it mansions that you might know the computation of years and the reckoning. Allah did not create it but with truth; He makes the signs manifest for a people who know.

Surah X, 5

He it is Who shapes you in the wombs as He likes; there is no god but He, the Mighty, the Wise.

Surah III, 6

. . . that I determine for you out of the dust like the form of a bird, then I breathe into it and it becomes a bird with Allah's permission . . .

Surah III, 49

e) Allah's creations as differentiated and potentially Renunciative:

And what He has created in the earth of varied hues; most surely there is a sign in this for a people who are mindful.

Surah XVI, 13

Do you not see that Allah makes the night to enter into the day, and He makes the day to enter into the night, and He has made the sun and the moon subservient (to you); each pursues its course till an appointed time; and that Allah is Aware of what you do?

Surah XXXI, 29

And the two seas are not alike: the one sweet, that subdues thirst by its excessive sweetness, pleasant to drink; and the other salt, that burns by its saltness; yet from each of them you eat fresh flesh and bring forth ornaments which you wear; and you see the ships cleave through it that you may seek of His bounty and that you may be grateful.

Surah XXXV, 12

And one of His signs is that He created mates for you from yourselves that you may find rest in them, and He put between you love and compassion; most surely there are signs in this for a people who reflect.

And one of His signs is the creation of the heavens and the earth and the diversity of your tongues and colors; most surely there are signs in this for the learned.

Surah XXX, 21–
22

And every one has a direction to which he should turn, therefore hasten to (do) good works; wherever you are, Allah will bring you all together; surely Allah has power over all things.

Surah II, 148

We appoint a law and a way, and if Allah had pleased He would have made you (all) a single people, but that He might try you in what He gave you, therefore strive with one another to hasten to virtuous deeds; to Allah is your return, of all (of you), so He will let you know that in which you differed.

Surah V, 48

f) Allah (alone embodying the Renunciative principle), is to be obeyed.

And who has a better religion than he who submits himself entirely to Allah? And he is the doer of good (to others) and follows the faith of Abrahim, the upright one, and Allah took Abrahim as a friend.

Surah IV, 125

Yes! whoever submits himself entirely to Allah and he is the doer of good (to others) he has his reward from his Lord, and there is no fear for him nor shall he grieve.

Surah II, 112

This Book (the *Qur'an*), there is no doubt in it, is a guide to those who guard (against evil).

Those who believe in the unseen and keep up prayer and spend out of what we have given them.

These are on a right course . . .

Surah II, 2–3, 5

g) And the Qur'an instructs:

1. <<Give much to those who have the least.>>

And what will make you comprehend what the
uphill road is?
(It is) the setting free of a slave,
Or the giving of food in a day of hunger
To an orphan, having relationship,
Or to the poor man lying in the dust.
Then he is of those who believe and charge one
another to show patience, and charge one another
to show compassion.
These are the people of the right hand.

Surah XC, 12–18

. . . and give away wealth out of love for Him to the
near of kin and the orphans and the needy and the
wayfarer and the beggars and for (the emancipation
of) the captives, and keep up prayer and pay the
poor-rate; and the performers of their promise
when they make a promise, and the patient in
distress and affliction and in time of conflicts—these
are they who are true (to themselves) and these are
they who guard (against evil).

Surah II, 177

If you give alms openly, it is well, and if you hide it
and give it to the poor, it is better for you;

Surah II, 270–
271

By no means shall you attain righteousness
until you spend (benevolently) out of what you love,
and whatever thing you spend, Allah surely knows
it.

Surah II, 92

Those who spend (benevolently) in ease as in
straitness, and those who restrain (their anger) and
pardon men; and Allah loves the doers of good (to
others).

Surah II, 134

And serve Allah and do not associate any thing
with Him, and be good to the parents and to the near
of kin and the orphans and the needy and the
neighbor of (your) kin and the alien neighbor, and

the companion in a journey and the wayfarer and those who your right hand possesses; surely Allah does not love him who is proud, boastful.

Surah IV, 36

And test the orphans . . . whoever is rich, let him abstain altogether, and whoever is poor, let him eat reasonably.

Surah IV, 6

2. <<Fast, but if not able, give to those who have least.>>

O you who believe! fasting is prescribed for you, as it was prescribed for those before you, so that you may guard (against evil).

For a certain number of days; but whoever among you is sick or on a journey, then (he shall fast) a (like) number of other days; and those who are not able to do it may effect a redemption by feeding a poor man; so whoever does good spontaneously it is better for him; and that you fast is better for you if you know.

Surah II, 183–
184

. . . do not kill while you are on pilgrimage, and whoever among you shall kill it intentionally, the compensation (of it) is the like of what he killed, from the cattle, as two just persons among you shall judge, as an offering to be brought to the Kaaba or the expiation (of it) is the feeding of the poor or the equivalent of it in fasting . . .

Lawful to you is the game of the sea and its food, a provision for you and for travellers, and the game of the land is forbidden to you so long as you are on pilgrimage, and be careful of (your duty to) Allah, to Whom you shall be gathered.

Surah V, 95–96

3) <<Men and women shall be (relatively) equal in their interdependence.>>

And do not covet that by which Allah has made

some of you excel others; men shall have the benefit
of what they earn and women shall have the benefit
of what they earn; and ask Allah of His grace; surely
Allah knows all things.

Surah IV, 32

It is made lawful for you to go into your wives on
the night of the fast; they are an apparel for you and
you are an apparel for them;

Surah II, 187

Men are the maintainers of women because Allah
has made some of them to excel others and because
they spend out of their property; the good women
are therefore obedient, guarding the unseen as Allah
has guarded;

Surah IV, 34

(Women guard the creative source while men provide
for them as they do, as in Aboriginal society)

4) <<Greed and selfishness are abhorred.>>
   (a Renunciative prerequisite for arresting
   technological and economic development in the
   interests of peace and order):

They said: How can he hold kingship over us while
we have a greater right to kingship than he, and he
has not been granted an abundance of wealth? . . .
And the prophet said to them: Surely the sign of
His kingdom is, that there shall come to you the
chest in which there is tranquility from your Lord
and residue of the relics of what the children of Musa
and the children of Haroun have left, the angels
bearing it; most certainly there is a sign in this for
those who believe.

Surah II, 247,
248

And do not swallow up your property among
yourselves by false means, neither seek to gain
access thereby to the judges, so that you may
swallow up a part of the property of men wrongfully

while you know.

Surah II, 188

The love of desires, of women and sons and hoarded treasures of gold and silver and well bred horses and cattle and tilth, is made to seem fair to men; this is the provision of the life of this world; and Allah is He with Whom is the good goal (of life).

Say: Shall I tell you of what is better than these? For those who guard (against evil) are gardens with their Lord, beneath which rivers flow, to abide in them, and pure mates and Allah's pleasure; and Allah sees the servants.

Surah III, 14–15

Those who swallow down usury cannot arise except as one whom Shaitan has prostrated by (his) touch does rise. That is because they say, trading is only like usury; and Allah has allowed trading and forbidden usury;

Allah does not bless usury, and He causes charitable deeds to prosper, and Allah does not love any ungrateful sinner.

Surah II, 275,
276

And whatever you lay out as usury so that it may increase in the property of men, it shall not increase with Allah; and whatever you give in charity, desiring Allah's pleasure—it is these (persons) that shall get manifold.

Surah XXX, 39

And wherefore did you not say you entered your garden: It is as Allah has pleased, there is no power save in Allah? If you consider me to be inferior to you in wealth and children,

Then maybe my Lord will give me what is better than your garden, and send it on a thunderbolt from heaven so that it shall become even ground without plant,

Or its waters should sink down into the ground so that you are unable to find it.

And his wealth was destroyed;

Wealth and children are an adornment of the life of this world; and the ever-abiding, the good works, are better with your Lord in reward and better in expectation.

Surah XVIII, 39–42, 46

5. <<Live in peace with non-Muslims so long as they do not attack you.>>

It may be that Allah will bring about friendship between you and those whom you hold to be your enemies among them; and Allah is Powerful; and Allah is Forgiving, Merciful.

Allah does not forbid you respecting those who have not made war against you on account of your (religion), and have not driven you forth from your homes, that you show them kindness and deal with them justly; surely Allah loves the doers of justice.

Surah LX, 7–8

. . . there should be no hostility except against the oppressor.

Surah II, 193

And whoever defends himself after his being oppressed, these it is against whom there is no way (to blame).

The way (to blame) is only against those who oppress men and revolt in the earth unjustly; these shall have a painful punishment.

Surah XLII, 41–42

Renunciation and its trappings, it seems, are as much a message of the *Qur'an* as they are of the scriptures and teachings of the other "major traditions" we have examined. However, they are, in the *Qur'an*, embodied in the person of Allah and Allah is decidedly "one" and "over and above" everything else. This monism is something that would have to be "subtracted" before we could consider the faith Renunciative in its fully developed Form(s). Perhaps we could proceed like the Gujar and consider the Oneness of Allah himself to be so far removed from human life that He (or It) is basically irrelevant; or, in Buddhist fashion, we could consider Allah as Nothing more than the sum of attributes he represents. considering these attributes, this would bring him back into our Renunciative ken.

Renunciation in Canadian Confederation and in the Way We Play?

Renunciation in Canadian Confederation

One aspect of a fully-developed Renunciative order is an ability to transcend "groundedness" to create institutions that afford people mutually respected jurisdictions in Place without actually having to be in place to enjoy those rights and obligations. The Hebrew idea of a Promised Land is a development in this direction. So too the Aboriginal Land/People, the Gujar Homeland. And also the State as we know it today. Citizenship permits one to enjoy rights and fulfil obligations within one's country while moving between countries in respect of the right and obligations of the people with citizenship there. A state can be conceived at the national level, but it can also be conceived at the local (as in the Greek city states).

In Canada the potential for a Renunciative framework of peace, order, and good government through mutually respected, bounded, jurisdictions was established at Confederation in 1867. Conceived in the circumstances of threat, Canada was born as a grid of abstract, "eternal" jurisdictions bounded in space and containing people and resources in separate but interdependent, part-of-one-in-the-other, if not wholly Renunciative, relation. As my reading of the founding documents of the country and my experiences growing up in Perth/Lanark County/Ontario (Plate 7) confirms, to live in this framework was, for a time at least, to settle differences by "separating and withdrawing" and moving into a relation of institutionalised interdependence as distinct from merging or dissolving into a larger unity or separating into warring factions.

In Canada as originally conceived, people's basic differences were to be settled first and foremost at the Municipal level. And these differences, once established, were to be interrelated through an interrelation of these Municipalities. That is, Canada was to be a federation of Municipalities at two different levels of representation, the Provincial and the National. Section 40 of the British North America Act, 1867, declares,

> 1. Ontario shall be divided into the Counties, Ridings of Counties, Cities, Parts of Cities, and Towns enumerated in the First schedule of this Act, each whereof shall be an Electoral District, each such District as numbered in that Schedule being entitled to return One Member.
> 2. Quebec shall be divided into Sixty-five Electoral Districts, composed of the Sixty-five Electoral Divisions into which Lower Canada is at the passing of this Act divided . . . each such Electoral Division shall be for the purposes of this Act and Electoral District entitled to return One Member.
> 3. Each of the Eighteen Counties of Nova Scotia shall be an Electoral District. The County of Halifax shall be entitled to return two Members, and each of the other Counties One Member.
> 4. Each of the Fourteen Counties into which New Brunswick is divided, including the City and County of St. John, shall be an Electoral District. Each of those Fifteen Electoral Districts shall be entitled to return One Member.

Though Canada was something more than this—there were also Provinces in complex interrelation with a National government—its primary focus was, I think, the Municipality-in-relation. That is, the Municipality was both a bounded jurisdiction in relation to other Municipal jurisdictions (linked first through Province and then through Nation) as well as a forum for bringing together the representatives of lesser bounded jurisdictions at the Town/ship and County levels within. Insofar as these representatives represented the jurisdiction as such and met to work out mutually beneficial arrangements between their respective citizenries, the potential for an Aboriginal/Renunciative way of life was established. Unfortunately, as we will see, this potential was established *despite* the conscious formulations and self-interests of many of its founders. This proved to be its principal weakness.

The founders of Canada created a framework for peace and order when what they were really interested in was rapid economic development. Theirs was an arrangement which took the form it did because they were under threat from elsewhere and when that threat vanished so would their commitment to that arrangement—that is, once they realised its arresting effect on economic development.

"Threat" represents the anticipation of "Nothingness" (*anti-thesis*). The "coming into being" in consequence, through a perception of Form, is *thesis*. The eventual outcome, given time and commitment, is part-of-one-in-the-other relationship through the renunciation of matter between Forms (*plurality*). This is one form of the process of Creation the Aborigines call *gemalyanggerranema*.

Anti-thesis —> thesis

Canada took the form it did, I think, partly because those who formulated it (or who elected representatives to formulate it) had been under siege in the countries from which they sprang, and ended up under threat in the Canada to which they emigrated. The Scots and Irish, for instance, arrived in the aftermath of the Highland Clearances in Scotland and the potato famines of Ireland, their lands there having been cleared for sheep, cattle, and English settlement. Another group, the Loyalists, arrived in Canada from the new United States fleeing the revolutionary war of 1776. Then more Scots and Irish followed from Britain in the aftermath of the Napoleonic Wars. French Canadians (not to mention the aboriginal people who had been here before them all), now found themselves under siege from an English-speaking North America internally subdivided into "American" and "British colonist." Under the circumstances, the Loyalist British colonists seemed the lesser evil compared to the predatory designs of the Americans to the south. Both

Loyalists and French, then, were willing to compromise.

In 1782 the Treaty of Paris afforded the 13 American colonies their formal independence from Britain. When the war ended, General George Washington refused to consider the American Loyalists who had sided with Britain during the war as part of the British regular army. Indeed, the British had not done so themselves, suspecting their true allegiances. They had maintained them in separate regiments wearing uniforms different in colour from those of the regulars. The Treaty of Paris was not to recognise the Loyalists' right to compensation for properties lost during the crisis; the Americans merely agreed to recommend to the various states that the Loyalists be given the opportunity to recover their belongings. Even had the states agreed, which they did not, it would have been a practical impossibility. Committees were already mobilising to "greet" those who tried to return.

Emigration north had begun even before war's end with Loyalists moving into Quebec or to the British stronghold at New York where they hoped to find passage to Nova Scotia. During this period some 3,000 found their way to what became Upper Canada, mainly to the Windsor area and Niagara-on-the-Lake. After the war this trickle became a flood as some 50,000 made their way north.

In 1783 some 10,000 Loyalists, mainly Scots, Aborigines, Quakers and Mennonites arrived on the north shore of the St. Lawrence from New York State. Between the fall of 1782 and November of 1783 some 35,000 arrived in Nova Scotia by sea. The head of each Loyalist family or enlisted man who settled in Britain's remaining North American territories received 100 acres of free land from the Crown. Each additional member of the family received 50. Non-commissioned officers each got 200 acres, subalterns 500 and on up to field officers who received 1,000. In addition, the Crown provided free supplies and the use of army personnel—masons and master builders and the like—to aid in the establishment of settlements.

Nova Scotia's population tripled overnight. The main body of settlers shied away from Halifax where the "Yankees" were concentrated. These were expatriate New Englanders who had come north to service the British garrisons. Instead they moved to the mouth of the St. John river across the Bay of Fundy in what is now New Brunswick where they demanded a separate colony. This was granted in 1784. Cape Breton too acquired that status and became home to mainly Scots Loyalists who came to join an earlier settlement of their countrymen and women there.

Meanwhile, in what would become Upper Canada, army surveyors were in the process of demarcating Lots, Concessions and Townships in anticipation of settlers. And when they arrived they settled according to their "differences": Royal Townships 1 to 8 from Glengarry to Leeds were given over to Johnson's Royal Yorkers, Township 1 to the Catholic Highlanders (most of them Macdonells), Township 2 to Scottish Presbyterians, #3 to German Calvinists, #4 to German Lutherans, #5 to Anglicans and #6–8 to "Major Jessop's Corps." The pattern continued westward all the way to Windsor where a community of French-Canadians was already established.

At this point the territories were part of Quebec and the eastern sector was occupied by French-speaking Catholics living under seigniorial land tenure binding landlord and tenant in mutual obligation. The new, predominantly Protestant, Loyalist settlers petitioned for a partition of the territory and for the establishment of their own, unique, institutions. First and foremost of these was the Town Meeting. A Loyalist petition dated January 1784 at Sorel read as follows (quoted in Cruikshank 1934, pp. 41–42):

And in as much as the said Associated Companies have for years past nobly contended for the support of that Constitution under which they have long Enjoyed Happiness, & for which they have at last sacrificed their All, Tis therefore their Earnest Wish & desire that His excellency for their Better Government & Good order when they arrive at the Place destined for their

Settlement would be pleased to establish among them, a Form of Government as nearly similar to that which they Enjoyed in the Province of New York in the year 1763 as the Remote situation of their new settlement from the seat of Government here will at present Admitt of And that Persons Chosen out of their own Body be appointed & vested with Power before their departure from hence to carry the same into Execution when there.

The town meeting was as necessary to the existence of these "conscious minorities" here in Canada as it had been in the old 13 colonies before. The British, however, realised the role they had played in mobilising revolutionary support in the 13 colonies and were reluctant to allow them. On the other hand, they could not risk losing the allegiance of their new settlers and perhaps their remaining colonies. But neither could these settlers return to their old homes in the United States. So there was a stand-off. The British authorities turned a blind eye to the informal Town Meetings that emerged in the newly surveyed Townships. As far as the Loyalists' petition for a separate colony went, the British granted it immediately. In 1795 a boundary line was established at Point au Baudet near Montreal separating the French-speaking Québecois on one side from the Anglos on the other.

—> *Plurality*

The Constitution Act of 1791 established the British North American Colonies of Upper and Lower Canada (now Ontario and Quebec, respectively), Nova Scotia, Cape Breton, Prince Edward Island and New Brunswick. Each colony would have an elected Legislative Assembly with the power to raise and spend taxes. Beside it would sit an appointed Legislative Council (intended to be hereditary but its titles were never activated) which could scrutinise but not veto legislation from the elected House. Over and above both sat the Governor appointed by the Crown with veto powers over the Legislative

Assembly. He was, however, to govern on the advice of an Executive Council appointed by himself from amongst the colonists. The Act further specified that constituencies were to be demarcated for the purposes of electing representatives to the Assembly. However, at this point, there was no provision for officially sanctioned local governments within their bounds.

The Royal Proclamation of 1792 divided Upper Canada into 19 Counties from Glengarry in the east to Essex in the west, grouped in turn into four Districts—Eastern, Midland, Home, and Western. Each of these jurisdictions was to return representatives to the new Assembly of Upper Canada but was not to contain local governments. However, in the first election almost all of the Governor's candidates—half-pay army officers—were defeated by what he referred to as "people of a lower order." And when the first Assembly of the elected representatives of Upper Canada met at Niagara the first item of business they placed on the agenda was a Bill to authorise the holding of Town Meetings within their respective Ridings. This passed as the Parish and Town Officers Act in 1793 and empowered local councils to appoint a Town Clerk, a Tax Assessor, a Tax Collector, a Roads Manager, a Fence Inspector, and a Poundkeeper and gave the councils the power to control roads, schools, and wildlife management. Taxes, though, were to be gathered and dispensed by the Upper Canadian Assembly.

The War of 1812 was, from the Canadian point of view, a defensive campaign against American aggression. Nevertheless, the Canadians managed to capture the State of Maine and lands west of Detroit in the process of defending themselves. But so anxious were the British to avoid future hostilities with the Americans that they ceded these lands back to them. Indeed, so arrogant were the Americans even in defeat that they demanded lands in Canada that they didn't even hold before the war.

With Canada's borders now secured, the British authorities began to ignore local grievances in the belief that their subjects would now not gravitate toward the United States. The major grievance in Upper Canada were the poor state of roads and canals, the vast tracts of land that had been set aside for the exclusive benefit of the Church of England and the unaccountability of the Governor's Executive Council to a majority in the Assembly, as well as the excessive powers of the appointed Courts of the Quarter Sessions which dominated local governments.

Giving voice to these grievances was a reform-minded member of the Assembly, William Lyon Mackenzie King. The more his demands were ignored, the stronger they became until finally he began to advocate joining the United States. It was at this point that many of his allies in the elected Assembly and most of the populace backed off his cause. On the other hand, were conditions to deteriorate any further in Canada, America may very well have become a practical alternative for many. The grievances had to be addressed and as early as 1832 the Crown began devolving the powers of the Courts of the Quarter Sessions to local councils. When Mackenzie and his counterpart Joseph Papineau in Lower Canada rose in rebellion in 1837 the people did not rise with them. Both men fled the country to the United States where, with some backing, Mackenzie mounted a counter-attack the following year but with no success. In order to prevent further outbreaks like this the British Government dispatched an emissary, Lord Durham, to investigate the basis of discontent in the colonies and recommend as to its alleviation.

The Earl of Durham was a nineteenth-century English liberal and, accordingly, against ethnicity and class but for individual liberty—in particular economic liberty. This led him to view French Canada as an ancient relic, something destined to be swallowed up in a tide of (English of course) individualism. But Durham recognised that this ethnicity was the very thing that prevented French-Canadians from falling into the waiting arms of the United States. Because of it the Americans would not have them! As he said in his *Report* (Toronto: Robert Stanton, p. 113):

There is no people in the world so little likely as that of the United States to sympathise with the real feelings and policy of the French Canadians; no people so little likely to share in their anxiety to preserve ancient and barbarous laws, and to check the industry and improvement of their country, in order to gratify some idle and narrow notion of a petty and visionary nationality.

And yet (p. 12),

The temptations which, in other states of society, led to offences against property, and the passions which prompt to violence, were little known among them. They are mild and kindly, frugal industrious and honest, very sociable, cheerful and hospitable, and distinguished for courtesy and real politeness which pervades every class of society.

The problem was more inter-, rather than intra-, ethnic relations and Durham perceived that this was a major issue dividing Canada. The French version of it prevented the English from dominating the elected Assembly of Lower Canada; the English version of it prevented the French from controlling the appointed Executive Council that advised the Governor.

The union of the two Canadas Durham proposed would merge both ethnicities within a single colony or Province, but it would not do so by dissolving all internal borders. Durham also perceived that a major grievance in Lower Canada was "the utter want of municipal institutions" in the colony "giving the people any control over their local affairs" (p. 50). Durham recommended that Municipal institutions on the Upper Canadian model be the "cornerstone" of the new united colony—indeed of all the colonies (p. 123). It was as if he was saying to French-Canadians, <<you can have your ethnicity so long as you assert it only on a local level>>. In addition,

Durham recommended Responsible Government—an Executive Council responsible to a majority in the elected Assembly, abolition of the Clergy Reserves and the Courts of the Quarter Sessions.

In his lament for this disunited nation we now call Canada Durham located its unique and, in my view, most progressive qualities (p. 65). I quote these at length:

The peculiar geographical character of the Province greatly increases the difficulty of obtaining very accurate information. Its inhabitants, scattered along an extensive frontier, with very imperfect means of communication and with a limited and partial commerce, have, apparently, no unity of interest or opinion. The Province has no great centre with which all the separate parts are connected, and which they are accustomed to follow in sentiment and action; nor is there that habitual intercourse between the inhabitants of different parts of the country, which, by diffusing through all a knowledge of the opinions and interests of each, makes a people one and united, in spite of extent of territory and dispersion of population. Instead of this, there are many petty local centres, the sentiments and the interests (or at least what are fancied to be so) of which, are distinct, and perhaps opposed. It has been stated to me by intelligent persons from England, who had travelled through the Province for purposes of business, that this isolation of the different districts from each other was strikingly apparent in all attempts to acquire information in one district respecting the agricultural and commercial character of another; and that not only were very gross attempts made to deceive an inquirer on these points, but that even the information which had been given in a spirit of perfect good faith, generally turned out to be founded in great misapprehension. From these causes a stranger who visits any one of these local centres, or who does not visit the whole, is almost necessarily ignorant of matters, a true knowledge of which is essential to an accurate comprehension of the real position of parties, and of the political prospects of the country.

On the basis of Durham's recommendations the British Government dispatched Lord Sydenham to the Canadas to negotiate the terms of a union. In the new, in theory, united, Parliament, Upper Canada, now to be renamed "Canada West" and Lower Canada "Canada East," were to be granted an equal number of seats—40. Canada East was granted its own school system, civil law and seigniorial land tenure. This meant separate attorneys-general for the in theory two, now non-existent, colonies. And while there would be no Responsible Government, the new Parliament would control all of the colony's finances in return for guaranteeing the salaries of the appointed administration. Finally, Sydenham recommended to the British Government that Municipal institutions be implemented on a uniform basis throughout the whole colony, as they were currently installed in Upper Canada.

The Act of Union passed through the British Parliament in 1840 implementing all of Sydenham's recommendations but one—Municipal institutions. These the class-conscious and working-class-fearing British authorities would not even grant to their own people. But Sydenham ignored this instruction and in 1841 allowed passage of the Municipal Act establishing District or County governments throughout the new Canada. By the terms of this Act, Town/ship councillors would be returned by popular election and they in turn would select representatives from amongst their number to sit on County or District Council. The Governor would then appoint one of them to act as Warden or head of government at this level. These last two provisions were amended in 1849 in the Baldwin Act that specified that a Reeve and Deputy-Reeve (where numbers warranted) would be elected on the Municipal ballot as voters' representatives to both Town/ship and County governments and that the Warden of the County would be elected by County Council itself. The Baldwin Act also gave County Council the power to raise property taxes, collect tolls from bridges and roads, hire public officials and operate schools and public works. In the end, the British government allowed both pieces of legislation to stand.

The new "union" was, of course, unworkable. An invisible boundary divided the House that separated representatives according to whether they came from constituencies in the old Upper Canada or in the old Lower. A principle of "double majority" evolved in which laws designed primarily for people in constituencies in one grouping could pass only with a majority vote of representatives from that grouping. Though Sydenham did his best to exclude French-Canadians from his appointed Executive Council his successors Baghot, Metcalfe, and Cathcart allowed them in under pressure from representatives on both (in theory non-existent) sides of the House.

In 1845 Britain was again preparing its Canadian colonies for war, again with the United States, this time over a boundary dispute on the west coast in sparsely populated British Columbia. The Americans had declared their Manifest Destiny to rule over the entire continent and wished a little more latitude for their population ("54/40 or fight"). It was under these circumstances that the government of the "united" Canadas began to break down.

With the achievement of Responsible Government in 1848 under which the powers of government devolved from the Governor to a majority in the House, the House became increasingly factionalised as special interests emerged and entered into coalition agreements so as to form a majority. These coalitions cut across the East-West division and grouped representatives first as Tory or Reformer, then as reformed-Tory and reformed-Reformer and so on as new issues arose. One particular coalition combination finally brought the business of the House to a standstill. This was a "reform the Reformers" movement led by Malcolm Cameron (of Perth and later Sarnia) on the Canada West side, and a reformist-nationalist movement led by A. A. Dorion on the Canada East side. They advocated abolition of the Clergy Reserves and Seigniorial land tenure (in Canada East) and wanted an appointed Legislative Council (Senate) with limited term rather than life appointments. Though they did not have enough support to form a majority they so depleted mainstream Tory and Reform ranks that neither was able to form a government. Finally, in 1857, a general election returned a majority of Conservatives from Canada East and a majority of reformers from Canada West. Now no one could predict the outcome of a vote on any issue.

While Parliament was coming to a standstill, the Americans were making their presence felt along the British North American border. American troops had been moved adjacent to Manitoba ostensibly to protect the interests of their merchants who were trading in the region; Yankee fortune-hunters had flooded into the Yukon in search of gold, and the British feared they would call for the annexation of that territory to the States. While the outbreak of civil war in the U.S. temporarily relieved the pressure, it only served to increase Canadian anxieties. The British had come out mildly in favour of the south ostensibly to protect their cotton interests there. A victorious north, its armies already mobilised, might turn its attention northward to Britain's remaining possession in North America.

In 1864, at the very climax of the American Civil War, Alexander Morris, Member for Lanark, successfully negotiated a coalition agreement between Tory leader John A. MacDonald and Reform leader George Brown committed to working out a new relationship between the two supposedly non-existent Canadas. Provincial boundaries would be reintroduced and a third tier of government would come into existence over and above the two. There was, however, disagreement as to how this third tier should be constituted, some arguing for an equal number of seats for both Canadas, others for representation according to a Province's share of total population. Under the latter scheme Canada West would gain a majority as the census showed that its population now outnumbered that of Canada East some 600,000 to 400,000.

At the same time as the terms of this coalition were being worked out the Maritime Provinces were in the midst of planning their own accord. They were to meet at Charlottetown P.E.I. in September of 1864 and the Canadian government asked if they could attend to discuss the possibility of a new arrangement involving them all. They did and agreed to meet in Quebec City later that August with absent Newfoundland invited to attend. At Quebec an agreement was reached.

Predictably under the circumstances of American threat, it was the governments of the colonies that did *not* border on the United States, namely, Prince Edward Island and Newfoundland, that rejected the proposal (indeed the Newfoundland delegates seem not to have submitted them to their legislature at all). New Brunswick ratified them, but then the government that did was defeated in a subsequent election. The Nova Scotia legislature seemed set to reject. But then if the Americans didn't arrive again in the nick of time to save the day.

In 1886 Irish-American Fenians struck at border points in the eastern Townships of Quebec and southern Ontario. As advocates of the Irish cause in the Old Country they had hoped to establish a second front in Canada, thereby diverting British troops to North America and paving the way for a general uprising in Ireland. But even the Irish in Canada did not respond to this call and the raids were repulsed. As a result of the threat, however, Nova Scotia quickly ratified the terms of the proposed Confederation, a new government was ushered into New Brunswick and it was ratified. On July 1, 1867, the new Dominion of Canada was proclaimed. It was to have been called "The Kingdom of Canada" but the name was changed so as not to offend the Americans.

In this new Dominion, Quebec's seats were to be fixed at 65 and the other Provinces' seats allowed to vary according to how their populations compared to Quebec's. No Province was to lose seats unless its population declined by more than

1/20th of the average Provincial population. This concern for protecting the integrity of "constituency" boundaries only makes sense once you realise that the Municipalities were to be the units of representation in the new Dominion (Section 40). Indeed, the Canadian delegates impressed on their Maritime counterparts the need for a uniform system of Municipal institutions in their region on the Canadian model if the arrangement was to work.

Confederation, then, was in many ways the duplication of the Municipal principle established in the Baldwin Act but at a higher level. As constituents were represented in Town/ship and County Councils, so now they would be represented in County constituencies (or comparable units) in Province and Nation. So precise, in fact, was the parallel that the same elected representative was permitted to serve in both governments, just as the Reeve served at the Town/ship and County levels. If you wanted to locate a truly significant difference from the American model, this would be it. There is no mention of Municipal institutions in the American Constitution. None at all. It is as if this level of existence was for all intents and purposes dissolved into higher levels of unification with Union. Though local governments remained in the new United States, they were not interrelated in any systematic fashion either in relation to each other or in wider spheres of jurisdiction.

If political jurisdictions in the Dominion of Canada were to be mutually embedded, powers vested in the various levels of government were to be as much overlapping and concurrent as separated in the American sense. Overlap and concurrence mean that the parties involved must take each other's interests into account *before* making a decision; separation of powers and checks and balances means that decisions are reached separately by each body and negotiations only entered into at the prospect of defeat. Overlap and concurrence, as we saw in relation to the concept of love in Christian Scriptures, isn't separation, it isn't unity, but it isn't quite part-of-one-in-the-other, Renunciative, relationship either. But it is close.

In the Canadian system, the Municipalities' powers were to be fixed by the Provinces, but then the Municipalities were to be the units of representation there. The Provinces were to be separate from the Dominion, but then the Municipalities were to be the units of representation there too. To the Dominion Government went the powers of Peace, Order, and Good government; the Provinces were to hold jurisdiction over property and civil rights. But with property embedded in jurisdictions at all levels and peace and order also a matter of civil rights, where one jurisdiction began and the other ended was (intended to be) unclear. The Provinces were granted control over their natural resources but the Dominion controlled their movement between Provinces and out of the country. Both levels of government (and in some areas the Municipalities) were to operate their own prison systems, their own courts, legislate their own criminal laws, regulate companies within their bounds and raise their own taxes. Both levels had their own Governors representing the Crown, both shared responsibility for agriculture and immigration. In respect of other matters, however, a division of powers was apparent: the Provinces would control hospitals, shipping, railways, canals, and telegraphs, and the Dominion would control fisheries, the money supply, banks, Aboriginal affairs, the military and other functions. The National government was to control inter-provincial trade and commerce and oversee completion of the inter-colonial railway linking the Maritimes to Quebec and Ontario (and later British Columbia). Section 118 of the Act also empowered the National government to distribute fixed and per capita grants to the Provinces "for the Support of their Governments and Legislatures." Nor was there strict equality here: special needs could mean special entitlements (Section 19).

Beside the elected Parliament was a Senate appointed by that Parliament. But it was to be constituted on a regional not a Provincial basis, though with (token) reference to the Municipalities. Each region (the Maritimes, Ontario, Quebec and the West when it joined) was to have 24 seats. The purpose of the Senate was not so much to check and balance the elected House but rather to act as a "House of sober second thought," reviewing legislation from a more didactic point of view than was possible in the elected Assembly.

Significantly (as significant as the lack of mention of Municipal Institutions in the American Constitution), there is no mention of Cabinet Government or Prime Ministers in the British North America Act. Canada was the work of a Coalition and was to herald the end of faction. Cabinet government is government by faction, by a special interest with a majority in the House. A Prime Minister is the head of the governing faction; a coalition, by contrast, has no single head.

Confederation was indeed, as my late friend and colleague John Holmes put it to a school principal's conference in Newmarket Ontario in 1977 "a framework of peace, order and good government to serve the needs of diverse colonies of people and allow them to collaborate" (personal communication):

> Their aim was not national unity, whatever that means. It was the provision of a more secure structure in which people could breathe as Nova Scotians or Quebeckers or British Columbians . . . the central principal was a recognition that our problem was not with demons or traitors, reactionaries and Bolsheviks, good guys and bad guys. We accepted the fact that for honest reasons and with legitimately differing interests people have different perspectives. What we sought were frameworks not for confrontations but for accommodation.

Unlike the Americans, or later the Soviets, Canadians did not try to make a New World Order but rather tried to remake the Old World Order (which included an Empire of Nations) in a new way.

In the April 1865 issue of *The Westminister Review*, a

British Journal, Canadian constitutional lawyer W. A. Foster had this to say about the proposed Dominion (*Canada First Movement,* p. 140):

> The complexity inherent in all federations will be increased by the fact of this one being of colonies. Above their government and vested with supreme authority, is the authority of Parliament and the Queen; below will be that of the lieutenant-governors of the Provinces, deriving their appointment and receiving their pay from the federal executive. Under this tertiary authority, in Canada at least, there prevails an elaborate and expensive, because extravagant, gradation of municipalities, beginning with the village and ending with the aggregation of towns and townships which form the County municipality.

As regards this "extravagance," Foster goes on to point out, "There was no choice in the matter. Confederation would not have proceeded without it."

If one reads the *Confederation Debates in the Province of Canada, 1865* (P. B. Waite ed., 1977), one gains the distinct impression that what was coming together here was something far from familiar given the models of political organisation current at the time. Foster, above, almost seems to be apologising for it. Confederation was not a legislative union at the National level without Provincial subdivisions. Nor was it a federation of Provinces as such or a combination of the two as was the American system (legislative in respect of the House of Representatives, federal in respect of the Congress). It *was* a federation—but a *Municipal* federation, something unheard of at the time. For this was a society that would be built from the ground up rather than the top down. But its creators were only dimly aware of what they had accomplished and why. "In the circumstances that led to Confederation," wrote P. B. Waite (p. vi), "some Canadians discerned the hand of God":

. . . the June coalition uniting men bitterly opposed, the accident of the Charlottetown Conference . . . the dazzling success of Canadians at Quebec, and all when the American union seemed broken in the holocaust of war. There were not a few in Parliament who vowed belief about the divine influence in Confederation.

Unfortunately this influence was not to last and today little remains of the original "Municipal focus" and accommodating spirit of the original. But it could be renewed and, with the proper "grounding" in a more transcendent awareness of boundaryForm, prepare the way for a truly Renunciative development if applied as well to other States and relations between States.

*   *   *   *

Renunciation in Sunday Morning Hockey

Finally, my favourite example of Renunciation: an example in which I participate as often as possible. This is Sunday Morning Hockey in my hometown of Perth, Lanark County, Ontario, one of those jurisdictions established in Canadian confederation. Ice hockey as an example of the lifeway of Renunciation? Indeed, as a *perfect* example of it? You must be kidding, you must be saying. Hockey is mayhem and violence— grown-up boys playing with their toys? It's two teams fighting each other to shoot the puck into their opponents' net, bashing and crashing each other in the process. And you are right. But that's Saturday night or N.H.L. hockey. I'm thinking, though, of Sunday Morning Hockey. You know, "*For years now, Bill and Greg and the lads have been getting together every Sunday Morning down at the Community Centre to engage in a little competition with the puck.*" We're 20 in all and, apart from Bill, Greg, Corky, Ryan, and a few others we're not very good. Some, though, were—like Gerry. But we have one saving grace—we try! The way we try is the lifeway of Renunciation. And the joy we experience in trying the way we do is what confirms that Renunciation is indeed present.

It all started over a decade ago when a bunch of the lads from the Brown Shoe and the Catholic School decided they'd had enough of Town League competitive hockey and wanted a more "civilised" alternative. So they started Sunday Morning Hockey. We represent all walks of life, from factory workers to tradesmen, to professionals, teachers, businessmen, "pseudos" (lads who have retired here on their ass-ets), and even the odd Professor. Half are Catholics and the other half of us Protestants or Indifferents. Right off, the Catholics have the upper hand. That's because they originally created the schedule. All games are played between 10 and 11:30 on Sunday Morning or just after Morning Mass but during the Protestant services at 11. For the Protestants, then, it's either Church or Hockey. Obviously we chose Hockey. Actually there's little difference between the two, except that Hockey may be the more truly Christian, that is more wholly Renunciative, institution.

Now you might wonder how dividing grown men up into two teams, putting lethal weapons in their hands and telling them to fight over a puck would have any other implications than mayhem and violence. Normally these would be the implications, but our game is different. You see, we play with Divine guidance. Our game is played through two Divine Forms, the Red and the Green Sweaters (Plate 8) It's the Sweaters that "compete," not the players inside them. Every week the Red Sweaters line up for the face-off in the zone to the west, the Green Sweaters in the Zone to the east. Then the puck is dropped and the Sweaters play until one team of them gets five goals. Then the Sweaters change ends but leave their goalies where they are and we play again. And if one Sweater starts winning too many games the Sweaters temporarily change some of the players around inside them, one from Green to a Red, one from Red to a Green and it's back to three games to two for Red one week, three games to two for Green the next.

Of course there are other things at work here too. In our game we have also come to some "understandings"—no slapshots and no bodychecks. Nothing defeats the point of the game more than disabling injuries. It not only means that you can't play, but that you may not be able to work either. Loft a puck too high, particularly if there's someone between you and the goalie, take a run at somebody (except if it's Paul Brisebois), and you get a warning "Watch it!" Do it again and you get an ultimatum: "Don't do it again!" A third time and you get a directive: "Don't you think you should be moving up to the Town League where your skills will be more appreciated?" The Town League is for players who haven't yet received Divine Grace—actually, I should have said "was." The Town League was eventually disbanded because it was getting a bit too rough, but then regrouped as the "Gentlemen's League" with understandings similar to our own. In between us and the Gentlemen's League is the "Geritol League" for those who are unable to get into Sunday Morning Hockey.

I won't say it's impossible to get into Sunday Morning Hockey, but the spares' list currently outnumbers the players on both teams. That's because we keep on adding new applicants each year without any vacancies appearing. They have to settle for the odd game here and there if one of us has to be away. Considering that we are training our children to succeed us in the future, the situation doesn't look like easing up for at least a generation or two. Some of the spares are taking the hint and moving to found new games of their own. Occasionally, however, someone from Sunday Morning does "die" of old age and a position opens up. It's then we bring in someone from the spares' list for a trial period to see if our judgement was right and he really is a candidate for conversion.

Successfully curb your excesses out there on the ice and you're honoured with an epithet. Me? I'm "The Hacker," which is just an affectionate way of saying, "Don't!" In the 10 years I've played, there's only been one serious injury, Peter Whitehead, who forgot to stop skating after taking a shot on the net when he broke in all alone on the goalie. Crashed into the boards and separated his shoulder. The only call to higher places came when this one lad arrived at the game slightly inebriated (on a Sunday morning) and caught someone with a puck around the eye. The reason we knew he was inebriated was because he drove to the rink in full equipment and wearing his skates. Sure what he did was an accident, but one that could reoccur with debilitating regularity under the circumstances. But even here, the lad realised this and retired himself. The only excesses we're reluctant to curb were those of Bob Thomas when he was manager of the rink. Cold showers and a freezing dressing room were not our idea of a good time after the game. But now that he's switched jobs we can clear up a few misunderstandings.

The job of the better players in Sunday Morning Hockey is to keep the game moving and the understandings in mind, all the while improving the standard of play, particularly among lesser lights like myself. Before we were called to Sunday Morning Hockey few of us had played anything more than river hockey down on the Tay when we were kids. Maybe a year or two of Pee-Wee but that was it. The better players, then, have their work cut out for them. First step is to make us look good, then, once we get the hang of it, to make us actually *be* good of our own accord. They start by putting us in the position we are best at regardless of whether anyone else on the team is better at that position. Then, once in position, a perfect pass when by some gross error of misjudgement you find yourself parked all alone in front of the net, can do wonders for your confidence— in my case if the pass is perfect and the goal tender is out of position (and it *isn't* Oscar Cordick. What I learned over time and repeated experience was that the reason I was all alone out there was because Bill Doyle had taken the play where he wanted it to go. Now I know where to be when he's doing it. I also know what it means to be able to take the play where you want it to go, even if I can't do it myself. This breeds respect.

You might think that this would lead to a situation where the poorer players all got better, but the better players stayed the same, or even got worse from lack of competition. Not so. Without the mindless violence to inhibit their play they can concentrate on perfecting their passes, their stick handling skills and play-making techniques. Come to think of it, isn't this what hockey's supposed to be all about?

With the better players controlling the flow of the game, and if we all keep our understandings constantly in mind, it's not too difficult to have it come out three games to two for Green one week and the other way around the next. Things only start getting complicated when some of the poorer players like myself or Ronnie Dickson start improving—like me learning how to shift to the right rather than the left to get around Jim Farrell; like Ronnie learning how to skate. Then we start interfering with the play—with the ability of the better players to control its flow. Crisis comes when the better players have to impress themselves on the game too much in order to be able to maintain the balance of wins and losses, or when the rest of us become so enamoured with our new-found abilities that we forget about the understandings. It's then that some of the Sweaters have to change bodies.

It's amazing what a change of team-mates can do to what you thought were your own newly-developed individual skills. It takes even the best of players time to adjust to a new set of gross inadequacies, and until they do to yours, you look positively atrocious. The experience is usually enough to curb your enthusiasm and it's back to three games to two for Red one week . . .

I should also add that by the last Sunday of the season everything is always "all even up to this point and it all boils down to one last Sunday Morning series." That series always ends in a tie, that is, one game for the Red, one game for the Green with the third game tied as the clock runs out. I don't know how we do it because none of it is conscious, but we do. I have a sneaking suspicion that Bill on the Red and Greg on the Green don't always keep proper track of the score .

As you must have realised by now, our game is only for the discriminating in taste. If you're watching from the sidelines you'll sense a certain monotony. No one seems to look all that good, and none all that bad. The play flows up and down the ice without a sense of urgency. But these are players who know each other's moves instinctively. If you're really observant, you might notice the half dozen truly great plays a game it takes to keep it all working this way. In principle, if not in level of execution, it's not that different from Team Canada versus the Russians.

The game, of course, has altered somewhat since its inception. We first began without goalies. Then, it was five games to three for Green one week, five games to three for Red the next. Goalies stepped up the pace a bit and also led us to wear some basic equipment—like shin pads and cups. Hoisting was permitted but not slapshots. As the all-round level of ability improved, the pace stepped up some more. Some of the players began wearing proper pants and helmets, though it wasn't really necessary. Others continued the old way. Then players began to form an attachment to their Sweaters, so much so that even when a player exchanged his for the other side's he still thought of himself (and was thought of by others) as, say, a Red player playing for the Green team. Donnie Currie switched his to Green seven years ago and he's still considered "really one of us."

So our game isn't really competitive, and it isn't really co-operative. I'll let Jimmy Buker explain what it is: our line was sitting on the bench after a shift with the score 4 to 1 for Green. We had already lost the first game 5 to 0. Jimmy was trying to exhort us to better things. "I don't mean we should try to be more competitive," he explained. "I mean we should try to keep up our end of the game." The level of our play was necessary to the level of theirs. If ours deteriorated, eventually theirs would too.

Actually, the main point of Sunday Morning Hockey is to get back to the dressing room for a beer after the game. The most popular player on either team for a long time was Jim Farrell. This was because he brought the Labatt's '50. Not that everyone liked '50, but everyone liked its being brought. If he will bring it, he can choose it. That's why Jim always looked so good out on the ice—we were always coughing up the puck to him and steering clear of his rushes, just to make sure he'd come back every week.

To give you some indication of how important the dressing room is, one week we learned that our ice time the following Sunday would be preempted by a figure skating competition. "Well, then, would you book the dressing room for us instead?", shot back one of the lads.

The dressing room's only place you're going to bump into somebody from the Hoof and Boot (Brown Shoe), the Trash and Can (Canadian Tire), the High School or wherever unless you're directly connected to them as a friend or a relative. And if you don't bump into them, just how are you going to find out who's been doing what to whom around town and in the country all week?

The problem at this point is that I really can't let you in past the dressing room door. Too revealing. Would be a breach of trust. Unless, of course, it just involved stories about me. Perhaps in that case a little peek wouldn't hurt.

If switching Sweaters can undermine your confidence, the dressing room can kill it altogether.

This one Sunday Jim and Ron were all agog about their recent trip to Toronto or the Little Apple (or Big Lemon, depending on your taste). They were going on about inadvertently stumbling into a gay bar and not being sure whether they'd get out unscathed, about the bright lights and very tall buildings when Greg McNally piped up, "Is that how come you got sunburned?" "Sunburned?" "Yes, on the roof of your mouth."

The image of two country bumpkins walking about the big city, their mouths agape at the sight of skyscrapers was too vivid for any of us to ignore. It's quite a sight seeing 18 grown men in various stages of undress rolling on the floor and crying with laughter. But we were. Stopped the conversation dead for half-an-hour. But then if a week later Ron wasn't coming back with,

"No need for me to go south this winter. Already got my tan in Toronto."

But you just don't come out with this to someone who hasn't been there with you before. Oops, I've gone and done it— let you in on something that didn't have me as its object. Sorry Ron and Jim, but Greg's to blame.

I can, however, talk about what we don't talk about and that's sex (in the sense of who's doing what to whom), religion (in the sense of passing judgement on any version of it), and politics (in any sense at all). No one is going to change anyone's mind on any of these subjects in the space of a conversation anyway, and you never know who might be connected to whom outside the dressing room, so why bring them up? Mere mention is likely to lead to a severing of connections. You can add "insult" to "injury" on our list of understandings. After all, we get along despite our various opinions of Liberals, of whether it's the Catholics and not the Protestants who are going straight to hell, or of the evils of American investment:

"At least you could have waited until he left the room before bringing it up! Shouldn't you be moving up a notch or two to the Town League?"

I've only seen this understanding breached twice, and since both instances involved me, I can tell you about it. They both involved a newcomer to Town through the Brown Shoe connection.

Myself and this other fellow, well, our dads don't get along all that well. In fact, they think they're enemies; and by Perth standards I suppose they are (they'd be mere rivals in Toronto). It's common knowledge. Both of us are aware of the problem, but we don't let it interfere with our own relationship. We both play for the Red team—or at least did. Well one Sunday Fred sits down and opens up a beer, turns to me with Harry present and says,

"Norm (my dad) and Joe (his dad) been at it again this week I hear."

Well you could have heard a pin drop on Gore Street, as the

saying goes.

Then Greg pipes up with something about Jimmy Buker letting one go at 90 miles an hour but since it hadn't left the ice we really couldn't call it a slap-shot and things went elsewhere from there. Fred got the message. It almost never happened again.

Then, a few weeks later, we had just come off the ice after a shift. Fred sits down beside one of the teachers from the Separate School and says, right out of the blue,

"I don't agree with the idea of extending separate school funding. There should be just one public school system. We should all be the same."

"Well, we're not," replied the tight-lipped teacher as he headed over the boards and onto the ice, giving us an immediate man advantage.

Fred, it seems, had spent too much time in the States.

Sunday Morning Hockey is just a game, right? Just a bunch of the lads getting together every week for a bit of fun. Well, yes and no. If you look more closely you'll see there's a lot more going on here. In the first place, there's no referee. Referees would be there to prevent the violence implicit in the very nature of the game from getting out of hand. Refereed hockey is crisis-management hockey. In our game we're beyond crisis-management to prevention. Yet, as I've said, we're two teams competing at high speeds in narrow confines. How do you account for this? As I said, I think it has a lot to do with the Sweaters.

"Red" and "Green" may be pitted against one another as two Sweaters of different colours but the players inside the Sweaters aren't opposed because the Sweaters keep shifting them about, one in the other. This is the Green goalie going over to the Red team and the Red goalie going over to the Green after every game; it is the Red player on temporary loan to the Green team and vice versa to correct any imbalances. When one of us or a team of us moves, then, it's not to be incorporated as a Red player into Green or a Green player into

Red. It's rather to be hosted or federated as a Red player temporarily on loan to the Green Team and vice versa. Looked at another way, it's a Red player from the Red zone to the east temporarily visiting the Green players and the zone to the west to help them out.

In all cases the same principle is at work: part of the one side is placed in the other and vice versa without loss of integrity—of Sweater—of either. Consequently, to destroy "them" would be to destroy a part of ourselves.

Given these factors, then, we don't defend as aggressively as we might when they come in over our blue line to "attack" us in our Red defensive zone; we don't attack them as aggressively as we might when we come over their blue line to "attack" them in their Green defensive zone. In N.H.L. hockey, by contrast, the aim of the game is to expand one's zone into the other's—literally blanket it with players until you score a goal. Here their defensive zone is your offensive zone.

In Sunday Morning Hockey, since we're not defending or attacking, again in contrast to N.H.L. hockey, gone is the need for all that protective equipment. Technological change, then, becomes unnecessary. Of course we have to take some precautions against "chance," hence shin pads and cups.

As I said, in our game you can't really say we're co-operating and we're not competing either. We're rather accommodating, one to the other. The result is three games to two for Green one week, three games to two for Red the next, all tied at the end of the season.

Of course, there are other moderating factors at work as well: the fact that we've come to know each other so well over the years, the fact that we come from the same community. But then the same could be said of players in the Town League (now Gentleman's League) and Geritol, yet their play is far more chippy than ours. The players here also change sweaters but it's on a *yearly* basis. That is, each player is incorporated into a new team each season. The relation between the teams as competing entities thus remains the same. In their case, local ties account for why their game is merely chippy and not violent. Still, they require referees. Ours, by contrast, requires neither referees nor prior local ties. Ours is the appropriate game for keeping the peace between friends and establishing it between strangers—even enemies.

Consider the range of differences we, as players and spares, in fact represent. These are nothing if not fundamental, namely differences of religion, ethnicity, and class. I am referring of course to the fact that we are Protestants and Catholics or Indifferents, Scotch/English and Irish in background (it's the community that's narrow in this respect, not us), owners and workers and public servants and various subdivisions of these differences. In fact, about the only major difference we don't contain is between male and female. That's because the women choose to separate out into a different game on their own, which is just as well because we're not certain that even our Sweaters can handle such an extreme incompatibility as this one. Nevertheless they'd be welcome to come on to our spares' list and wait for a Sweater to become vacant just like anyone else.

Now it's not that these differences have been eradicated or eliminated before they come to the game—the incident over separate school funding illustrates that. The differences are still there and clung to tenaciously. It's just that we've found a way to transcend them while leaving them more or less intact. But now they're not extreme.

There's also a peculiar mode of thought going on in our game. When trouble does look like brewing, such as when Paul Brisebois starts forgetting he really is just a Green player on temporary loan to the Red team (getting more temporary all the time) and begins becoming more and more attached to his new Sweater, we "back off." What thought is doing is temporarily removing the Sweaters and the player-loans between them to see what really lies below the surface. And when it discovers that all hell will break loose without them, it sends out the message "separate and withdraw." It's a message that in practical terms has a certain survival value. We avoid Brisey even if he doesn't know enough to avoid us. This is a mode of thought appropriate to a human environment of institutionally, Sweater-mediated, ties such as our game and Aboriginal Renunciative society represents.

Our accomplishment is reflected in the logo chosen to symbolise Sunday Morning Hockey on our Sweaters, two crossed sticks separating the letters S M from H L (Sunday Morning Hockey League) enclosing a segment of the sun. Just a picture, right? Well, yes and no. It's two lines enclosing part of a circle. Line is the most efficient, elegant, way of indicating boundary, two-sidedness, as well as exclusive association with the same boundary over time (as in passing your boundary, your Sweater, from father to child). Circle, by contrast, expresses unity, gravitation towards a centre, pent-up energy waiting to explode, incorporation as "my team" as opposed to "your team." In Sunday Morning Hockey, line compartment-alises or subdues circle and situates it as one in a block of four grouped into two. That's separation into interdependence—the way we play. Not that there's anything wrong with N.H.L. hockey as such. I enjoy watching it myself. It's only when it becomes a model for life outside the arena that we have a problem. Which means, today, we have a problem.

Sunday Morning Hockey is based on the same principles as a society that achieved peaceful co-existence on a continent-wide basis for many thousands of years—that of the Australian Aborigines. There, though, the Sweaters were "Promised Lands," the material parts-of-one-in-the-other between them were resources bounded exclusively for the purpose, men and women on marriage, ceremonial items and symbols.

VII

Conclusion

It is much easier to find evidence of the lifeway of Renunciation in the present than in the past. The difficulty is that the lifeway in question leaves little in the way of material remains, hence little in the way of a record of its existence. People living according to the lifeway of Renunciation have either arrested technological development at a particular stage of its progress or have rejected development outright and set about "regressing." Renunciative societies are in a very real sense "invisible Realities" whose existence must be deduced, not induced, from material evidence. Archaeology has contributed little to their discovery by focusing on material remains as such as the basis of their discipline. The people who leave the most "data" behind in the way of material evidence for archaeologists to find are, of course, the ones who produce the most material evidence namely the accumulators and incorporators—the predators—and they have little to teach us except how to destroy others and, eventually, themselves. The peaceful, by contrast, are more or less invisible to history.

The problem of searching for evidence of Renunciation in the Aboriginal sense in the texts left by people is that if these texts were likely composed by people in one ambience of awareness (monism) being drawn into another (pluralism), the terms of the latter will be very difficult to formulate, being as they are beyond the parameters of their previous experience. Communicating what exactly this new thing *is* that they are now "on about" will be very problematic indeed. Perhaps this explains the ambiguities and incompletenesses in the sacred texts of the Hebrews, the Christians, the Muslims, the Hindus, and the Buddhists, as far as articulating the terms of Renunciation goes. Perhaps this was the source of the confusion on the part of the Fathers of Canadian Confederation as to what they were formulating when they came up with the British North America Act.

Perhaps the founders were clear but their followers were not; and it was the followers in most cases who did most of the recording.

*   *   *   *

A key insight that emerges out of this discussion of the lifeway of Renunciation and its manifestation in various traditions is the relationship it posits between peace and order and economic and technological development. The Aboriginal evidence suggests, and the insights of the major religious traditions seem to support the view that the relationship between them is an inverse one. That is, the more you have of the one the less you have of the other. This is because the competitive, individualist/corporatist forces that fuel the one (economic and technological development) is the very one that undermines the other (peace and order). This is not to say that competitive individualism/corporatism is the *only* force behind economic and technological development, but it is to say that it is the major force behind rapid *rates of change* in economy and technology.

Another key insight that emerges from this discussion of the lifeway of Renunciation is the paradox of re/Creation. The very engine of progress that would destroy the lifeway of Renunciation contains within itself the prerequisites for its emergence. In the circumstances of competition, selfishness, and domination the "losers" in the struggle are drawn together in a spirit of accommodation as an alternative to their predicament. Vision *outside* the bounds of the mainstream tradition is now possible; reason deduces the implications for a new way of life and imagination formulates the possibility.

I put it that one of the major paradoxes, if not *the* major paradox of the human condition, is the perpetrator-become-victim-become-perpetrator cycle. How to emerge out of the situation of victim while still face-to-face with the source of the perpetrators of your predicament? To respond passively and peacefully means continued oppression. To fight back and overthrow the source of that oppression—to appropriate what your oppressors have, namely wealth and power—is to enter yourself into the perpetrator stream of history and, if victorious in the struggle, to transform those who formerly oppressed you into victims.

I cannot help but think of the biblical account of Jesus' agony on the cross and his apparent feeling of abandonment by his "Father" in this connection. Perhaps this dramatisation reflects the realisation that even the unconditional love one extends to one's enemies cannot transcend the paradox in question, as one may have been led to believe. Perhaps that is why the Jesus of Scriptures resigned himself to a peaceable kingdom only in heaven—though leaving open the possibility of an earthly transformation in the apocalyptic upheaval of his return.

Recognising the "eternal nature" of the paradox in question (which Aborigines are now experiencing at the hands of Europeans), the only way out, it seems to me, is for the *oppressors*, not the victims, to grasp its nature, anticipate their own demise, and to prevent it from happening by providing the "have nots" with what they need *before they come to demand it*. In other words, it is in the interests of both the "haves" and "have nots" to arrest the forces of technological progress at their current stage of development in the interests of interdependence, co-determination, and peace and order through mutual accommodation while providing adequate and sustainable existence for all. This would be another expression of the *anti-thesis* —> *thesis* —> *plurality* scenario where *anti-thesis* is the prospect of death or "material-less-ness," *thesis* is "my continued existence," and *plurality* is Renunciation of the means of existence from me to you.

The paradox eliminated (or rather transcended), implementation of the lifeway of Renunciation means reversing the very order of our present priorities away from science and technology toward the arts and humanities. Following the Aboriginal example, this would be to enhance our sensitivity to the living world around and within us, to get in touch with the Presences that define us as something more than "carbon-based entities," that define the animate and inanimate "others" around us as something more than objects to be exploited for our own gain. This would be to see, hear, feel, the Presence of everything, experience the giving up of a part of yourself to those with whom we interact, to feel the relief of detachment from material things that would enable you to give everything of something you have to someone who has it not.

Apart from education in the means of perception (music, art, meditation), developing this awareness would entail adopting a certain personal lifestyle approximating that of the Aborigines prior to contact: no polluting intrusions into the body—no alcohol, no drugs, no tobacco (a prescription today's Australian Aborigines in particular would find hard to reintroduce); a diet low in red meat, high in fish, root vegetables and fruit; regular physical exercise; creativity (art, letters, and, most importantly, music, particularly polyphonic, multi-dimensional music). Live this way and you will begin to cultivate a sense of the aesthetic, a sense of the Formal, the proportional, a sense of the "other" outside yourself—perhaps even a sense of the spiritual—and you will see/hear the basis of Renunciation for yourself.

At an institutional level, re-create the political jurisdictions within which we govern ourselves in concert with others according to the principle of differentiate and federate rather than unite and incorporate. Maintain systems of governance close to people on the ground by internally subdividing existing jurisdictions (the State, the Province, the Municipality) when they become too large, too remote, and too out of control. The initial terms of Canadian confederation and the process of its formation are a good blueprint here. But political jurisdictions need not be bounded Spaces. They may be any boundable differences such as a class, an ethnicity, a creed to be represented as such and accommodated one to the other. Whether these institutions turn into "churches" rather than "states" will depend on the degree of "transcendence" achieved in the Formation in question.

But whether we realise Renunciation or not, the Eternally unCreated with which the Aborigines are in tune will, they say—and based on experience I believe them—still be there awaiting the appearance of someone, some time, some place, for its realisation. Let us hope that these others are not just the few survivors of a global holocaust or the members of other species as yet unanticipated in history.

These statements are not prophetic but conditional. They are of the "if this, then that" variety. There is no compulsion, no inevitable force in history or elsewhere that leads us to peace and order. If history shows us anything it is the opposite. That technological and economic change, and with them competition and violence, are the norm. But they are a norm out of ignorance rather than rational choice. Most people, I believe, engage in this kind of behaviour in this kind of pursuit, reluctantly for the very good reason that the world into which they are born and raised has already established the rule that if you don't behave this way and pursue these things you will yourself end up a "loser" and go to the bottom of the pack. Most people, I guess, would choose to opt out of the game altogether if they could. The enormous popularity of "disaster movies" in our society—for example, the recently released *Titanic*—is symptomatic here.

As an audience we respond vicariously to the pain and suffering of the characters; a bond of camaraderie grows between us as the threat "they" experience on the screen also becomes a threat to us. We weep together on the impending death of a child, of an aged couple, of young lovers. We curse the cold and calculating "me-first" villains of the piece—in fact the very kind of people many of us are in our own everyday business lives. But for a moment we realise a different kind of relationship to the people with whom we are sharing the experience, no longer impersonal and detached but personal and engaged; as so many of the victims we view on the screen are realising a new or deeper kind of relationship to each other at the prospect of their mutual demise.

A Renunciative outcome does not rely on human nature nor on circumstances but rather on choice. Not a choice between utopian ideals which no-one could live by because no-one ever has but of real lifeways that have appeared on the human horizon and persisted for however short a time. The Australian version of Renunciative living lasted thousands of years; could not we? With this book I hope I have made more explicit the nature of the real choices at issue in the human condition as we know it to date, if I have not been so clear on realising a Renunciative outcome.

*   *   *   *

I claim to have located evidence of the lifeway of Renunciation in the "world religions" and in certain episodes of history and contemporary society. The lifeway is a framework for accommodating differences by providing yours for me and mine for you. It would be appropriate then if this proved to be the "common ground" for accommodation between these religious traditions. It would be appropriate if these religious traditions could set the tone for a different kind of future than we in the West in particular have represented in our past.

The religious traditions addressed here all recognise the "Presence of No-thing when everything is taken away," that is, of spirituality. In varying degrees they recognise the process of "being" and "relationship" that flows from the initial, "Emptying," starting-point. Significantly, the Creative process in question (which forms the basis of the Aboriginal lifeway of Renunciation), that is, *anti-thesis* —> *thesis* —> *plurality*, "codes" the pivotal events of the "major traditions."

Gautama the Buddha experienced Enlightenment

(Nothingness or *anti-thesis*), followed by —> an experience of ego-less self (being or *thesis)* followed by —> teaching and practising compassion to all living things (relationship or *plurality*). In Jesus' case, his death (Nothingness or *anti-thesis*) is followed by —> resurrection (being or *thesis*) is followed by —> re-relationship with his disciples and instruction to love one another (relationship or *plurality*). In Mohammed's situation a direct encounter with presumed-to-be God (Nothingness or *anti-thesis*), is followed by —> re-identification of Mohammed as prophet (being or *thesis*) is followed by spreading God's message of love amongst the people (relationship or *plurality*).

In the case of Nambirrirrma, the man who appeared to Aborigines on Bickerton Island adjacent to Groote Eylandt before European contact, he incarnated directly out of Creation-substance (Nothingness or *anti-thesis*) to be identified as belonging to a particular Land/People (being or *thesis*) and re-establish mutually Renunciative relations between those of different Lands (relationship or *plurality*, specifically of a part-of-one-in-the-other kind).

The path to accommodating all these traditions, then, lies in the realisation that they have Nothing in common and that each may be a different path toward the understanding of a profoundly Creative, life-affirming, process.

Epilogue:
A Way to Renunciation?

We began by introducing the Aboriginal concept *gemalyang-gerranema*, which I translated "*anti-thesis* —> *thesis* —> *plurality*," or Nothingness —> being —> relationship. This means the something emerges from Nothing (an active or spiritually-based "Nothing") and is "cut off" and becomes "twisted in" to something else). The Aborigines apply the concept to "original Creation" or ultimate Creation, to re-Creation in the sense of people reproducing the terms or order of original Creation and to a type of relationship—the result of this process—I termed Renunciative. In its second meaning we come to another sense of *gemalyanggerranema*, and that is as "*anti-thesis*" or "Nothingness" as "imagination" and "anticipation." In other words, the sense that people "dream things up" out of "nowhere" or anticipate things that do not yet exist and plan for them accordingly.

In the process of examining Christian Scriptures in particular we developed another possible meaning of *gemalyanggerranema*, one that apparently did not occur to the Aborigines. This is "*anti-thesis*" or "Nothingness" as the anticipation of non-existence in the circumstances of threat and suffering. In this context, the "*thesis*" that emerges is the affirmation of one's existence in accommodation with others in like-circumstances, if not with the perpetrators of one's suffering. This extended understanding of the process at issue is an important addition to our understanding of historical processes in general. We realise (or are now in a position to test the hypothesis) that at least two mutually interacting forces are at work in our world to determine its character at any given moment in time. These are the force of "*thesis* —> *anti-thesis* —> *synthesis*" or the "me-first" clash of individuals and groups with opposing wants, interests, values, and so forth, and the force of "*anti-thesis* —> *thesis* —> *plurality*" or the "you-first" accommodation of what otherwise would be opposing wants, interests, values, and so forth. Insofar as the former process provides the pre-condition, in terms of threat and suffering, for the emergence of the second, and insofar as the former continues on in its original form alongside its Renunciative offspring, it is unlikely that the Renunciative "slip-stream" will remain in existence for long precisely because of its accommodation, peaceful nature (witness the fate of today's Aboriginal people). And yet it seems, theoretically, that the Renunciative stream is the only stream that can lead us to permanent peace.

If we wish to now interject into the discussion the value judgement that permanent peace is a good thing, how is it to be achieved? The answer lies in choice, but choice informed by knowledge of two interpenetrating forces at work in society and history. In other words, there is no determination; we cannot simply sit back and wait for some evolutionary process to work it out in this direction. While we may not comprehend, as Aborigines do, how the *anti-thesis —> thesis —> plurality* scenario generated Renunciation as part of original creation, we can see that our imaginations are able to "incarnate" this scenario in anticipation of the disastrous consequences of remaining subject to the mainstream *thesis —> anti-thesis —> synthesis* alternative of competition, conflict, and potential violence.

We can conceive, then, of implementing Renunciation as a rational act, either wholesale or in a set of stages. Each stage would take us one step further away from the extreme of conflict and violence stemming from selfishness and hoarding, toward a state of peaceful co-existence and mutual accommodation through a transcendence of material determination to determination by institutionalised Forms expelling "content" from one to the other, that is, Renunciation. In between would be a stage of unstable accommodation of "crisis-management" where one seeks to preserve one's own self-interest against that of others by a certain degree of compromise. Here practices of reciprocity, sharing, and charity would prevail. Hence,

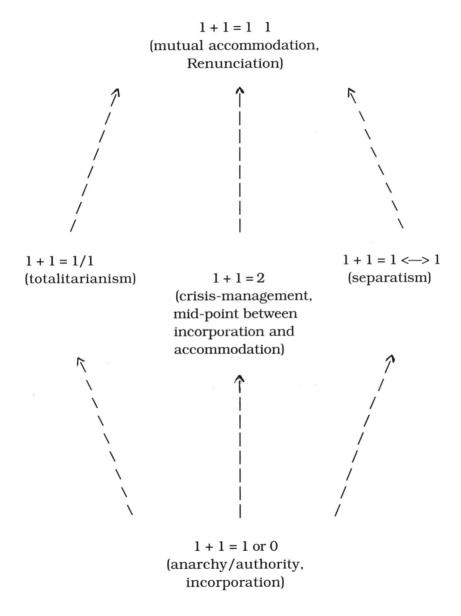

$1 + 1 = 1 \quad 1$
(mutual accommodation,
Renunciation)

$1 + 1 = 1/1$
(totalitarianism)

$1 + 1 = 2$
(crisis-management,
mid-point between
incorporation and
accommodation)

$1 + 1 = 1 <\!\!-\!\!> 1$
(separatism)

$1 + 1 = 1$ or 0
(anarchy/authority,
incorporation)

There is no evidence to suggest that history takes us "naturally" through these stages, nor that we are capable of moving from one to another through an act of rational choice. We seem buffered toward and away from Renunciation as a way of life by circumstances of oppression and suffering. When these circumstances wane we easily slip back into selfishness and old habits. Only occasionally are we moved towards Renunciation by imagination, foresight, and realisation of its necessity if we are to live peacefully together-apart on this planet.

Select References

Aboriginal Land Rights (Northern Territory) Act, 1976. Commonwealth of Australia, Canberra.

Adams, Charles. J. 1971. "Islam." In *Man and His Gods: Encyclopaedia of the. World's Religions*. Edited by Geoffrey Parrinder. London: Hamlyn.

Adlam, Robert, Glen. 1985. *The Structural Basis of Tahltan Indian Society* (PhD thesis, University of Toronto).

Andrews, Lynn. 1987. *Crystal Woman*. New York: Warner Books.

Arnheim, R. 1974. *Art and Visual Perception*, Berkeley: University of California Press.

Berndt, R. M., and C. H. Berndt. 1964. *The World of the First Australians*. Sydney: Ure Smith.

Beteille, André. 1969. *Caste: Old and New*. Bombay: Asia Publishing

Blainey, Geoffrey. 1975. *The Triumph of the Nomads*. Melbourne: Macmillan.

Bradley, A. G. 1932. *The United Empire Loyalists, Founders of British Canada*. London: Thornton, Butterworth.

The British North America Acts: 1867 to 1975. Ottawa: Department of Justice, Government of Canada.

Brown, Wallace. 1969. *The Good Americans*. New York: William Morrow.

Buber, Martin. 1958. *I and Thou*. New York: Charles Scribners Sons.

Calhoon, Robert McCluer. 1973. *The Loyalists in Revolutionary America*. New York: Harcourt and Brace Jovanovich.

Chatwin, Bruce. 1984. *The Songlines*. London: Penguin.

Cornford, Francis MacDonald, ed. 1962. *The Republic of Plato*. London: Oxford University Press.

Craig, Gerald M. 1963. *Upper Canada: The Formative Years*. Toronto: McClelland and Stewart.

Creighton, Donald. 1964. *The Road to Confederation*. Toronto: Macmillan.

Cruikshank, E. A. 1934. *The Settlement of the United Empire Loyalists on the Upper St. Lawrence and Bay of Quinte in 1784*. Toronto: The Ontario Historical Society.

Donaldson, Ian, and Tamsin Donaldson. 1985. *Seeing the First Australians*. London: George Allen and Unwin.

Dumont, Louis. 1970. *Homo Hierarchicus*. London: Weidenfeld and Nicolson.

Dumoulin, Heinrich. 1979. *Zen Enlightenment*. New York: Weatherhill.

Durham, the Earl of. 1839. *Report on the Affairs of British North America from the Earl of Durham, Her Majesty's High Commissioner*. London, Jan. 31, 1839, 4th Sess., 13th Parl., 2nd Victoria. Toronto: Robert Stanton.

Eliade, Mircea. 1960. *Myth of the Eternal Return*. New York: Harper Torchbooks

_____. 1973. *Australian Religions: An Introduction*. Ithaca: Cornell University Press.

_____. 1974. *Shamanism: Archaic Techniques of Ecstasy*. Princeton: Princeton University Press.

_____. 1979. *Pattern in Comparative Religion*. London: Sheed and Ward.

Elkin, A. P. 1977. *Aboriginal Men of High Degree*, Brisbane: University of Queensland Press.

Flood, Josephine. 1995. *Archaeology of the Dreamtime*. Sydney: Angus and Robertson.

Foster, W. A. 1890. *Canada First, Our New Nationality*. Toronto: Hunter, Rose and Co.

Frankenberry, Nancy. 1987. *Religion and Radical Empiricism*. Albany: State University of New York Press.

Ghurye, G. 1932/57. *Caste and Class in India*. Bombay: Popular Book Depot.

The Gospel According to Thomas. 1959. Trans. A. Guillaumont *et. al.* San Francisco: Harper and Row.

Grant, George M. 1967. *Lament for a Nation*. Toronto: McClelland and Stewart.

Guillet, E. C. 1937. *The Great Migration*. Toronto: Thomas Nelson and Son.

Harney, Bill. 1976. *Life Among the Aborigines*. Sydney: Rigby.

Havel, E. B. n.d. *Aryan Rule in India*. New Delhi: K.M.N. Publishers.

Herrigel, Gustie. 1987. *Zen in the Art of Flower Arrangement*. London: Arkana.

Hocart, A. M. 1950. *Caste: A Comparative Study*. New York: Athenium.

Hume, R. E. 1931. *The Thirteen Principle Upanishads*. London: Oxford University Press.

Ingold, Tim. 1988. "Comment" on Alain Testart's "Some Major Problems in the Social Anthropology of Hunter-Gatherers," *Current Anthropology*, vol. 29, no. 1: p. 15.

Kadowaki, Kakichi. 1982. "God as a Problem in the Dialogue between Zen and Christianity." In *God: The Contemporary Discussion*. Edited by Frederick Sontag and M. Darrol Bryant. New York: Rose of Sharn Press.

Kolenda, Pauline. 1978. *Caste in Contemporary India*. Mento Park, Cal.: Benjamin/Cummings.

Langer, S. 1953. *Feeling and Form*, New York: Charles Scribner & Sons.

Lanoue, Guy. 1983. *Continuity and Change: The Development of Self-Definition Among The Sekani of Northern British Columbia*. Ph.D. dissertation, University of Toronto.

Lee, Richard, and Irven De Vore, eds. 1972. *Man the Hunter*. Chicago: Aldine.

Mack, Burton L. 1995. *Who Wrote the New Testament? The Making of the Christian Myth*. San Francisco: Harper.

Macknight, C. C. 1972. "Macassans and Aborigines," *Oceania*, 42: 283–321.

Maddock, Kenneth. 1972. *The Australian Aborigines: A Portrait of Their Society*. London: Penguin.

Maquet, J. 1986. *The Aesthetic Experience: An Anthropologist Looks at the Visual Arts*. New Haven: Yale University Press.

Martin, Barry. 1988. *Kinship and Culture: A Study of the Kanesatake Mohawk*, Ph.D. dissertation, University of Toronto.

Mauss, Marcel. 1990. *The Gift: The Form and Reason for Exchange in Archaic Societies*. New York: W. W. Norton.

McDonald, J. Ian H. 1995. "Interpreting the New Testament in the Light of Jewish-Christian Dialogue Today." *Studies in World Christianity*, vol. 1, part 1.

McMillan, Andrew. 1992. *Strict Rules*. Rydalmere: Sceptre Books.

Morgan, Marlo. 1995. *Mutant Message Down Under*. New York: Bantam

Morphy, Howard. 1989. "From Dull to Brilliant: The Aesthetics of Spiritual Power Among the Yolngu," *Man* 24: 21–39.

_____. 1991. *Ancestral Connections: Art and Aboriginal Systems of Knowledge*. Chicago: University of Chicago Press.

Narayana, Vasudha. 1996. "The Hindu Tradition." In *World Religions: Eastern Traditions*. Edited by Willard G. Oxtoby. Toronto: Oxford University Press.

254

Nelson, W. H. 1961. *The American Tory.* Oxford: Clarendon Press.

O' Connell, Joseph T. 1989. "Hindu Views on Human Person, Human Rights and Human Duties." *Studies in Sikhism and Comparative Religion* (*Journal of the Guru Nanak Foundation*), edited by Mohinder Singh. 3 Parts.

Pagels, Elaine. 1981. *The Gnostic Gospels.* New York: Vintage Books.

Prebble, John. 1963. *The Highland Clearances.* London: Penguin.

Pretty, Graeme. 1976. *The Excavations at Roonka Flat, South Australia: An Insight into Ancient South Australian Society.* Adelaide: South Australian Museum.

The *Qur'an.* Trans. M. H. Shakir. New York: Tahrike Tarsile Qur'an.

Radhakrishnan, S. 1953. *The Principle Upanishads.* London: George Allen and Unwin.

Renou, Louis. 1963. *Hinduism.* New York: Washington Square Press.

Rose, Deborah Bird. 1992. *Dingo Makes Us Human: Life and Land in an Australian Aboriginal Culture.* Cambridge: Cambridge University Press.

Rose, F. G. G. 1960. *Classification of Kin, Age Structure and Gerontocracy Amongst the Groote Eylandt Aborigines.* Berlin: Akademie Verlag.

_____. 1976. *Australien und seine Ureinwohner.* Berlin:: Akademie Verlag.

Rouja, Philippe. 1997. *Fishing for Culture: Toward an Aboriginal Theory of Marine Resource Use Among the Bardi Aborigines of One-arm Point, of Western Australia.* Ph.D.. dissertation, Durham University.

Rowatt, Donald. 1969. *The Canadian Municipal System.* Toronto: McClelland and Stewart.

Singh, Balbir. 1986. *Indian Metaphysics.* New York: Humanities Press.

Singh, K. S., ed. 1991. *The Anthropological Survey of India.* Delhi: Government of India Publications.

Smith-Eivemark, Philip John. 1996. *Beyond Language: Mystics and the Language Trap.* Ph.D. dissertation, University of Toronto.

Stanner, W. E. H. 1979. *White Man Got No Dreaming.* Canberra: Australian National University Press.

Strauss, Lehman. 1964. *The Book of the Revelation.* Neptune New Jersey: Loizeaux Brothers.

Strehlow, T. G. H. 1971. *Songs of Central Australia.* Sydney: Angus and Robertson.

Strehlow, T. G. H. 1965. "Culture, Social Structure and Environment," in *Aboriginal Man in Australia.* Edited by R. M. and C. H. Berndt. Sydney: Angus and Robertson.

_____. 1971. *Songs of Central Australia.* Sydney: Angus and Robertson.

Subrahamanian, N. S. 1985. *Encyclopaedia of the Upanishads.* New Delhi: Sterling Publishers.

Sullivan, Lawrence E. 1988. *Icanchu's Drum: An Orientation to Meaning in South American Religions.* New York: Macmillan.

_____. 1989. *Death, Afterlife and the Soul.* New York: Macmillan.

Sutton, Peter, 1996. "The Robustness of Aboriginal Land Tenure Systems: Underlying and Proximate Customary Title," *Oceania,* vol. 67, no. 1: 7–29.

Suzuki, D. T. 1970. *Zen and Japanese Culture.* Princeton: Princeton University Press.

_____. 1987. *The Awakening of Zen.* London: Shambhala.

Swain, Tony. 1993. *A Place for Strangers: Toward a History of Australian Aboriginal Being.* Cambridge: Cambridge University Press.

Swain, Tony, and Deborah Bird Rose, eds. 1988. *Aboriginal Australians and Christian Missions.* Adelaide: The Australian Association for the Study of Religions.

Taylor, Charles. 1982. *Radical Tories: The Conservative Tradition in Canada.* Toronto: Anansi.

The Teachings of Buddha. 1966. Tokyo: Kosaido Printing Co.

Thomson, Donald. 1949. *Economic Structure and the Ceremonial Exchange Cycle in Arnhem Land.* Melbourne: Macmillan.

Thorne, A. G. 1977. "Separation or Reconciliation? Biological clues to the development of Australian Aboriginal Society." In *Sunda and Sahul: Prehistoric Studies in South East Asia, Melanesia and Australia.* Edited by J. Colson and R. Jones. London: Academic Press.

Trautmann, Thomas. 1971. "Hinduism." In *Man and his Gods.* Edited by Geoffrey Parrinder. London: Hamlyn.

Trott, Christopher Geoffrey. 1989. *Structure and Pragmatics: Social Relations Among the Tununirrusirmiut.* Ph.D. , dissertation, University of Toronto.

Turner, David H. 1978. "Ideology and Elementary Structures." In *The Social Appropriation of Logic: Essays presented to Claude Lévi-Strauss on his 70th birthday.* Edited by Pierre Maranda. Special edition of *Anthropologica,* vol. 20, nos. 1 and 2: 223–47.

_____. 1979. "Hunting and Gathering: Cree and Australian," In *Challenging Anthropology,* 17–26.

_____. 1980a. *Australian Aboriginal Social Organization.* New York: Humanities Press.

_____. 1980b. "Les Adaptations à la Mode: Découvrir les Australiens," *Anthropologie et Sociétés,* vol. 4, no. 3: 3–27.

_____. 1985/87. *Life Before Genesis: A Conclusion (the Significance of an Understanding of Australian Aboriginal Culture).* New York: Peter Lang.

_____. 1986. *Transformation and Tradition: A Report on Aboriginal Development in/on the Northern Territory of Australia.* Darwin: Government Printer.

_____. 1989/1996. *Return to Eden: A Journey Through the Promised Landscape of Amagalyuagba.* New York: Peter Lang.

_____. 1991. "Brahmanform: The Vedic-Hindu Tradition in Aboriginal Perspective," *Man in India* (Special issue in commemoration of the 70th Anniversary of the Journal), vol. 71, no. 1: 47–65.

_____. 1992. "'We Will Always be Gujar': the Politics of Nomadism in Himachal Pradesh." Special issue of the *India International Centre Quarterly* for the Earth Summit Conference, Rio, August, edited by Geeti Sen. Reprinted in *Indigenous Vision*, edited by Geeti Sen., London: Sage.

_____. 1993. "The (S)Pacific Effects of Sunday Morning Hockey: a Participant's Observation," *Culture*, vol. 12, no. 1, 77–85

_____. 1995. "Reaching In and Reaching Out: Prayer in Anthropological Perspective." In *The Human Side of Prayer* by L. R. Brown. Birmingham, Alabama: Religious Education Press.

_____. 1997. *Afterlife Before Genesis: An Introduction (accessing the Eternal through Australian Aboriginal Music)*. New York: Peter Lang.

Turner, David H., and Paul Wertman. 1977. "A Model of Band Societies." In *Shamattawa: The Structure of Social Relations in a Northern Algonkian Band*. Ottawa: National Museums of Canada.

Ueno, Yuji 1995. Eastern Philosophy and the Rise of the Aikido Movement. Ph.D. dissertation University of Toronto.

Upanishads. Trans. Patrick Olivelle. 1996. New York: Oxford University Press.

Upton, L. S. F., ed. 1967. *The United Empire Loyalists*. Toronto: Copp Clark.

Vithoulkas, George. 1986. *The Science of Homeopathy*. New Delhi: B. Jain Publishers.

_____. 1987. *Homeopathy: Medicine of the New Man.* New Delhi: B. Jain Publishers.

Waite, P. B. 1963. *The Confederation Debates in the Province of Canada, 1885.* Toronto: McClelland and Stewart.

Watt, Alan. 1989. *The Way of Zen.* New York: Random House.

Weaver, E. P. 1913. *The Story of the Counties of Ontario.* Toronto: Bell and Cockburn.

Wilson, Ian. 1996. *Jesus: The Evidence.* London: Weidenfeld and Nicolson.

Worsley, P. M. 1953. *The Changing Social Structure of the Warnindilyaugwa.* Ph.D. dissertation, Australian National University.

Zeitlin, Irving, M. 1988. *Jesus and the Judaism of His Time.* New York: Polity Press.

Index

TORONTO STUDIES IN RELIGION

Donald Wiebe, General Editor

This series of monographs is designed as a contribution to the scholarly and academic understanding of religion. Such understanding is taken to involve both a descriptive and an explanatory task. The first task is conceived as one of surface description involving the gathering of information about religions, and depth description that provides, on the basis of the data gathered, a more finely nuanced description of a tradition's self-understanding. The second task concerns the search for explanation and the development of theory to account for religion and for particular historical traditions. The series, furthermore, covers the phenomenon of religion in all its constituent dimensions and geographic diversity. Both established and younger scholars in the field have been and will be included to represent a wide range of viewpoints and positions, producing original work of high order at the monograph and major study level.

Although predominantly empirically oriented, the series encourages theoretical studies and even leaves room for creative and empirically controlled philosophical and speculative approaches in the interpretation of religions and religion. Toronto Studies in Religion is of particular interest to those who study the subject at universities and colleges but is also of value to the general educated reader.

For additional information about this series or for the submission of manuscripts, please contact:

Peter Lang Publishing, Inc.
Acquisitions Department
516 N. Charles St., 2nd Floor
Baltimore, MD 21201

To order other books in this series, please contact our Customer Service Department:

800-770-LANG (within the U.S.)
(212) 647-7706 (outside the U.S.)
(212) 647-7707 FAX

or browse online by series at:

WWW.PETERLANG.COM